Books, Bluster, and Bounty

Books, Bluster, and Bounty

Local Politics in the Intermountain West and Carnegie Library Building Grants, 1898–1920

Susan H. Swetnam

Utah State University Press
Logan Utah
2012

Published by Utah State University Press
An imprint of University Press of Colorado
5589 Arapahoe Avenue, Suite 206C
Boulder, Colorado 80303

The University Press of Colorado is a proud member of
The Association of American University Presses.

The University Press of Colorado is a cooperative publishing enterprise supported, in part, by Adams State College, Colorado State University, Fort Lewis College, Metropolitan State College of Denver, Regis University, University of Colorado, University of Northern Colorado, Utah State University, and Western State College of Colorado.

Manufactured in the United States of America
Printed on recycled, acid-free paper
Cover design by Barbara Yale-Read
Cover photo by Dan Miller: Carnegie library in Richmond, Utah

978-0-87421-842-8 cloth
978-0-87421-852-7 paper
978-0-87421-843-5 e-book

Library of Congress Cataloging-in-Publication Data

Swetnam, Susan H.
Books, bluster, and bounty : Local Politics and Carnegie Library Building Grants in the Intermountain West, 1890-1920 / Susan H. Swetnam.
pages cm
Includes bibliographical references and index.
ISBN 978-0-87421-842-8 (hardback) — ISBN 978-0-87421-852-7 (paper) — ISBN 978-0-87421-843-5 (e-book) (print)
1. Carnegie libraries—West (U.S.)—History. I. Title.
Z732.W48S94 2012
027.478—dc23

2012000173

To the Idaho librarians who have supported and
continue to support "Let's Talk About It" book discussion programs,
especially to Peggy McClendon, whose work as the program's founder
and long-time director has made LTAI a living demonstration of the
perennial power of books and reading.

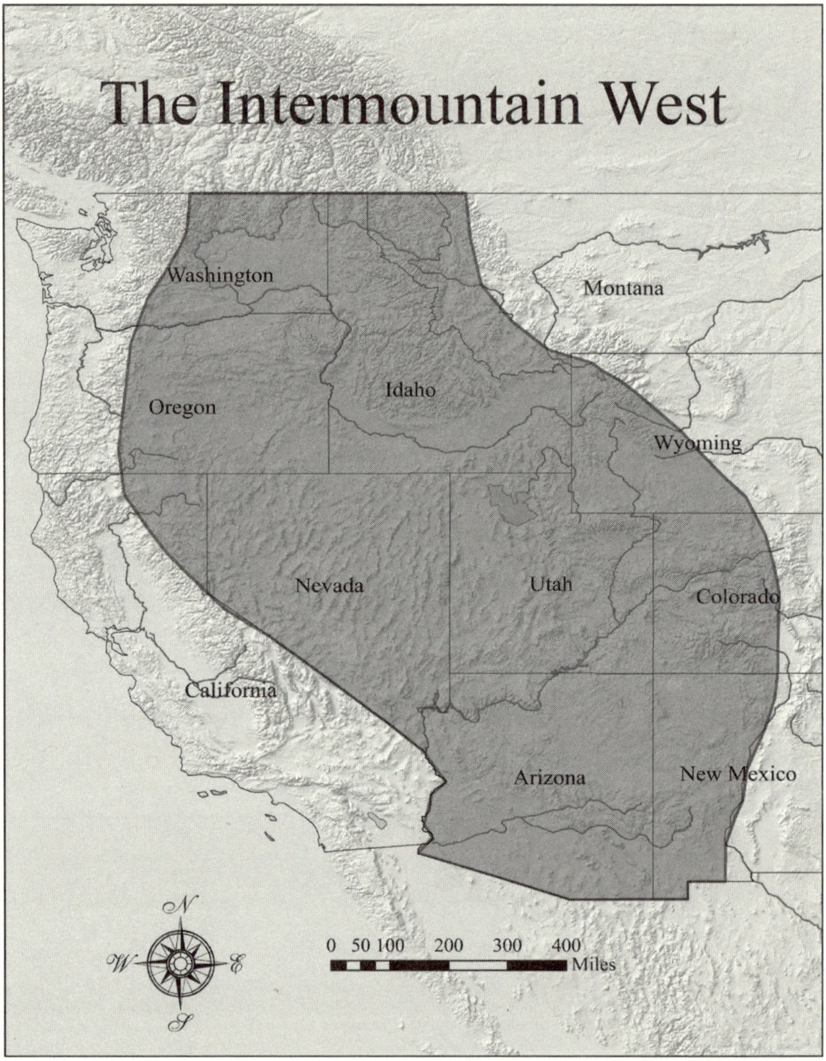

Cartography by: Adam Clegg

Contents

Acknowledgments

GLADYS MCQUEEN OF THE CARNEGIE CORPORATION LIBRARY in New York City and Brenda Hearing of Columbia University's Rare Book and Manuscript Library got this study off the ground by allowing me on-site and interlibrary loan access, respectively, to the microfilmed reels of original correspondence between Andrew Carnegie and applicant communities. Numerous staff members tirelessly fetched materials for me at research libraries and historical societies across the West, including the Oregon Historical Society Library in Portland, the Montana and Idaho State Historical Societies, the Utah State University Library, the University of Utah Library, the Utah State Historical Society, the Arizona State University Library, and the library of the University of Nevada, Reno. I received wonderful assistance in public libraries both large (Spokane, Reno, and Salt Lake City) and small (Steamboat Springs and Delta, Colorado; Pocatello, Idaho; Green River, Wyoming; and Prescott and Yuma, Arizona). Staff granted me access to rare book rooms and special collections archives in the Norlin Library at the University of Colorado, the University of Washington Library, the Provo, Utah, Idaho Falls, Idaho, and Durango, Colorado public libraries. This project has given me a permanent respect for the work that librarians do and for the riches that they superintend.

I have also received financial support from various institutions. This project began with a sabbatical and Faculty Research Committee Grant from Idaho State University in 1989. Later phases of research were supported by travel-to-collections grants from ISU's Department of English and Philosophy and its Office of Graduate Studies and Research, and by a Research Fellowship from the Idaho Humanities Council (IHC). This book has been vastly improved by the many people who have commented on my evolving conclusions. I've presented papers at the Rocky Mountain American Studies Association's annual conference, at Idaho State University colloquia, and, most recently, at the New England American Studies Association's annual meeting in October 2010. In a less formal context, I've given numerous IHC Speakers Bureau talks on the subject of Carnegie library social history at public libraries across Idaho—now and then (always movingly) in the very structure whose genesis I was describing. *Journal of the West* published an article based on chapters 3 and 4 in 1991 and *Nevada Magazine* published an article based on chapter 7 in 2003. The two people who reviewed this manuscript for Utah State University Press (Daniel F. Ring and a woman whose name I do not know) gave useful critiques and suggestions. This project has also been influenced by the hundreds of Idaho librarians who have heard me give keynote addresses at Idaho Library Association state conferences, at regional meetings, and at summer institutes over the past twenty years. In answering their questions and articulating how my findings related to their work, I discovered this book's thesis.

My late husband, Ford Swetnam, contributed more to this project than I can begin to articulate in the space available here. Over the long tenure of this study, Ford came to know more than he ever wanted to know about Carnegie libraries. Deeply knowledgeable about regional culture and libraries himself, he listened, asked, suggested, and read endless drafts. He sympathized with my frustration when responsibilities as faculty senate chair and graduate director all but halted my work soon after it began, and celebrated when I had time to resume. He understood when I left for long research road trips, and he once took time from his own sabbatical to surprise me during a Valentine's Day blizzard in Portland, where I was working in the Oregon Historical Society. When we traveled together, he cheerfully accepted detours so I could visit Carnegie library towns, and he found ways to occupy himself when I disappeared into tiny public libraries as soon as their doors opened in the morning, emerging only when those doors closed, babbling about some secret of local history, some wonderful gossip dead and buried for many decades. Living with another writer wasn't easy, but he always managed with grace, good humor, and love. This book reflects his love—as well as mine—of the quirky, maddening, sublime Intermountain West.

Carnegie Library Applicant Communities in the Northern Intermountain West

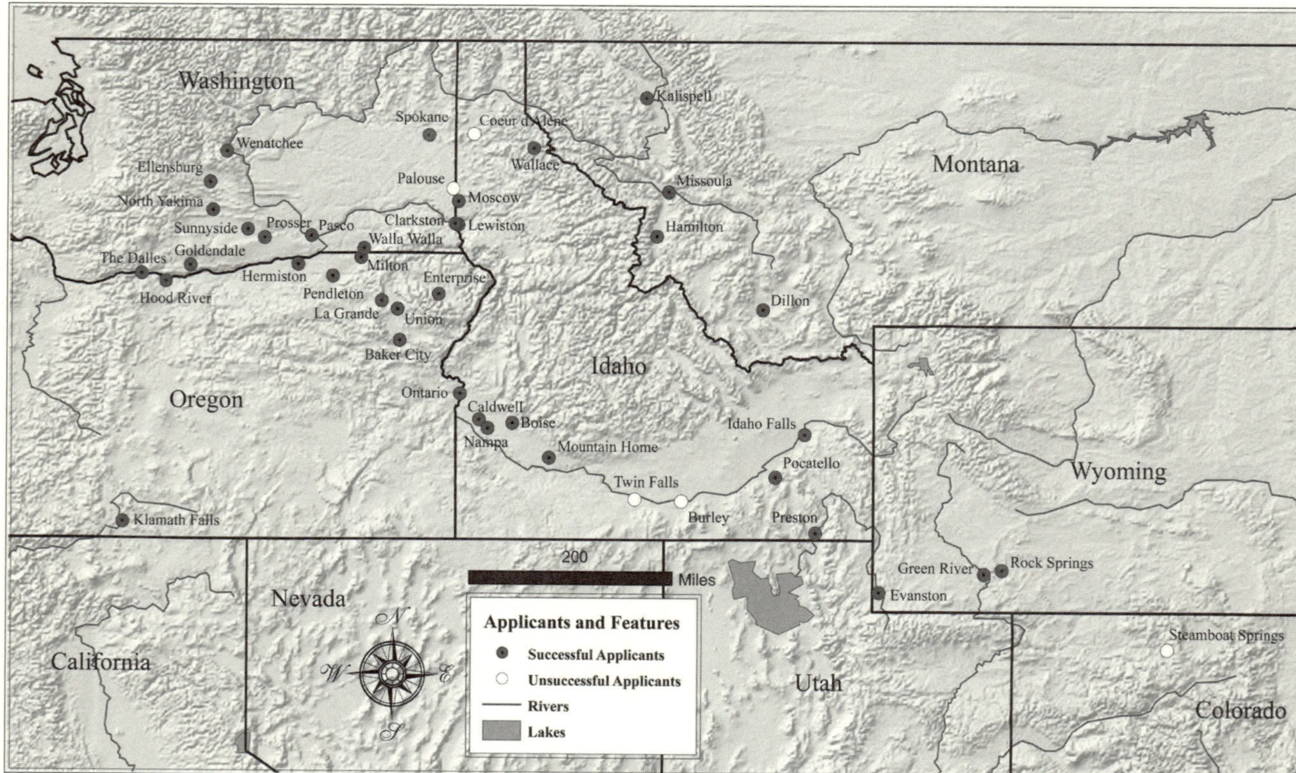

Cartography by: Adam Clegg

Carnegie Library Applicant Communities in the Southern Intermountain West

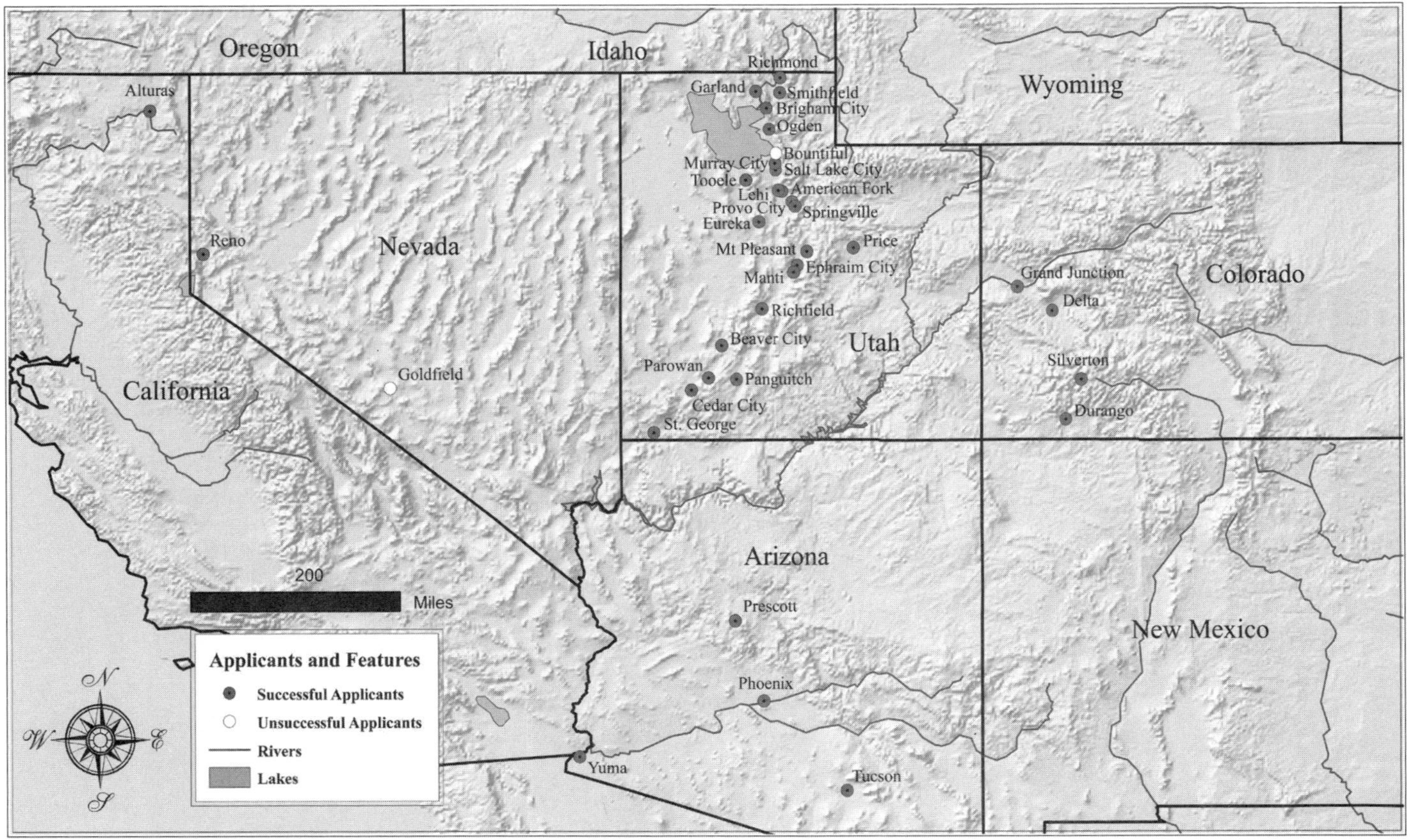

Cartography by: Adam Clegg

Introduction

ON THE AFTERNOON of July 28, 1910, citizens of Prosser, a small young town in eastern Washington, gathered for the dedication of a new public building. This was "an event of great importance in the history of the city," a speaker remarked, "marking the upward trend of the educational and social life in the history of Prosser."[1] Much of the town's population was able to attend, since stores and offices had been closed by municipal order and the local court had been adjourned. Attorneys and clergymen spoke; a quartet and a soloist sang; entertainers performed dramatic readings, recitations, and sleight of hand stunts. Enthusiastic speakers proclaimed Prosser a place "distinguished for the high character, moral worth, and continued enterprise of its citizens." This new construction signaled the dawn of a new era for Prosser, they asserted, an era of regional prominence.

What were they celebrating? Not the dedication of a grand cathedral, not a magnificent theater, an institution of higher learning, or a giant sports arena. Instead, the structure being dedicated was one that nearly every town holds today: a public library. Prosser had just joined the approximately 1,400 cities and towns in the United States that successfully constructed public library buildings between 1898 and 1919 with funds granted by Andrew Carnegie.[2]

Communities across the United States celebrated at Carnegie public library dedications, but Intermountain West communities like Prosser had particularly justifiable cause for pride, for they were not the sort of places one might have expected to find people enthusiastically pursuing cultural amenities. As the next chapter will discuss in detail, the turn-of-the-twentieth-century Intermountain West—a high, dry region between the

1 An account of this ceremony appears in the *Prosser (WA) Record*, July 29, 1910.

2 Carnegie library statistics can be found in Bobinski's foundational study in the field of Carnegie library history, *Carnegie Libraries: Their History and Impact on American Public Library Development*, and in Jones's more recent *Carnegie Libraries Across America*, both of which tabulate numbers of successful and unsuccessful applications, distribution by states, grant sizes, grant dates, etc.

Continental Divide and the crest of the Cascades—was truly "new country" from the perspective of Anglo settlers,[3] only recently settled, short on human resources, and economically tenuous. As a consequence of the area's climate, rugged landscape, lack of infrastructure, Native American presence, and a variety of other factors, most early travelers on overland trails had either stopped short of the Intermountain West or rushed through it to the more temperate west coast.[4] The region's communities were, on the whole, newly established; few (certainly not Prosser) had celebrated their twenty-fifth anniversaries when Carnegie began his general offer of public library building grants in 1898.[5]

According to census records, the Intermountain West's population density was the lowest in the United States in 1900 since figures indicate only 3.9 people per square mile, contrasted to 7.6 for the West as a whole and 35.5 for the US. Furthermore, while the 1900 census listed 2787 American communities with populations above 2,500 people, the Intermountain West contained only 79 such places. In contrast, the Pacific coast and eastern slope of the Rockies (the segments of the West that lie outside the Intermountain West)

3 This phrase, written about Grand Junction, Colorado, appears in a letter from Mrs. B. F. Jay to Andrew Carnegie, Oct. 9, 1899, Carnegie Corporation Archive, hereafter CCA. All primary correspondence between applicants and Carnegie cited in this book is stored in the CCA, Archive, described later in this introduction's text. "Mrs. Jay" is cited by her husband's name rather than by her own given name because the latter proved irretrievable; this study always uses women's given names where women used them or research revealed them.

4 This study defines the Intermountain West by geography rather than strictly by state boundaries because settlement history and economic circumstances—the variables whose influence on Carnegie library establishment it traces—are distinctive in the interior west, compared to the regions west of the Cascades/Sierras and east of the Rockies. In the pages that follow, the term "Intermountain West" thus should be understood to include not only the states that lie wholly between the Continental Divide and the crest of the Cascades/Sierra chain (Idaho, Utah, Arizona, Nevada) but also the subsections of states encompassed within this geographical area: the western portions of Montana, Wyoming, and Colorado; the eastern portions of Washington and Oregon; and a sliver of extreme northeastern California. Though western New Mexico is also geographically within the Intermountain West, that part of the state received no Carnegie grants and is thus not discussed in this book.

5 Prior to 1898, Carnegie had offered libraries to a few communities with which he had personal ties, including Pittsburg, Pennsylvania, and his birthplace in Scotland. This first, "retail" phase of giving (as Carnegie termed it) was superseded in 1898 when the "wholesale" public library grant program that forms the subject of this book began. Bobinski discusses Carnegie's "retail" public library gifts in *Carnegie Libraries*, 13, 76–78; see also Wall, *Andrew Carnegie*, 815–17.

Courtesy of History Colorado, Orig. Photos collection, scan #20004424.

"New County": Grand Valley, Colorado around 1910.

held 238 communities with populations above 2,500 in an area collectively half as large. Just 39 towns in the Intermountain West boasted more than 5,000 people, and only Salt Lake City and Spokane numbered over 25,000.[6]

As Carnegie was instituting his library building grant project, however, new development was beginning to change the face of the region. Federally funded and privately capitalized irrigation projects were making large-scale agriculture possible in vast tracts previously dismissed as desert; new rail lines were providing access to districts that had seemed impossibly remote. Yet life was still economically uncertain. Fluctuations in distant markets could abruptly drop the price of crops or bankrupt a timber company. Railroad companies could astronomically raise the price of transporting goods. Reports of mineral strikes could prove chimerical, established mines could

6 The figures come from the author's calculations based on the twelfth (1900) census. Where whole states lie in the Intermountain West, comprehensive state figures were used. Where a state's landmass lies partially inside the region and partially outside (as in the case of Colorado, which includes territory east of the Continental Divide as well as west), the "Area and Population of Counties" charts were used.

play themselves out, and strikes could cripple operations. Irrigation projects could fail to materialize or fail to deliver the water they promised. County seat or state capital designations could be lost due to politicking.

In this volatile atmosphere the region's new communities worked feverishly to develop the basic civic infrastructures that might help insure their continued existence. Around the turn of the twentieth century many were building (or had very recently completed) their first municipal waterworks, modern schools, city halls, courthouses, sewers, paved sidewalks and streets, fire departments, and electric lighting plants. Taxes were consequently high and citizen complaint common. Harried city officials struggled to stay on top of multiple ongoing projects even as they lobbied for support of future ones, and tried to forget that their tax bases could abruptly erode if a local economic downturn or a rumor of good times elsewhere triggered a mass exodus.

Carnegie's application procedure was not friendly to such demographic and economic variability, as chapter two will document. It assumed a stable population, awarding a particular level of funding to an individual town based on the most recent census count.[7] This formula posed a serious problem in mushrooming Intermountain West communities, where even recent tallies bore no relation to current populations. When North Yakima, Washington, applied to Carnegie in 1903, for example, city leaders could document only 3,500 people from the 1900 census—though the tax city's valuation had doubled since that count was taken and the 1910 census would record 14,000 inhabitants. At least North Yakima could show a large enough population to qualify for a minimal grant. Communities founded in a census year or immediately before were forced to submit federal tallies below Carnegie's minimum requirements, though they actually held double or triple that number of people at the time of application. A number of bourgeoning Intermountain West Carnegie library towns could demonstrate no population at all, for they hadn't even existed during the previous census.

Applying for a Carnegie library building grant also posed significant economic challenges for cash-poor Intermountain West towns. Carnegie's gifts were in no way "free," though they helped pay for "free" public libraries, for application communities were required to invest a great deal of what we'd now call "matching funds." Before Carnegie would issue a promise of

7 See Bobinski, *Carnegie Libraries*, 34–75, for a comprehensive discussion of application procedures.

forthcoming monies, community officials were obliged to submit a legal document pledging to support the library through taxation at a rate equal to 10 percent of his total gift—*every year, in perpetuity*. Moreover, communities were required to secure a building site at their own expense, to supply all books, magazines, and documents, and to fund all landscaping, furniture, and staff.

To complicate matters, the library support taxes Carnegie demanded weren't legal in many parts of the Intermountain West at the turn of the twentieth century. In 1898 Nevada and Idaho had no state laws at all enabling towns to levy taxes for public library service. Arizona, Utah, and Washington had set their levy amount so low that only the very largest communities could achieve funding adequate to meet 10 percent of Carnegie's offer. The first applicant towns in these new states (or territories, in the case of Arizona) were required to begin their Carnegie campaigns in their own state legislatures.[8]

The amount of local, hands-on activity a Carnegie grant required posed a further obstacle to overworked and sometimes amateurish officials in the interior West. Exact census and valuation figures were required, along with data about any existing library. The site title had to be documented as free and clear and the tax contract had to be worded exactly as Carnegie wished. After some early applicants appeared to take advantage of loopholes, more and more information began to be demanded and oversight became more rigid during the first decade of the twentieth century.[9] Carnegie's exacting private secretary James Bertram reviewed architectural plans, inspiring protracted correspondence and much negotiation—a cumbersome process when one communicator lived three-thousand miles from the other and discussion took place via mail. Funds were released in stages while building committees struggled to time construction to clement seasons. The smallest discrepancies between bids and actual costs had to be justified.

Successfully winning a Carnegie public library grant thus constituted a victory against great odds for an Intermountain West community like Prosser—a victory arguably justifying a great deal of bluster. But what's more likely to surprise those who advocate government fiscal support

---

8 The US Bureau of Education's *Statistics of Libraries and Library Legislation in the U.S. 1895–96* presents an overview of extant state library laws just before the turn of the twentieth century. See also Bobinski, *Carnegie Libraries*, 44–45.

9 Bobinski discusses the evolution of Carnegie procedures in chapters three and four of *Carnegie Libraries*.

for cultural institutions in the early-twenty-first century is that Prosser's citizens were willing to incur *any* hardship at all in the cause of a public library.

Public libraries haven't been exactly high on the list of local and state government priorities in recent years. Most people will voice a vague, affectionate attachment to public libraries, and some of them will even attend programs at their local public libraries, if the programs are free. But where money is involved, public libraries have been in trouble for some time, as I know from experience as a former Chair of the Idaho Humanities Council and thirty-year program scholar for the state-library-supported "Let's Talk About It" book discussion program. In my own state in fiscal year 2010, the Idaho Commission for Libraries suffered a 9 percent staff cut; its state appropriation for 2011 totals 34 percent less than its appropriation for 2009.[10] On the local level, taxpayers routinely oppose bond issues for enhanced library services. "Where will it stop?" demanded a letter to the editor of the *Idaho State Journal* when my adopted home town, Pocatello, sought funds thirty years ago to replace its antiquated, cramped library with a new building. "Ordinary citizens pay and pay and pay for such frills. We've had enough."[11] Only after much haggling, multiple referendums, and considerable bitterness was a new library constructed. And things haven't changed much. In lieu of adequate municipal support, our local library was recently forced to ask its "Friends" organization to raise funds for a much-needed bookmobile.

Yet in 1906, when Pocatello was much poorer, the city successfully negotiated a Carnegie library building grant, with backers mustering such overwhelming grassroots support that a reluctant city council was forced to proceed with the project, as chapter 6 will document. Towns with a more tenuous grasp on existence than Pocatello (including Prosser) also passed levies and incurred sizeable debts in the library cause. Even communities in the midst of rebuilding from catastrophic fires or floods staunchly worked for Carnegie libraries. Amazingly, seventy-one of the seventy-eight Intermountain West towns which cleared the initial hurdle with Carnegie successfully constructed their libraries. The success ratio in the Intermountain West was actually slightly *higher* than the national average,

---

10 Performance Measurement Review, Idaho Commission for Libraries (n.d.). www.dfm.idaho.gov/cdfy2012/publications/perfreport/PerfRpt_libraries.pdf.

11 *Idaho State Journal (Pocatello)*, March 20, 1982.

Citizens of Tooele, Utah, lay the cornerstone of their Carnegie library-to-be.

despite daunting region-specific difficulties that complicated the process.[12]

I first calculated those figures in the late 1980s, after "Let's Talk About It" sessions at charming, still-operating Idaho Carnegies inspired me to read George S. Bobinski's *Carnegie Libraries: Their History and Impact on American Public Library Development*. To say that the Intermountain West's enthusiastic embrace of the program amazed me would be a decisive understatement, given the difficulties we were then having in funding public humanities programming. How, I wondered had those long-dead advocates of books and reading been able to muster such enthusiastic and tangible support from their local governments and fellow citizens in difficult times, with so many competing obligations? Who *were* those people, and why were they so dedicated to establishing public libraries? Was it possible that the alleged books-in-every-wagon frontier ethos so popular in sentimental regional folklore wasn't

12 Bobinski identifies 1,412 communities which successfully pursued Carnegie libraries and 225 failed applications in *Carnegie Libraries*. The national success rate was thus 86 percent. In the Intermountain West, where 71 of 78 applicant communities successfully completed their libraries, the rate was 90 percent. The 225 figure, it is important to note, represents only communities which did not build after receiving a provisional promise of funding from Carnegie. It is *not* a total of all communities which merely inquired and never reached the promise stage. Undoubtedly some additional Intermountain West communities beyond the 78 were interested in the program (Hepworth mentions Logan, Moab, Heber, and Pleasant Grove, Utah in "Carnegie Libraries in Utah," 40), but in the absence of documentation (Carnegie kept only records from communities which received promises) identifying and discussing them was beyond the scope of this study.

a myth after all? Or—a possibility more encouraging for a contemporary public humanist—had those turn-of-the-twentieth-century library proponents employed some forgotten persuasive tactic we might steal?

So began the two decades of research that led to this book. In reviewing the extensive literature on library history, I discovered that a wide range of hypotheses have been posited about why Americans have valued libraries since colonial days. Jesse Shera suggests that educational and cultural motives inspired public library establishment, including self-education for both vocational and enrichment purposes, concern with conserving intellectual and historical resources, and desire to pursue scholarship. Numerous other writers have emphasized middle- and upper-middle classes' concern with social control and acculturation of immigrants and the working class. The library's perceived role in a democratic society has been argued. Several historians have noted that desire for economic development could inspire libraries; many suggest that women were particularly interested in founding public libraries out of a concern to enhance their communities' cultural resources for themselves and their families.[13]

Studies that explore in depth why a *particular community* might have chosen to emphasize a *particular argument* from this list, however, are less common. Among the writers who have correlated the social histories of specific locales with their library histories are Abigail A. Van Slyck (who discusses the architecture of large city Carnegie branch libraries relative to their anticipated working class users); Barbara Jones (who suggests the connection between the establishment of Buhl, Minnesota's public library and the region's heavily immigrant population); and Daniel F. Ring (who argues for social control and image-remaking as impetuses in Butte, Montana's library foundation).[14] Such studies typically discuss the establishment of only one

13 Shera, *Foundations of the Public Library.* Writers who have discussed public libraries as instruments of social control include Ditzion, *Arsenals of a Democratic Culture* and Garrison, *Apostles of Culture.* Economic development has been suggested as a motive for library development by Ring, "Men of Energy and Snap," "Carnegie Libraries as Symbols for an Age," Van Slyck, *Free to All,* and Swetnam, "Pro-Carnegie Library Arguments." Among those who have discussed women's importance in establishing public libraries are Haarsager, *Organized Womanhood,* Scott, *Natural Allies,* and Blair, *The Clubwoman as Feminist.* For a variety of perspectives in a convenient package, see the essays "American Libraries and Agencies of Culture," in a special issue of *American Studies* edited by Augst.

14 Van Slyck, *Free to All,* 110–24; Jones, "The Center of Culture and Helpfulness"; Ring, "The Origins of the Butte Public Library."

or a few libraries rather than comparing and contrasting a larger set. Ring's "Carnegie Libraries as Symbols for an Age: Montana as a Test Case" is one important exception relative to the library history of the American West, for it correlates the economic and social circumstances of eighteen communities with the prevailing rhetoric and demographics of support that accompanied their attempts to win Carnegie grants.[15]

The study that follows turns a wider lens on Ring's core question—"Why were Carnegie libraries supported so enthusiastically in Montana?"—by investigating the local politics that inspired and shaped a region's worth of campaigns to establish Carnegie public libraries. The research on which it is based began with an investigation of the forty reels of microfilm in the archive of original Carnegie library building grant correspondence, now held at Columbia University. That collection includes letters to and from all Carnegie applicant communities, along with forms and other documentation (though not always a comprehensive record of all correspondence from an individual town), arranged alphabetically. Using these primary records from the seventy-eight Intermountain West Carnegie applicant communities, I identified the dates and correspondents for each application and noted what writers claimed about their communities and how individual applications progressed. I then turned to local sources: period newspapers;[16] locally written library histories; community, county, and state histories; library board and city council minutes; club and church records; biographies, autobiographies, and obituary collections; state legislative records; and a variety of miscellaneous sources depending on individual applications' contours. Scholarship in library history (especially Carnegie library history), American studies, western history, and women's studies provided theoretical framework and background.

---

15 Ring, "Carnegie Libraries as Symbols for an Age." The essays in Robert Stanley Martin's *Carnegie Denied* present the largest comparative sample to date, discussing the circumstances regarding the failure of library establishment in a nationwide sampling of Carnegie applications.

16 Because I was interested in the broad context of each application, I began my newspaper scans several months before the initial letters to Carnegie and continued through the negotiation period (with particular attention to dates of most active correspondence) until the library was dedicated or negotiations broke off conclusively. In addition to stories relating directly to local Carnegie libraries, I used a variety of other newspaper sources to construct the larger narratives of Intermountain West Carnegie applications, including editorials, general news stories, city government reports, club, society, church columns, obituaries, business advertising, and police logs.

What has resulted might be described as an interdisciplinary piece of detective work, an attempt to construct seventy-eight social-historical narratives from partial (and sometimes contradictory) sources. Because this study's methodology involved bringing disparate sources into conversation with each other, it inevitably yielded some surprises. Celebratory local accounts of the history of beloved libraries, I discovered, sometimes left out compelling back-stories, stories with rich implications about what it must have been like to live in particular Intermountain West communities at particular times.

Such stories reveal that Carnegie library history should not be considered simply a minor footnote to Western history but a subject that can significantly enhance the revised picture of regional history that new western historians have been building for the past thirty years. In the interior West Carnegie library applications bear little resemblance to the democratic, egalitarian decision making posited by "old" Western history as a feature of the frontier.[17] While many applicants did cooperate and some even seem to have acted from noble motives, venial competition appears much more common than the bland myths of western town-building might suggest. Communities contested for power with rival communities during Carnegie library campaigns; citizens contested with their neighbors. People formed special-interest coalitions and they lobbied, bullied, and manipulated other people. They occasionally even cheated (or attempted to cheat) each other and/or Carnegie, though usually in polite ways and often for admirable reasons. Taken as a whole, regional Carnegie library application history also debunks the notion that the West held a unified and hegemonic "white middle class" at the turn-of-the-twentieth-century. In reality, not only did men's and women's interests sometimes clash, but even within genders long-standing rivalries, pragmatic hope of personal gain, religious affiliation, and even neighborhood loyalties could divide people who inhabited essentially the same socio-economic niche. To study Intermountain West Carnegie library applications is to understand that diversity in the interior West came not just from the people of color who have drawn so much recent and justified scholarly interest, but also from

17 The classic stereotypes of the West have, of course, been under attack since the 1980s from scholars including Patricia Nelson Limerick, Donald Worster, and David M. Wrobel. Worster's *Rivers of Empire*, which suggests that the American West had a colonial status, is especially relevant to this study, as is Wrobel's *Promised Lands*, which explores conflicting visions of the region presented by promoters vs. "reminiscers."

the numerous and nuanced Anglo-American middle class "cultures" the region contained.

The history of how Carnegie libraries came to the Intermountain West also turns out to be a subject with considerable relevance to those who dream of mustering grassroots support for the arts and humanities today. It's not that these stories reveal the sort of simple "forgotten persuasive tactics" I once imagined finding. Still, this book will contend that today's advocates of cultural "frills" *can* learn something useful from the people who helped secure Carnegie libraries for their communities a hundred years ago. For their stories offer a simple unerring precedent: their libraries succeeded where supporters were able to connect the institutions to locally relevant questions of civic identity. "What do we stand for?" people asked themselves during this period of rapid change. "What distinguishes us from other communities?" Carnegie libraries garnered general grassroots buy-in where proponents were able to identify them symbolically in the public mind with a shared consensus about "who we are" (or "who we want to become"). Applications succeeded at particular points in particular places during the grant program's twenty year span precisely because the institutions were understood as relevant to the immediate Zeitgeist, as institutions that would solidify a desirable identity and communicate it to the outside world. And that, this book will suggest, is a precedent with living relevance.

To illustrate how the rhetoric of successful pro-Carnegie library applications correlated with particular local circumstances, this book is organized around clusters of applications that shared similar socio-economic profiles and pro-library rhetoric. A handful of Intermountain West Carnegie libraries do not receive much discussion, either because the resources necessary to reconstruct their application stories do not exist (as with Wallace, Idaho, where a devastating forest fire destroyed records from that period in community history), or because they do not fit clearly into one of the paradigms the book discusses.[18] In the great majority of the seventy-eight communities, however, history, contemporary preoccupations, Carnegie library leadership, and local pro-Carnegie library rhetoric align decisively.

This study begins with two introductory chapters establishing contexts essential for understanding the applications. The first describes the social and economic history of the Intermountain West at the turn of

18 One such application, Dillon's, has previously been identified as "an oddity" among Montana Carnegie libraries because of its atypical rhetoric and demographics of support (Ring, "Carnegie Libraries As Symbols for an Age," 14).

Photo by the author.

Carnegie library, Silverton, Colorado.

the twentieth century; the second outlines the Carnegie library application procedure. Chapter 3 takes up the first cluster, a set of communities where Carnegie libraries were championed as adjuncts to economic booms and where businessmen were the prime movers. Chapter 4 moves to a very different set, applications from Mormon agricultural settlements in Utah and on its borders, where Mormon Church officials supervised the projects and the libraries were promoted as safeguards for youthful morals. Chapter 5 describes Carnegie applications from Utah communities containing significant non-Mormon ("gentile") populations. It includes two sub-paradigms; one for small towns, where citizens studiously sidestepped the divisions which might have prevented them from cooperating in ways necessary to secure a grant; the other for Utah's two largest cities, where Carnegie libraries were championed by gentiles as correctives to Latter-day Saint influence. Chapter 6 considers a group of economically stable, relatively sophisticated communities where women's clubs took and retained charge of Carnegie library applications—in contrast to the majority of Intermountain West applications, where the women who had founded and maintained initial community libraries yielded control of Carnegie applications to men. Chapter 7 describes communities where oligarchies of like-minded men and women sought Carnegie libraries in the service of several kinds of reform. Chapter 8 describes a cluster of towns where Carnegie libraries became pawns in the service of individual men seeking to consolidate personal power. The ninth chapter focuses on a small group of applications that sparked bitter internal feuds within communities, arguing that such dissention reflected deeper intramural cultural divisions. The tenth summarizes conclusions and makes suggestions.

Back in 1966, in the very first issue of *The Journal of Library, Philosophy, and Culture*, Frank Woodford argued that "the organic growth of a library itself . . . reflects the social evolution of the community it serves."[19] The study that follows offers new evidence to show just how accurate and nuanced that truth is.

19 Woodford, "Second Thoughts on Writing Library History," 34.

1

The Culture of the Intermountain West, 1890–1920

"New Country"

RESIDENTS OF STEAMBOAT SPRINGS, COLORADO, rode a crest of excited optimism in 1907, certain that prosperity was finally about to arrive in their community. For twenty years Steamboat Springs had made its living as a modest commercial center serving a far-flung ranching and mining district in northwestern Colorado. The town did boast a hot springs, but its isolation from major population centers limited potential as a health resort. Now news had come that the Moffat Railroad was building a standard gauge line through the Rockies. It was just a matter of time, boosters claimed, until Steamboat Springs became "the main town between Denver and Salt Lake City."[1] Flush with anticipated prosperity, businessmen initiated projects designed to draw tourists and encourage in-migration. Most of these ventures were unambiguously commercial as a new hotel was capitalized and the hot springs were modernized. But one item on this booster wish list was not quite like the others. Steamboat Springs also dreamed of a Carnegie library, an institution that would demonstrate the place to be "refined" as well as "coming."

The early steps of Steamboat's Carnegie library building grant application progressed smoothly. Citizens were fortunate to have an ally in a friend of Carnegie's who had vacationed there. The community soon obtained a promise of $5,000. Though this number was smaller than the sum the

1 John Rolfe Burroughs, *Steamboat in the Rockies*, 33–36; *Steamboat (CO) Pilot*, April 19, 1908, Sept. 11, 1907, April 27, 1910.

commercial club members spearheading the application had desired, their boosterish spirit remained undimmed, and this figure was inflated in the public press to "a strong probability for . . . a $10,000 library" within "a year."[2]

But Steamboat's fortunes fell apart, and with them the town's enthusiasm for a Carnegie library. Mountainous terrain proved more difficult to negotiate than Moffat Road builders had anticipated and the most expedient path was discovered to cross a tract already tied up with reservoir survey claims. Lawsuits, logistical difficulties, and bad weather stalled building. By the time track construction reached Steamboat (a year later than anticipated), the railroad was heavily in debt, its founder dead, and its future right-of-way challenged. The track stopped just beyond Steamboat, never to become a through-line.[3] The anticipated influx of new settlers and their money never came. When the 1910 census was counted, the town's population was closer to 1,000 than to the 2,500 which library applicants had claimed to Carnegie, and citizens struggled with taxes incurred in the cause of promoting pre-empted prosperity. For the first time in four years, in 1910 the *Steamboat Pilot*'s last issue in December did not include a chronicle of the year's progress and a prediction of a glowing future. Steamboat Springs' boom was over before it began, and with it the town's Carnegie library campaign. City leaders quietly abandoned the application, and no one seems to have noticed, much less clamored for its renewal. Steamboat Springs never built a Carnegie library and did not construct a purpose-built library until 1967.[4]

While Steamboat Springs' Carnegie library story is distinguished by particularly bad luck, many other Intermountain West communities faced similar challenges at the time of their applications due to unpredictable economic and social change. Between 1898 and 1919, the period when Andrew Carnegie offered funds for the construction of public libraries, the Intermountain West was a zone self-consciously in transition—a place which variously anticipated, dreamed of, or dreaded change, but which could not ignore that change was occurring. In a substantial number of the region's towns, many people remembered community beginnings.

---

2 Letter from M. E. Houston to James Bertram, Dec. 13, 1908, CCA and *Steamboat (CO) Pilot*, Sept. 29, 1907.

3 Bollinger and Bauer, *The Moffat Road*, 80, 83, 94, 139 and *History of West Routt County*, 14.

4 Richards, *Steamboat Round the Bend*, 77.

Of the seventy-eight Intermountain West communities which applied for Carnegie public library building grants, a third were established after 1890 and a half dozen after 1900. Citizens voiced a sense of inhabiting land where no civilization had previously existed. They also emphasized their sense of rapid municipal transformation. "The town is . . . passing from the village class to the city class," an editorial in the *Eastern Oregonian* proclaimed of Pendleton during that community's Carnegie library application and an inquiry letter to Carnegie from Nampa, Idaho, spoke of that town's "remarkable transformation" in the previous few years.[5] Even in the pockets of the region that had been settled for decades diversity increased: Eastern Europeans arrived to work in mines and new industries; Russians immigrated to labor in beet fields; an influx of non-Mormons infiltrated Mormon country; and Anglo-Europeans colonized towns long dominated by Hispanic influences.

The narratives of individual communities' Carnegie library histories, this book will argue, are integrally tied to just such circumstances, mirroring both larger trends in regional social history and specific local variations. As a foundation, this chapter offers a brief overview of the specific economic and cultural circumstances that led residents to call the region "new country" at the time of Carnegie's offer.

The European Settlement of the Intermountain West

Before Lewis and Clark's expedition in 1804–6, the Intermountain West was a land of mystery to Euro-Americans, isolated between rugged mountain chains reaching to 14,000 feet. Spanish explorers and missionaries had operated in New Mexico in the sixteenth century, French fur traders had traveled in Canada, and British and American ships had explored the coast of the Pacific Northwest. The interior west, however, was so little-known that the Corps of Discovery set out expecting to find the mythical great "river of the west," a conduit to the Pacific Ocean just one day's portage west of the Missouri River. Most of the region wasn't even technically in American hands at the time of the Lewis and Clark expedition. Northwestern Montana, Idaho, Eastern Washington, and Oregon belonged to Oregon Territory, jointly controlled with the British. The Spanish controlled Nevada,

5 *Eastern Oregonian (Pendleton, OR)*, Nov. 29, 1913 and letter from Mrs. E. H. Dewey to Andrew Carnegie, Jan. 10, 1907, CCA.

Utah, Arizona, western Wyoming and Colorado, and most of New Mexico. Venturing into contested territory, Lewis and Clark became the first men to map the northern Rockies, floating rivers and recording wonders that no whites had ever before seen. And yet, monumental as their expedition was, it only passed through a tiny fraction of the region.[6]

Further exploration followed on the Corps' heels. Mountain men (several of whom had traveled with Lewis and Clark) pushed into new country in the northern and central Rockies. Zebulon Pike led an expedition into Spanish territory in 1806. Jedediah Smith wandered through present-day Colorado, Oregon, and California in the 1820s. In the 1840s, after Oregon and some former Mexican territories became US possessions, the newly established federal Corps of Topographical Engineers systematized exploration. John C. Fremont's expeditions crossed Utah, Colorado, New Mexico, and California. Howard Stansbury explored the Great Basin. Expedition surveyors mapped the 17th, 19th, 38th, 35th, and 32nd parallels. After the Civil War, geologist Ferdinand Hayden and scientific adventurer John Wesley Powell surveyed particularly remote sections of the interior west, including the Grand Canyon and northwestern Wyoming.

Though artists including Thomas Moran and Albert Bierstadt celebrated the interior West's landscape, chronicling its expansive light, sweeping panoramas of basin and range, and huge sky, it was not a region particularly inviting to agriculture. The region's geography offered numerous barriers to internal travel including precipitous basin-and-range-style ranges, and river canyons hundreds or thousands of feet deep. It also held numerous zones uninviting to cultivation including immense ossified lava fields, alkaline deserts, and wind-swept plateaus. Even most of the relatively level ground lay over 3,000 feet in elevation. Compared to the land immediately east of the Continental Divide and west of the Cascade/Sierra crest, the interior west was distinctively arid and subject to more extreme temperature swings.[7] Several Eastern Oregon counties lying within the Intermountain West, for example, received less than 10 inches of rain in 1910, compared to 40 inches in the Willamette Valley. Rainfall in Delta and Grand Junction, Colorado, was calculated in 1910 as about 8 inches, compared to the 14–18 inches for foothills east of the Colorado Rockies.

6 White offers a concise history of the exploration of the American West in *It's Your Misfortune*, 119–36. See also Ronda, "Passion and Imagination."

7 The climatological detail which follows has been calculated by the author from the figures reported in *Summary of Climatological Data*.

Even in dust-dry Wyoming, the southwestern, Intermountain West, part of the state recorded significantly less rain in 1910 than counties east of the divide. States whose boundaries were wholly within the region were particularly arid. Nevada counties received between 5–10 inches of rain a year and the towns in southern Idaho's Snake River Plain averaged around 11 inches. Clear skies fostered especially hot and especially cold weather. In many sections (including parts of Washington, Oregon, Wyoming, and Idaho in the north) summer temperatures regularly neared or surpassed 100 degrees, while winters routinely threw thermometers far below zero. Furthermore, frost could also strike in any month in the region's northern reaches, or even in its southern high country, including Arizona's mountains.

Home-seekers on the Oregon and California trails thus tended to hurry as quickly as they could through the region. With their gaze fixed ahead to the temperate, fertile ground of the Pacific slope, they registered their disgust at the unpromising nature of the interior West. "The country all the way down the Snake River [in Idaho] is one of the most desolate dreary waste in the world," wrote one Oregon Trail traveler. Sixty years later even the boosterish mayor of Rock Springs, Wyoming admitted the region's deficiencies in terms of obvious incentives to settlement. "If there is a place that merits recognition from those interested in the upbuilding of humanity," he wrote to Andrew Carnegie in 1907, "certainly it is here. Nature has not been kind except to give us a wonderful coal basin, lying in the heart of the Great American Desert, sans water, sans vegetation of any kind."[8]

By the 1850s the Intermountain West saw only scattered settlement. Although communities grew up around former forts, including Tucson and Boise, and around Indian missions, including Walla Walla, those who ranched and farmed lacked the means to transport their goods to larger markets. Only in Utah, where Latter-day Saints fleeing persecution collectively migrated under Brigham Young's leadership in 1847, did a significant network of interlocking settlements develop.[9]

Then a series of mineral strikes explosively initiated town-building. Miners on their way to California discovered gold on Nevada's Carson River in 1851 and populated the Comstock district in 1859. Precious metals were discovered in northern Idaho's Clearwater/Salmon region in 1861, then in

8 The Oregon Trail traveler, E. S. McComas, is quoted in Eide, *Oregon Trail*, 166. Letter from A. Kendall to Andrew Carnegie, July 5, 1907, CCA.

9 Arrington describes settlement and economic development in pre-Civil-War Utah in *Great Basin Kingdom*.

Wyoming State Archives, Department of State Parks and Cultural Resources.

"Nature Has Not Been Kind": Green River, Wyoming, near Rock Springs.

Idaho City, and then in the Coeur d'Alene district. Miners rushed to Utah's Bingham Canyon in 1863, introducing a gentile (non-Mormon) presence to Utah territory. Utah's mining expanded with new strikes in the 1870s in Park City, in the Tintic region, in Little Cottonwood Canyon, in Silver Reef/American Fork, and in the Beaver and Cedar City vicinities. Silver and copper drew miners to Butte, Montana, in 1875 and 1880. In western Colorado, the future Carnegie library towns of Durango and Silverton began as silver mining camps.[10]

Adjacent settlements grew to support these enterprises. Corinne boomed as a freighting center connecting Utah and the Montana mines. Farmers and ranchers settled in valleys where they could raise crops and meat for miners, including Montana's Bitterroot Valley and Idaho's Boise, Payette, and Weiser valleys. New towns (including the future Carnegie library communities of Lewiston, Idaho; Spokane, Washington; Reno, Nevada; and Prescott, Arizona) functioned as market centers for such areas.

But several problems limited full-scale development in the Intermountain West. Crucially, no rail network existed before the Civil War to supply settlers and carry the region's products to distant market. Then, in 1862, Congress approved the Pacific Railroad Act chartering the Central Pacific to build east from Sacramento while the new Union Pacific built west from Omaha. Land grants for railroad right-of-way were authorized, and the nation's first transcontinental railroad was completed at

10 For histories of mining in the West, including specifics about various Intermountain West communities, see Greever's *Bonanza West* and Paul's *Mining Frontiers.*

Courtesy of History Colorado, William Henry Jackson collection, scan #20100753.

Silverton, Colorado and the Sultan Mountains, late 19th century.

Promontory Summit, Utah, in 1869. By the 1880s numerous feeder lines had snaked into previously isolated parts of the interior West. The Oregon Short Line was built through Idaho and eastern Oregon; the Northern Pacific through Montana, northern Idaho, and eastern Washington; the Denver and Rio Grande through western Colorado and eastern Utah; and the Atlantic and Pacific and the Southern Pacific through Arizona and New Mexico.[11]

A string of settlements grew up alongside the tracks. Some had their genesis as railroad service communities, including the railroad shop centers (and future Carnegie library towns) of Pocatello, Ogden, and Missoula, Montana. All three of the future Carnegie library towns in southwestern Wyoming began as company towns. Rock Springs was established to supply coal to the Union Pacific, Green River to supply water, and Evanston to act as a switching point. In other cases, new agricultural towns were platted by development companies beside new rail lines and promoted for their "inevitable" growth given this connection to the outside world. Typical of such communities was the future Carnegie library town of Caldwell, Idaho, platted in 1883 when the Idaho and Oregon Land Improvement Company offered bare ground along the Oregon Short Line Railroad. Within four months the new settlement contained a hotel, a millinery shop, two

11 White describes railroad development in *It's Your Misfortune*, 246–58.

Courtesy of Washington State Historical Society.

The arrival of the first train, Yakima Valley, Washington, 1910; a community celebrates.

blacksmiths, three doctors, a newspaper, a post office, several general mercantile operations, several lawyers, and numerous saloons.[12]

American Indian presence constituted another impediment to European-American settlement in parts of the interior West—but only temporarily, for any rumor of hostility, even the most unfounded, was seized as an excuse for Indians' removal from desirable districts. In the 1860s and 1870s settlers who saw agricultural potential in eastern Oregon's Wallowa Valley and in northwestern Idaho pressured the government to remove the Nez Perce. An excuse for removal came when young Indian men clashed with settlers. Fearing reprisal, the band fled, then garnered a reputation for "viciousness" by defending itself when attacked by militia and federal cavalry. The Nez Perce journeyed hundreds of miles in their attempt to seek refuge in Canada, only to be caught by federal agents and relegated to a reservation.[13] The future Carnegie library community of Enterprise, Oregon was platted in 1887 on land taken from the tribe.

The Utes of western Colorado received especially bad treatment since they were removed not once but twice. The first displacement came after a few tribal members attacked an Indian agency and kidnapped a white

12 "Caldwell Revisted 1883–1923."

13 West chronicles the Nez Perce War in detail in *The Last Indian War*.

family in 1879. The second came just three years later, after would-be settlers pointed out that the new reservation included potentially prime land for farming at the confluence of the Gunnison and Grand Rivers. "The Utes Must Go!" demanded newspaper headlines, and commissioners confiscated 150,000 acres around the confluence and opened them to settlement in 1882. Some eager settlers even staked claims while the land still technically belonged to the Indians.[14] The Carnegie library town of Grand Junction became the market center for this new district.

The federal government similarly removed Apaches from ancestral grounds in Arizona after the United States assumed control of the territory from Mexico in 1848/1853, allowing the development of the future Carnegie library communities of Tucson and Yuma. Last of all in the region to be removed were the Modocs of Northeastern California, Southern Oregon, and Western Nevada, whom the government sent to reservations in 1873. Among the communities settled in the territory the Modocs had roamed was Alturas, California, which obtained a Carnegie library grant a few decades later.[15]

Perhaps the most needed thing for widespread settlement in the Intermountain West, however, was irrigation water.[16] While the Homestead Act of 1862 did lead to widespread development elsewhere in the United States, its requirements proved unworkable in the arid interior, offering in the words of historian Richard White, "not a ticket to independence but to starvation."[17] Small-scale irrigation projects thrived in limited districts along reliable rivers and streams, especially in Mormon Utah and southeastern Idaho, where settlers united by religion organized themselves to plow common ditches and to self-police water distribution.[18] In large portions of the region, however, distance from water sources and lack of a coherent social structure made such projects impossible.

The Carey Act of 1894 offered a breakthrough in irrigation development, though it did not prove the panacea it was hoped to be. Under its terms the federal government ceded a million acres to each western state,

14 Underwood, *Town Building*, 2–12.

15 For a history of the conflict, see Murray's *The Modocs and Their War*.

16 For a history of irrigation in the West, see Worster, *Rivers of Empire* and Fiege, *Irrigated Eden*.

17 White, *It's Your Misfortune*, 142–43.

18 See Arrington, *Great Basin Kingdom*, 52–53, for early Mormon irrigation .

Courtesy of Washington State Historical Society.

Irrigation Comes to Eastern Washington; Pasco Power and Water operations.

intending that the states would hire private construction companies to construct irrigation works. The land, thus "improved," was sold to farmers who paid fees to the developers and taxes to the states. A great deal of south-central Idaho and eastern Washington was irrigated under the terms of this Act, sparking the establishment of Carnegie library applicant towns including Twin Falls and Burley, Idaho.

In 1901 the National Reclamation Act instituted another strategy for irrigating the West. The Newlands Act, as it was called for its sponsor, Nevada Congressman Francis Newlands, created a federal agency (later named the Bureau of Reclamation) charged with constructing large-scale irrigation projects. Its first effort, the Salt River Project in Arizona, led to the boom in Phoenix, which inspired construction of that city's Carnegie public library.[19] Backed by federal dollars and infrastructure, the Newlands Act eventually succeeded in bringing water to other parts of the interior

19 See chapter 7 for an account of the connection between the Salt River Project and Phoenix's library.

West also. However, in many sections lying beyond its projects' reach, settlers remained dependent on private, speculative companies.

Population Growth and the Economy of the Turn-of-the-Twentieth-Century Intermountain West

Once railroads had improved access, Indians had been banished to reservations, and large-scale irrigation had begun, land-hungry migrants began to regard the interior West with greater interest. While the US population as a whole increased 20 percent between 1900–1910, Idaho's population increased 101 percent and Nevada's 85 percent. Intermountain West segments of other states also saw disproportionate growth. Delta County and Mesa County on Colorado's western slope recorded population increases of 149 percent and 139 percent respectively during that decade, compared to Colorado's overall 48 percent increase. Wasco and Hood River Counties in eastern Oregon grew by 84.5 percent. Both the region's larger cities and its small towns experienced population explosions. Phoenix swelled from 1,900 people in 1900 to 5,544 ten years later, Tucson from 7,531 to 13,103 and Salt Lake City from 53,500 to 92,777. On a more modest scale, Nampa, Idaho, grew from about 800 in 1900 to 4,205 in 1910. Pasco, Washington, grew from 254 in 1900 to 2,082 in 1910. The most remarkable increase came in brand-new irrigation-project towns, notably Twin Falls, Idaho, which had not existed at the 1900 census but recorded a population of 5,258 in 1910.[20]

Promotion conducted by railroads, irrigation companies, states, and speculative townsite developers encouraged much in-migration. Brochures, magazines, and special edition newspapers were sent to the East, the Midwest, and Europe. Some were written in German or Russian to target particular populations, some featured classically draped women reminiscent of agricultural goddesses, and some promised overnight riches from new mines or rail development. All proclaimed the praises of this new "American Eden," suggesting that a virgin land lay waiting to make fortunes, though Frederick Jackson Turner and others had lamented the closing of the American frontier after the 1890 census.[21]

20 Population data about growth in the Intermountain West has been compiled by the author from the *Thirteenth Census of the U.S. Taken in the Year 1910*.

21 Wrobel discusses promotional rhetoric in *Promised Lands*, 58–60, including developers' exploitation of the closing-frontier motif.

Courtesy of Washington State Historical Society.

Promotional brochure cover.

What these migrants often found when they arrived was less idyllic. One historian has termed the economic development of the West as "a rickety wonder," due to the process's vast scope, its inefficiency, and its dependence on forces beyond itself.[22] The Intermountain West was hardly "open land" in economic terms, for great chunks of natural resources had already been secured by private hands. Mining speculation and railroad right-of-way had tied up large tracts of country and immense ranches had fenced open ground. In Nevada in 1900, one hundred corporations and individuals, largely based outside the state, owned 75 percent of privately held land.[23]

Such outside concerns could hold the power of life or death over new towns, as several future Carnegie communities discovered to their advantage. Green River, Wyoming, came into being when the Union Pacific chose its location for shops, thanks to a reliable water supply. A nearby community that had been hoping for railroad patronage, Benton, became a ghost town overnight. Similarly, Kalispell, Montana, supplanted the flourishing town of Demersville when the Northern Pacific changed its mind about right-of-way and enterprising residents literally picked their buildings up and relocated them to the former.[24]

Mining communities were notoriously insecure. Intermountain West history includes a litany of ghost towns once "boomed" fraudulently or on the basis of soon-played-out claims. Limited technology, labor unrest, instability in the price of minerals, accidents, and natural disasters could cripple operations. Rumors of competing bonanzas could lure whole populations away, as happened in Idaho's Clearwater in 1862, when reports of new strikes in Idaho City reduced Florence's population from 8,000 to 2,000 in one week. Florence's merchants were left with $40,000 of unsold inventory, and small businessmen went bankrupt along with their community.[25] Forty or fifty years later such high hopes and catastrophic downturns could still impact mining community history, as the Carnegie library application stories of Baker City, Oregon; Beaver, Utah; Goldfield, Nevada; and several other Intermountain West communities reveal.

---

22 White, *It's Your Misfortune*, 285.

23 Ibid., 268.

24 Parker, *Early Days of Green River Schools*, 1 and Elwood, *Montana and the Upper Flathead Valley*, 12–14.

25 Conlin discusses this migration—and its attendant disaster for storekeepers—in *Bacon, Beans, and Galatines*, 107–8. See also Elsensohn, *Pioneer Days in Idaho County*, 49, 54.

Despite romantic stereotypes of the small independent American farmer in the West, even those who secured their own agricultural land found their fate tied to factors beyond their control. Undercapitalized private irrigation companies often promised more—and sooner—than they delivered. Farmers deeply in debt for start-up supplies waited impatiently for dams, canals, and headgates to be constructed as their grubstakes dwindled. When works were up and running, less water than anticipated might be delivered due to corporate ineptitude or drought. During the dry years in the first two decades of the twentieth century, even Idaho's Snake River sometimes ran out of water before it reached the irrigated tracts of the Magic Valley. Farmers in the Minidoka and Twin Falls areas were left to watch their crops parch. As more farmers went bankrupt, irrigation fees skyrocketed in a vicious circle.[26] "Long and acrimonious . . . quarrels" between water users and water suppliers were common, and one estimate suggests that 90 percent of Carey Act companies were "in financial distress" by 1900.[27]

Changes to the ecosystem introduced by overgrazing and irrigated agriculture further undermined farmers' and ranchers' efforts. Useful bunchgrass disappeared and land eroded. Seepage brought toxic salts to the surface and made land unusable. Weed and invasive tree species, rabbits, and destructive insects flourished in the new conditions.[28]

Moreover, farmers found their ability to profit from their crops compromised by their dependence on middlemen and distant markets. Railroad freight charges were unregulated and subject to abrupt escalation, leaving farmers with the choice of either paying or failing to sell their crops. National panics and depression dropped wheat prices repeatedly in the late-nineteenth and early-twentieth centuries. Borrowing and foreclosures became endemic; beginning in the 1880s Western states led the nation in per capita debt.[29] "Only the one-in-a-thousand [irrigation-project farmers] ever succeeds," wrote Idaho's Annie Pike Greenwood, a memoirist whose family lost its Carey Act holding.[30]

---

26 Fiege documents broken promises and economic difficulties associated with irrigation in *Irrigated Eden*, 81–116, 143–70. Gentry gives details on Twin Falls' citizens' struggles with the Twin Falls Land and Water Company in *In the Middle and on the Edge*, 203–4.

27 White, *It's Your Misfortune*, 403.

28 Fiege, *Irrigated Eden*, 42–80.

29 White, *It's Your Misfortune*, 263.

30 Greenwood, *We Sagebrush Folks*, 6.

The populations in agricultural districts consequently shared the restlessness which historians have identified as characteristic of American frontiers.[31] When settlers deemed that lands in the Boise Valley "seemed to promise as much wealth as the mines," according to Dean May, "they were quick to stake a claim" but were also "quick to sell if they found that the soils were being depleted or if a new opportunity beckoned elsewhere."[32] Even professional men in the Intermountain West frequently relocated to seek better opportunities and/or greater security, as Carnegie library application correspondence demonstrates.[33]

Sunnyside, Washington, provides an instructive case study of the effect of outside economic influences on Intermountain West communities. Sunnyside was incorporated with high hopes in 1893 after new irrigation projects seemed to indicate that land in the Yakima Valley of eastern Oregon would soon prove a profitable investment. Before the year was out, however, the national panic of 1893 halted development and all but seven families fled. The townsite company declared bankruptcy, and the area languished. Five years later, as economic conditions slowly improved, a Christian cooperative bought Sunnyside as a speculative venture. In 1907, as irrigation construction began in earnest nearby, the town was re-incorporated. The chief engineer of the Washington Irrigation Project fortuitously bought property in Sunnyside and became a booster; his wife assumed leadership of the new women's civic improvement club. Businessmen formed a commercial club, produced a promotional brochure, and lobbied for a rail connection. When a Northern Pacific line actually arrived, a burst of civic improvement projects began, including a Carnegie library application. By 1910 Sunnyside boasted a comfortable 1,379 people—and a Carnegie library under construction. Visitors expressed amazement at the "rapid development" of the town, "which seven years ago was practically a sage brush desert."[34]

31 Hines, *Community on the American Frontier*, 152.

32 May, *Three Frontiers*, 282.

33 Boorstin notes the "transferable loyalties" of community builders on the American frontier (*The National Experience*, 122). Such mobility was not limited to a single class: one of the most respectable men described in subsequent chapters of this book, Judge James Beatty (husband of Mary Beatty, who was active in Idaho Carnegie grants [chapter 6]) moved frequently, as did one of the most shady, J. Challen Smith (chapter 8).

34 Sheller, "Sunnyside at Sixty," *Sunnyside (WA) Sun*, Aug. 26, 1909.

As the introduction to this book suggested, establishing the infrastructure necessary to support such rapid growth strained local resources and inflated tax burdens. Though more abruptly developed than some other Intermountain West communities, Sunnyside was hardly alone in incurring debts for multiple civic improvements (including a water system, an electric light plant, and a city hall) at the time of its Carnegie library application. Union, Oregon, had just issued bonds for a $50,000 high school and Klamath Fall, Oregon, was constructing a county courthouse.[35] Municipal debt in Hamilton, Montana, was so large that the newspaper editor offered special pleading as the town considered a Carnegie library application. Readers should not be afraid to support the project on fiscal grounds, an editorial asserted, because the city's deficits were temporary, the result of multiple worthy one-time improvements. Moreover, the city was economizing by discharging the night watch officer and turning off streetlights on moonlit nights.[36]

Hamilton's citizens were apparently quieted by such arguments, for they added a library levy to their tax burdens. In other communities, however, applications foundered on what we'd call today tax payers' rebellions—grass-roots protests in the Tea Party style. In Bountiful, Utah, citizens balked at supporting not only a library but also a new irrigation district in 1910, complaining that they were already overtaxed for new waterworks and cement sidewalks. Some old-timers in the community are reported to have remarked that "the railroad and telegraph had not been particularly beneficial to them, so why should they support other proposed changes?" "The council meetings were one continual complaint after another," a historian concludes, and civic leaders never brought the Carnegie application up for a vote, even though they'd received a promise.[37] In Coeur d'Alene, Idaho, citizens protested a Carnegie library tax when the city council simultaneously proposed building a municipal electrical plant (the private contractor the city had been using had just raised rates exorbitantly). "The public funds have been spent with a lavish hand in county, city, and school district," proclaimed an editorial in the local newspaper, predicting that any official who promoted higher taxes would "be spotted by the people for slaughter at

35 Letter from Mary L. Hill to Andrew Carnegie, Apr. 3, 1911, CCA and Drew, *The Great Courthouse Battle*, 28.

36 *(Hamilton, MT) Ravalli Republican*, Aug. 21, 1914.

37 Foy, *The City Bountiful*, 149–65.

the next election." When the city's librarian suggested that, since Carnegie had already issued a tentative promise, the city should move ahead with a library, the editor turned his discontent on that project. Even the city's currently modest public library, he wrote, "is proving quite a burden on account of the expense of upkeep . . . Carnegie libraries are expensive luxuries that should not be fastened upon the public." In such a hostile climate of opinion the city council would not act on Carnegie's promise, and even a 1914 mayor enthusiastic about the project advised library supporters that it would be unwise to call for a vote since success was so "unlikely" at that time. No municipal action was taken until 1922, when a new crop of officials who apparently did not know about the promise advised the library board to contact Carnegie and obtain a grant. By then, of course, the program was over. Like Bountiful, Coeur d'Alene had forfeited its Carnegie library through municipal inaction.[38]

Community Self-Promotion

The rapidly changing, economically volatile nature of life in the Intermountain West led to a paradoxical combination of braggadocio and anxiety in citizens' attitudes about their towns. Promotional bluster about western communities had been a feature of frontier settlements for many decades. Stanley Elkins and Eric McKitrick have described the intense sense of rivalry that occurred in the Old Northwest of Ohio, Illinois, and Indiana, as new small towns (500 were platted in 1835–37 in Illinois alone) competed for immigrants. "It was the promotion which gave the tone to the entire life of the town," write Elkins and McKitrick. "The town must be made attractive; it must be a suitable place to live in . . . The town must grow—it was vital to get people there and keep them there."[39]

The same spirit activated many Intermountain West communities which applied for a Carnegie library. In the region's newest, rawest towns, rhetoric supporting Carnegie libraries presented questionable superlatives. Applicants from Union, for example, sent Carnegie a promotional newspaper asserting that the community possessed "an ideal climate" in which

38 *Coeur d'Alene (ID) Evening Press*, Sept. 10, 1913, Oct. 23, 1913; letter from Mrs. Kate Hammond Fogarty to James Bertram, Jan. 14, 1914, CCA and letter from Helene G. Norton to the Carnegie Corporation, Jan. 3, 1922, CCA.

39 Elkins and McKitrick, "A Meaning for Turner's Frontier," 136–37. See also Boorstin, *The National Experience*, 115–34, 161–68.

"crop failure [was] unknown." Delta was not only termed "one of the most beautiful, prosperous, and energetic small cities in the State of Colorado," but also "one of the richest counties in the world."[40] In longer-established places, high schools (Price, Utah), county seat designations (Manti, Utah), state capital status (Boise), and self-proclaimed regional capital status (Baker City, Oregon) became the subject for bluster.

And yet insecurity lay oddly co-mingled in these claims. Two issues of the *Dillon (Montana) Examiner* published less than two months apart in 1901–02 illustrate this dissonance. The first, published on December 18, 1901, promotes the community's growth as a Northern Pacific distribution point for the Beaverhead mines. Dillon, the editor claimed, had become "the Queen City of Southern Montana," completing "one of the most progressive years in her history." With oil drilling nearby, only a city waterworks plant was missing "to fill our cup of happiness." On January 29, 1902, however, the same editor warned citizens that nearby communities were also on the make. In order to secure a permanent footprint on the ground, he cautioned, Dillon had to get busy and distinguish herself as an "attractive[ ] . . . residential town."[41]

Prosperity was the most common source of pride echoed in community self-promotion in the turn-of-the-century Intermountain West. But as the chapters that follow demonstrate, it was not the only one. Communities in rural, mostly Mormon Utah strutted their moral soundness. Longer-established communities once infamous for gambling, prostitution, and crime—including Spokane and Reno—worked to reassure the world that those "wide-open" days were over. Several Arizona communities emphasized that they were no longer Hispanic "mud villages" but true "American cities." The constant is that all these campaigns, like those that were economically based, were inspired and fueled by the perception of rapid change.

The Role of Women in Civic Improvement

While businessmen and city authorities raised the loudest voices about municipal growth, it was the women who typically contributed the kinds of civic improvements that the Dillon editor called for. As historians including Anne Firor Scott, Karen Blair, and Sandra Haarsager have documented,

40 Letter from Millard Fairlamb to Andrew Carnegie, July 1, 1907, CCA.

41 *Dillon (MT) Examiner*, Dec. 18, 1901, Jan. 29, 1902.

late-nineteenth-century and early-twentieth-century women in the West, like their counterparts across America, formed associations that deeply impacted not only their own lives but also the nature of their communities and the politics of their states. In the recently settled Intermountain West, these women's clubs played an especially important role.

Multiple roots of the club movement have been suggested, including early nineteenth-century benevolent societies, charitable groups associated with the Civil War, reforming organizations including the WCTU, a woman's literary society in Michigan, and New York's Sorosis Club, founded by a prominent female journalist in 1868. What is clear is that by 1890 enough clubs existed to inspire the organization and first biennial meeting of the General Federation of Women's Clubs. By 1910, as the movement spread across America and states and larger cities organized their own federations, more than a million women belonged to a woman's club.[42]

These organizations typically began as self-improvement ("self-culture") study clubs but transitioned into activist organizations targeting the larger community. They worked to bring civic improvements that would enhance the quality of life on a local level and on the state level; they became political activists supporting protective laws crucial to women and children. Scholars have suggested that such clubs enhanced their members' political astuteness and power long before the nineteenth amendment. As the women presented results of study and debated social questions, as they lobbied for causes and learned the process by which laws were made or changed, they inevitably gained confidence and claimed a more public presence. And they achieved incredible success, though their contributions have received little notice until recent years. They lobbied for laws protecting workers, for reform in the treatment of the insane, for pure food legislation, and for public education. They established children's hospitals, kindergartens, settlement houses for immigrants, and women's dormitories at universities. They also supported "comfort stations" for women in downtown districts and public parks.[43]

Women's clubs' often established particularly high contemporary profiles in the new communities of the Intermountain West, where city officials had little time for or interest in quality-of-life improvements. In Idaho

42 Wilson, *American Women in Transition,* 100.

43 Many of these activities are described in Haarsager's discussion of Seattle and Tacoma women's clubs in *Organized Womanhood,* 208–25.

Idaho State Historical Society, photo #61.178.8

The Caldwell, Idaho, Women's Study Club.

Falls, for instance, the "indefatigable" Village Improvement Society members "planted the trees on C street, turned the sagebrush and weed-filled cemetery into an attractive oasis, planted flowers, cleaned canal banks and numbered the houses in the residential districts so mail delivery could be established."[44] Intermountain West women's clubs also deeply influenced judicial and legislative processes. Boise's Columbian Club invited a famous Denver judge to speak to citizens on the need for a separate juvenile justice system, an appearance that seems to have inspired the city to hire its first probation officer. Additionally, the Idaho Federation of Women's Clubs influenced civil service reform and uniform divorce laws.[45]

Initial Community Libraries in the Intermountain West

Most relevant for this study, though, is women's central role in establishing initial community libraries in the interior West. Paula D. Watson has described women's "zealous and persistent work" founding community libraries, crediting women as a gender with "the spread of the public library idea" across

44 Crowder, *Tales of Eastern Idaho*, 126.

45 Haarsager, *Organized Womanhood*, 204, 306.

America. Several sources credit women's clubs with founding the majority of public libraries in the country; one estimate goes as high as 75 percent.[46]

In Intermountain West Carnegie library applicant towns, women also played a dominant role in the establishment of pre-Carnegie libraries, though the proportion does not seem quite as high as the estimates above. Of the 78 Intermountain West Carnegie library applicant communities, 59 held pre-Carnegie libraries, but information about who founded them is available for only 47. Still, of those 47 pre-Carnegie initial community libraries where agency can be attributed, an impressive two-thirds were women's club projects (31 of 47).

Such early libraries were almost always subscription libraries, institutions that charged modest dues for the privilege of taking out books (as opposed to "free libraries" where any resident was granted free access). Maintaining such private libraries inevitably burdened those who staffed them, almost universally volunteers rather than paid professional librarians, almost universally women. In club-run libraries, members typically took turns during the scattered hours of opening—a few evenings or afternoons a week and perhaps Saturdays. Quarters were makeshift: a room located in private home or merchant, a vacant building nobody else had use for, or—for the fortunate—a room in city hall. Space was at a premium in most early libraries. Pocatello patrons, for example, could not read their books in the actual "library"—a club member's fourteen-by-fourteen-foot front room—because there was no room for tables and chairs.[47]

Money to support the operations was also limited, and women's clubs worked tirelessly to support their beloved libraries. Typical of them were the women of Union, Oregon, who, as Amy Scibird wrote to Carnegie with a mixture of pride and desperation, had kept their library open "by a hard struggle and without any help from the town authorities. . . . We gave cooked-food sales, teas, dinner, socials, home-talent plays, everything we could think of to raise money to buy books and to pay a competent person to take charge."[48]

Despite such heroic patronage, women like Scibird typically did not direct Carnegie library applications when it became time to turn a

46 Watson, "Founding Mothers," 235.

47 Schedule of Questions from Pocatello, ID, CCA and letter from Dr. Minnie Howard to Andrew Carnegie, Dec. 11, 1903.

48 Letter from Amy Scibird to Andrew Carnegie, Mar. 11, 1911, CCA.

pre-existing community library into a grander institution. In only about 20 percent of Intermountain West communities (16 of 78) did women take and retain charge of ongoing correspondence with Carnegie (though many wrote initial inquiry letters or supporting letters). Neither did they claim roles as lead public spokespeople for the projects, or shape the local "spin" put on the institution, or lead building committees, or make key decisions about library architecture or site.

Chapter 6 of this book will examine why those 20 percent of communities might have formed an exception to this rule, arguing that women's dominance in Carnegie library building applications was not the result of chance. Rather, it will suggest that (as in the other paradigms of support for Carnegie libraries in the Intermountain West) a particular constellation of features involving local history, population, and economic and cultural life—as well as the nature of the women themselves and their clubs—aligned in these sixteen communities to make female leadership seem not just appropriate, but inevitable.

"Local Elites"[49]

One final feature of Intermountain West culture particularly relevant to Carnegie library building grant applications involves demographics. Who were the citizens of this new and rapidly evolving region? Did they have a distinctive intellectual affinity for books and reading that might account for the high rate of success of applications in the interior West?

If one attempted to answer these questions by reading only application letters to Carnegie, one might well conclude that the region did indeed hold an extraordinarily high percentage of exceptional citizens—people who, if they weren't yet wealthy, constituted an intellectual, cultural, and moral elite. A correspondent from Hood River, Oregon asserted to Carnegie that the town's inhabitants came "mostly from the cities of Eastern and Middle United States, and have been accustomed and trained to the use of large libraries. The high average grade of intelligence of the citizens is a matter of general comment in a complementary way." He assured Carnegie as evidence of this claim that 700 copies of Portland's three daily newspapers were "sold regularly in this city."[50] A letter from Hamilton, Montana, similarly

49 The phrase "village elites" is Hine's (*Community on the American Frontier*, 150).

50 Letter from J. O. Laughlin to Andrew Carnegie, Dec. 18, 1901; Jan. 29, 1902, CCA.

boasted that its population was "almost entirely eastern people of a superior class who appreciate books and the advantages of an older country."[51] Even tiny Milton-Freewater, Oregon, one of the newest of the region's agricultural towns, claimed to hold citizens "in moderate circumstances but above average in culture and reading habits."[52]

In fact, a small layer of true "eastern people of a superior class"—truly cultivated and wealthy people—did exist in some Intermountain West communities. Phoenix's Carnegie library application leaders were particularly distinguished: Benjamin Fowler, a wealthy landowner with enough clout to personally influence federal reclamation policy, and developer Dwight B. Heard, heir to the largest hardware company in America, both of whom had come to Phoenix for their health.[53] The same was true in Evanston, Wyoming, where influential US Senator Clarence Clark engineered a Carnegie grant, and in Prescott, Arizona, where cosmopolitan Julia Goldwater, daughter-in-law to the famous family, was a prime mover.

In most communities, however, the top tier constituted what has been more properly called a "local elite"—a group of solidly middle- and upper-middle class families and individuals. Some had helped found their communities and dominated local politics, like Nampa, Idaho's "pioneer horticulturist" Mark Anthony Kurtz and his wife Belle, who drew their wealth from large landholdings, and Belle's compatriot in Nampa's Carnegie library application, Mrs. E. H. Dewey, married to the son of the man who organized the town.[54] Professional men and women who supported Carnegie libraries also numbered in this group, among them were doctors Minnie Howard (Pocatello) and C. T. Hackett (Enterprise, Oregon); lawyers Emmett Callahan (Baker City, Oregon) and Bertha Stull Green (Mountain Home, Idaho); teachers S. P. Eggertsen (Provo, Utah) and Ethel Bear (Delta, Colorado); and clergyman P. R. Keplinger (Rock Springs, Wyoming). Many prosperous small businessmen also claimed membership in village elites, including W. Zenas Smith (Twin Falls, Idaho) and Rufus Woods (Wenatchee, Washington). In rural Utah, holding a leadership position in the Mormon Church (as did D. H. Morris of St. George) was as important as income level.

51 Letter from Mrs. J. F. Sullivan to Andrew Carnegie, Aug. 31, 1912, CCA.

52 Letter from Sabra L. Nason to James Bertram, Sept. 29, 1921, CCA.

53 Johnson, *Directing Elites*, 17–20.

54 White discusses civic leadership and local politics in the West in *It's Your Misfortune*, 363–64. Kurtz and Dewey are described in F. G. Cottingham's "History of Nampa and Vicinity."

Many of these people were indeed cultured, but evidence from some letters to Carnegie should inspire skepticism about claims of universal sophistication. Consider, for example, Ray Gundmunsen, a Cassia County Recorder living in Burley, Idaho, who first misspelled Carnegie's private secretary's name as "James Burtram," then complained, "I suppose that it will be necessary to send you tentative plans for inspection" after he had already received very clear instructions to that effect. When presented with a routine request for accurate assessment figures, Gundmunsen protested the effort involved: "We would have to go to the old books and compile it every bit and the corporation stuff and all personal property."[55] Others elected by their communities to communicate with Carnegie were charmingly unprofessional, including the woman from Goldendale, Washington, who signed her letters "Your Friend, Louise Dorman," and the librarian from Cedar City, Utah, who included stamps for Carnegie's reply.[56] Beyond correspondents' own words, the ever-present patent medicine advertisements and tabloid-style gossip on the front pages of community newspapers across the region suggest a gullibility and sensational taste in at least some of the "superior class" of citizens who consumed these pages.

The people who led Carnegie applications in the Intermountain West seem to have been very much like the middle class people whom library history scholars have identified as the moving forces behind the vast majority of libraries across America. While these people varied in the exact stratum of the "middle class" they inhabited, they were clearly not the "most aspiring poor" Carnegie had sought to reach through his libraries.[57] Nor were they ever people of color, Native Americans, or recent immigrants to the United States, a pattern of ethnic homogeneity of library application leadership consistent with other regions.[58]

That wasn't because the interior West's communities weren't diverse. New western historians long ago established that fact, and the data is still

55 Letter from Ray Gundmunsen to James Bertram, Feb. 19, 1916, CCA, May 18, 1917, CCA.

56 Letter from Louise Dorman to Andrew Carnegie, Jan. 20, 1913, CCA and letter from Mrs. E. C. Watson to R. A. Franks, Feb. 1, 1912.

57 This phrase comes from Carnegie's essay "Wealth," it is quoted in Wall, *Title of Work*, 808.

58 Carnegie did provide grants for a number of "Negro branch libraries" in southern towns, but requests for such institutions came not from African Americans themselves but from white city officials (Bobinski, *Carnegie Libraries*, 80–82).

accumulating. Some Intermountain West Carnegie communities were actually among the most diverse in the region. The mining town of Price, Utah held not only Eastern Europeans, Italians, and Finns, but enough Greeks to warrant construction of an elaborate Orthodox church.[59] African Americans lived not only in the region's larger cities (Salt Lake, Spokane, and Reno) but in railroad towns like Pocatello. Hispanic men and women made up substantial segments of the populations of Arizona applicant communities. But these groups did not participate in Carnegie library applications.

Nor did the underclass present in these communities. One doesn't hear much about the working class, the unemployed, or the disorderly in Carnegie library application correspondence outside of vague contentions that the requested library will morally benefit wintering miners, young working men with no wholesome places of recreation, and the occasional delinquent youth. But somebody had to be going to all those saloons that community histories document, and it couldn't have been just transients. Somebody had to be patronizing the brothels in Boise that the Columbian Club helped close down, and regularly visiting the much more extensive red light districts in Reno and Spokane.

Piecing together Carnegie library application stories from disparate sources reveals that significant cultural fractures could exist even between the village elites and other solid Anglo citizens. The oligarchy that directed the application in allegedly reader-rich Hood River, Oregon, for example, found its progress toward "an emblem of the intellectuality of our community" abruptly halted by a taxpayers' revolt they hadn't seen coming. Their library rally supporting municipal bonds to purchase a site had seemed such a success that the *Hood River Glacier*'s editor had gushed that "If but an atom of the enthusiasm" shown at the meeting manifested itself in the vote, the library was a sure thing. The tally, though, was 254 against issuing bonds, with only 235 in favor.[60] While Hood River's Carnegie library proponents managed to buy a site themselves and donate it to the city, grassroots obstruction killed applications in several other Intermountain West communities, including Bountiful, Utah, and Coeur d'Alene, Idaho, as noted above.[61]

59 Powell, "Coal Industry," 132.

60 *History of Hood River County*, 121 and *Hood River Glacier*, April 3 and 17, 1913.

61 See chapter 7 for more detail on the Hood River application.

These, then, were the socio-cultural circumstances that Intermountain West Carnegie library applicants faced when they attempted to garner local support for their projects. The next chapter suggests a further set of challenges imposed by Carnegie himself via the multi-part, labor-intensive formal application process, a system some Intermountain West library supporters found every bit as obstructionist as the most obtuse members of their own communities.

2

The Challenging Process of Applying for a Carnegie Library Building Grant

"A hard matter for amateurs"

ANDREW CARNEGIE CHANGED AMERICAN PUBLIC LIBRARY HISTORY IN 1898 when he began offering funds "wholesale" from his vast fortune for the construction of free public library buildings. Before that date Carnegie had donated library construction funds on an *ad hoc* basis to a few towns and cities well known to him, including his home town of Dunfermline, Scotland, and Allegheny and Homestead, Pennsylvania, where he had business interests. Now the possibility of a grant existed for any community in America which would apply. Over the next twenty years, Carnegie public library building grants had funded construction of 1,679 new public library buildings in 1,412 communities, many of them places that had never before possessed a purpose-built library.

The need for Carnegie's assistance was particularly great in the Intermountain West, where in 1898 only *one* applicant community, Salt Lake City, housed its public library in a building constructed with library service in mind.[1] As the previous chapter suggested, a quarter of Intermountain West applicant communities had no library at all when they approached Carnegie. Of the communities that did offer library service, only about half of the institutions were municipally supported and free to borrowers. The

1 Salt Lake City sought Carnegie funds not to replace this extant library—which was relatively new and perfectly adequate—but to fund construction of a branch library in a working-class neighborhood, as discussed in chapter 5.

rest led a tenuous existence, relying on subscription fees, fundraisers, and overworked volunteers.

Carnegie library building grants were consequently desirable to public library proponents in the Intermountain West. But they weren't easy to win. As applicants walked through the rigid and complex set of steps Carnegie required, they found their abilities to find facts, persuade, organize, negotiate, and calculate tested, and their reservoirs of patience plumbed. Some became furious at what they perceived as unnecessary obstacles and deliberate obfuscation. Few emerged to stand at dedication ceremonies as naïve and energetic as when they began.

Carnegie's requirements strained the capacities of applicants from every region of the United States.[2] The circumstances of life described in the previous chapter, though, made the process particularly complicated in the interior West.

The Genesis of Carnegie Public Library Building Grants

Born in Scotland in 1835, Carnegie immigrated to the United States with his working-class parents in 1848. An energetic young man, he rose quickly from messenger boy to telegraph operator and then to division manager of the Pittsburgh Division of the Pennsylvania Railroad. He invested in oil, sleeping cars, and bridges. He added iron, steel mills, and railroads to his business interests. By 1901 he had assembled such a fortune that he sold the Carnegie Company (including Carnegie Steel and other concerns) and retired from business, embarking on a career as a philanthropist.[3]

Why Carnegie decided to become a philanthropist is much debated. He himself said that as a young man he had consciously chosen to live "that life which will be the most elevating in character." He even provided himself with a tangible reminder to stay the course of virtue: a famous memo, long preserved, that registered his youthful vow to give away his surplus, should he ever become rich. "The amassing of wealth is one of the worst species of idolitary [sic]," the young idealist wrote to his future self. Once that wealth

2 Bobinski provides many brief examples of such difficulties in *Carnegie Libraries*. See also Martin's *Carnegie Denied*, which provides extensive case studies of application failures.

3 Biographical detail about Carnegie can be found in Wall's standard work, *Andrew Carnegie*, and in Nasaw's recent *Andrew Carnegie*, which draws on newly available sources.

had been achieved, Carnegie offered this credo to others. In two essays published in the *North American Review* in 1889 (titled "Wealth" and "The Best Fields for Philanthropy"), Carnegie articulated his theory of stewardship. This "Gospel of Wealth" contended that rich men had an obligation to act as trustees for their less fortunate but worthy brethren.[4]

Some commentators have suggested that Carnegie's philanthropy was driven by less idealistic motives. In particular, the public library building grant program inspired cynics to accuse Carnegie of donating money to earn acclamation and lasting fame, and grounds for such suspicion existed, for applicant communities frequently so emblazoned their buildings with his name and hung the donor's portrait in a prominent location, though Carnegie never stipulated that such things be done.[5] J. F. Wall suggests a more subtle motive: Carnegie may have been attempting to assuage internal guilt, justifying himself *to* himself as a man who had not forgotten his roots. Carnegie came from a long line of working-class laborers. Born in a Scottish village where hand-weavers like his father had fallen in status and wage-earning capacity due to the industrial revolution, he saw early the wretchedness that oblivious manufacturers could inflict on their workers.[6] The youthful Carnegie became a supporter of the Chartist movement, a radical organization advocating of the rights of labor. Thus, Wall speculates, as an adult Carnegie might have felt guilty about his success as a capitalist who necessarily exploited labor.[7]

Whatever Carnegie's motives, he was indisputably munificent during the later years of his life, ultimately giving away nine-tenths of his wealth to causes including church organs, simplified spelling, and international peace. But it was public library philanthropy that took "first place" in his affections, as he once wrote.[8] Reading, Carnegie emphasized repeatedly in speeches and noted in his autobiography, had been valued in his family, working class though it was. His grandfather had founded an informal discussion group which functioned as the "College" of Pattiemuir, Scotland, and his father had helped establish Dunfermline's first circulating library, encouraging fellow workers to pool money for books and to read aloud

4 Wall, *Andrew Carnegie*, 224–25, 806–9.

5 Bobinski, *Carnegie Libraries*, 13, 105.

6 Nasaw, *Andrew Carnegie*, 19–22 and Wall, *Andrew Carnegie*, 47–60.

7 Wall, *Andrew Carnegie*, 812–15.

8 Ibid., 808 and Bobinski, *Carnegie Libraries*, 3.

to each other as they worked.[9] Carnegie attributed his personal interest in books to an informal godfather, Colonel James Anderson of Allegheny, Pennsylvania, a wealthy man who opened his library to working boys.[10]

Carnegie's interest in public libraries also had an ideological basis in Carnegie's abiding admiration of American democracy. It was that system, Carnegie insisted in writings including *Triumphant Democracy* (1886), that had allowed him to make his fortune after his family immigrated to America. In a democratic country, opportunities for bootstrap self-improvement existed that would have been unthinkable in the old world.[11] Possessing ambition was of course crucial, as was hard work. But another key to seizing American opportunities, Carnegie believed, was the kind of education only books could provide. He'd been lucky to find a patron who allowed him such access and now he'd become such a patron providing access for others. The public library, he assured one grant applicant, "outranks any other one thing that a community can do to benefit its people . . . It is the never failing spring in the desert."[12]

Whatever his motives, Andrew Carnegie moved from the "retail" giving phase he'd begun in 1886 to the "wholesale" opportunity he announced in 1898. Report of the proffered largesse spread through newspapers, magazines, and the channels of the new American Library Association organized by Carnegie's friend Melvil Dewey. Soon applications were flooding in at the rate, one biographer suggests, of four hundred to five hundred every day.[13]

Carnegie's Assistants

During the earliest years of the program Carnegie personally reviewed requests for public library building funds. As the number of applications bourgeoned, however, he authorized his trusted private secretary James Bertram to make recommendations, although Carnegie continued to vet grants. Born in Scotland in 1872, Bertram became Carnegie's secretary in 1897, immediately before the second phase of library giving began. He'd returned to Scotland after ill health forced him to retire from railroad administration work in South Africa. Back in the northern hemisphere he

---

9 Bobinski, *Carnegie Libraries*, 11–12.

10 Wall, *Andrew Carnegie*, 19–20.

11 Ibid., 106–7.

12 Ibid., 106–7, 443–47.

13 Ibid., 118–19, 824.

caught the eye of the Chief Librarian in Edinburgh, whom Carnegie had commissioned to hire a "confidential secretary" for him. Bertram quickly became one of Carnegie's most trusted advisors, serving as Secretary of the Carnegie Corporation from its inception in 1911 until his sudden death in 1934. Bertram considered himself "a buffer between the applicants and Mr. Carnegie"—a position he took seriously indeed.[14]

Another assistant, R. A. Franks, became Financial Officer and helped process applications after the Carnegie Corporation of New York was formed. As Financial Officer, Franks had the responsibility for distributing funds and evaluating budgets once awards were approved. In summers when Carnegie retired to his estate in Scotland, taking Bertram with him, Franks's duties broadened to the general advising of grantees. This overlap in responsibilities could cause difficulties for applicants, particularly where library design was concerned. Bertram's and Franks's views about what constituted an appropriate design sometimes varied, and applicants could find themselves forced to defend an already approved plan after Bertram returned to New York.[15] To make things more complicated, both Bertram and Franks were now and then over-ridden by Carnegie himself as he awarded a community a larger-than-allotted grant or an increase to an extant award based on the request of an influential correspondent.[16]

The Application Procedure

Though vagaries crept into actual decision-making, the application procedure itself was highly standardized, much like a federal or foundation

14 A biographical sketch of Bertram appears on the website of the Carnegie Mellon University Library, which holds an archive of his papers: http://brie.library.cmu.edu/Research/Archives/UnivArchives/BertramAid.html. See also Bobinski, *Carnegie Libraries*, 25–27.

15 Bobinski, *Carnegie Libraries*, 34. Pocatello, Idaho, became the victim of such disagreement when the city requested funds in 1917 to expand its original 1907 Carnegie library. Bertram rejected the request for expansion, arguing that the original design had been flawed, resulting in unnecessarily cramped quarters. Although a correspondent pointed out that Franks (who had approved the original plans) had called the arrangement "admirable," Bertram stood fast, arguing that he himself "would not then have commended" the plans, and the request died. See letter from R. A. Franks to Dr. Minnie F. Howard, July 5, 1907, CCA and letter from James Bertram to Walter E. Siders, April 24, 1917, CCA.

16 As later chapters describe, several Intermountain West communities, including Boise and Phoenix, benefitted from such largesse.

grant application today. The exact steps did change over time as Carnegie and Bertram became aware of potential confusion, loopholes, and outright exploitation on the part of particular communities, but all applicants at any given point in time had to satisfy the same requirements in the same order.

The Initial Inquiry Letter

During the wholesale phase of library giving Carnegie did not approach communities; they were required to approach him. Applications began with inquiry letters requesting that a community be considered for funds. Bertram would respond to anyone who composed an inquiry letter, including curious private citizens as well as public officials, library board members, or club members.

Like their peers in other parts of the United States, Intermountain West correspondents tended to compose these initial letters as if these simple documents alone could win grants.[17] In truth Carnegie hardly cared about the detailed profiles of their communities and earnest arguments many presented; his awards were ultimately based on objective measures including current state of library service, population, and ability to meet financial requirements.

But present such arguments they did, detailing why their communities needed and would clearly use a library. One of the most common themes was a community's moral status, though the writers of inquiry letters in the Intermountain West, like their counterparts elsewhere, apparently disagreed about the relative effectiveness of claiming high and low ground. Some, including writers from Moscow, Idaho, and Delta, Colorado, cited the number of churches in their communities to impress Carnegie. Others trumpeted their lack of saloons, and places like Sunnyside, Washington, that had somehow managed *never* to hold a saloon, emphasized that distinguishing fact.

Other correspondents, in contrast, seem to have believed that suggesting immanent moral peril would be the most effective strategy. The initial inquiry letter from Rock Springs, Wyoming, informed Carnegie that the town was full of single working miners and clerks, men who had "no place to spend their evenings, except in Public places, particularly saloons or dance halls, where they are exposed to the drink habit more than is best for

17 Bobinski presents an overview of typical rhetoric in *Carnegie Libraries*, 35–36.

them."[18] Other writers guessed that as a capitalist Carnegie would be more concerned with the economic status of applicant towns than with their virtue, that he was looking for go-getter sorts of places likely to offer a good return on his money. Such letters tend toward the enumerative, like this one from Kalispell, Montana:

> Kalispell has Macadamized streets, a complete system of Waterworks and sewerage, both drainage and sanitary, which cost over two hundred thousand dollars, Telephone, Electric Light, power for which is furnished by a recently developed water power of 2000 Horse Power . . . During the past year thirteen 2 and 3 story brick business blocks have been erected, and over one hundred dwellings, and in 1900, half as many business blocks and an equal number of dwellings were erected . . . It has nine Churches, two large brick School buildings, and a new and thoroughly equipped free County High School occupying a building of its own, with a total school enrollment of twelve hundred in the three school buildings; two National Banks with a combined capital and surplus of $200,000.00, and deposits of nearly $1,000,000.00 . . . The agricultural output for 1901 is conservatively estimated at one million dollars. The lumber output for the year will be one hundred and twenty-five million feet. Twelve miles from Kalispell, Mr. J. J. Hill, President of the Great Northern Railway Company has just completed an extensive plant for preserving Ties for his Railroad whose output will be one million ties per annum.[19]

To supplement such narrative documentation, Intermountain West correspondents frequently enclosed the "booster editions" of their newspapers alluded to in the previous chapter. Hyperbolic by nature, booster editions featured impressive profiles of leading citizens and illustrations of churches, schools, and flour mills which made those structures look as impressive as possible. They made improbable assertions about the community's ideal climate and presented best-case statistics about tons of apples grown or of copper shipped. They alleged population growth that census figures do not bear out. Bertram's eyes must have often glazed over.

A contrasting strain of economic rhetoric emphasized need rather than current prosperity. Like their peers who frankly confessed that their communities were not morally perfect, these writers apparently worried that

---

18 Letter from Millard Fairlamb to Andrew Carnegie, July 1, 1907, CCA and letter from Col. R. Harvey Reed to Andrew Carnegie, Mar. 13, 1903, CCA.

19 Letter from J. K. Edwards to Andrew Carnegie, Nov. 29, 1901, CCA.

Courtesy of Washington State Historical Society.

"Conspicuous Prosperity": shipping apples, Wenatchee, Washington.

presenting themselves as too accomplished might suggest they didn't really need Carnegie's money. Writers in this category took pains to demonstrate that their communities were cash-poor (though, of course, worthy in all other ways). An initial inquiry letter from Grand Junction, Colorado, informed Carnegie that "There is not one rich person or capitalist here, every citizen works for his living, and for the development of the country. There is not one able to give us a donation."[20] A correspondent from Twin Falls, Idaho, tempered his description of new school buildings and paved roads by pleading that such improvements had left the town cash-poor. "The burden of taxes," he wrote, "is very heavy as it is bound to be where so many improvements have to be built all at once—improvements that many other towns spend 20 or more years in building."[21]

A third bifurcated theme in initial inquiry letters was cultural resources or their lack. To demonstrate to Carnegie that his community deserved

20 Letter from Mrs. B. F. Jay to Andrew Carnegie, Nov. 29, 1901, CCA.

21 Letter from W. Zenas Smith to Andrew Carnegie, July 17, 1913, CCA.

a library, one correspondent described the town's recently constructed $60,000 high school.[22] Others emphasized the scarcity of such institutions, including the writer from Evanston, Wyoming, who informed Carnegie that "Here . . . is a region as large as the State of New York without a college, an academy, or a public library."[23]

As they constructed their arguments, the writers of initial inquiry letters from Intermountain West communities anticipated that negative regional stereotypes might cripple their applications. In a period when fraudulent Western investment schemes were common and notorious, they took pains to assure Carnegie that their communities were not speculative ventures, but stable entities. "I assure you that you have a live place substantially built and not feeding on any speculations like a great many new towns in the West, in the town of Burley," wrote Cassia County Recorder Ray Gundmunsen about a dusty southern Idaho settlement carved by Carey Act funds from the desert only a decade before.[24] Correspondents from mining towns, a genre of communities especially given to being "bubbled," sounded the theme of stability with particular emphasis. The correspondent from Wallace, Idaho, assured Carnegie that the town was located "in the heart of the Coeur d'Alene mining district which is, as you know, the greatest lead producing district in the United States. The stability of the district is assured for years to come, as new prospections are being opened up constantly, and old ones are showing fresh veins of the metal."[25]

Assertions of an exceptional citizenry addressed the stereotype of westerners as rough frontiersmen or rubes. Correspondents seemed especially sensitive on this point, lashing out at any hint of condescension, as did Ellensburg, Washington's, J. C. Hubbell:

> It seems to be necessary in some cases to let you people back east know who you are dealing with. I was graduated from Williams College in the class of 1885, and my family live in New York state. I have a brother who is manager at Garden City of the Garden City Company,

22 Letter from Frank Stanley to Andrew Carnegie, June 13, 1917, CCA and letter from J. K. Edwards to Andrew Carnegie, Nov. 29, 1910, CCA.

23 Letter from C. S. Baker to Andrew Carnegie, Feb. 7, 1902, CCA.

24 Letter from Ray Gundmunsen to James Bertram, Feb. 19, 1916, CCA.

25 Letter from Sabelle W. Gyde to Andrew Carnegie, Jan. 31, 1908, CCA. A correspondent from Rock Springs made an argument for his community's exceptionality by contrasting it to "the average Western Coal Mining Town," whose mines are quickly "worked out," see letter from George A. Murphy to James Bertram, Nov. 25, 1907, CCA.

Rail station in Burley, Idaho.

> and you can find out all about me from Mr. Edmund Seymour, 45 Wall St., New York City.[26]

No matter what claims or defenses they offered, all writers of initial inquiry letters received the same treatment. Return mail eventually brought a form termed the "Schedule of Questions."[27] This matter-of-fact request for objective information formed a crux in the application process. If a community provided satisfactory answers, it would win a conditional promise of a building grant. If not, the case was hopeless without considerable further argument.

Filling out the "Schedule of Questions" with even the vaguest attempt at accuracy required consultation of public records, so municipal officials were brought into the process at this point, even if a private citizen or a club had submitted the initial letter.[28] Required information included

26 Letter from J. C. Hubbell to James Bertram, Nov. 16, 1908, CCA.

27 "Eventually" could stretch to months due to the volume of mail Bertram handled or to his visits to Scotland in summers with Carnegie, as Intermountain West communities including Rock Springs discovered.

28 This is the point at which the majority of women who had nurtured pre-Carnegie libraries lost control of the process. As Bobinski notes, however, Bertram *did* sometimes condescend to continue corresponding with many applicants who were not "proper authorities," so long as city officials signed the necessary paperwork. In the Intermountain West, both men and women received this privilege.

population at the last census, presence or absence of a current public library and municipal support if one existed, availability of a library building site, and money collected locally for supporting library construction. Over time, the Schedule evolved, and applicants were also required to describe an extant library's housing and the number of its books, to cite the amount the city was willing to pledge to support a Carnegie library, and to clarify the level of support allowed by state law. In some cases an annual municipal financial report was also requested along with the schedule.[29]

The seemingly innocuous population report was the schedule's make-or-break question. Towns that did not meet a minimum figure (under one thousand) were judged too small and thus not eligible for a building grant. Towns that bettered that number were offered monies at a rate based on the number of people they held, generally about $2 a head. This population-based funding soon became wide public knowledge, and applicant communities nationwide tended to exaggerate their populations out of guesswork, wishful thinking, and/or greed. In his employer's defense, James Bertram regularly verified self-reported figures against actual census records. "The local population statements, if believed, would give the United States a population of 150 million [instead of 75,994,575]," he complained in 1903.[30] When Bertram found discrepancies, he was curt. The "451" written across the top of a letter which claimed that ten thousand people lived in Wenatchee, Washington,[31] is written with ruthless precision and underlined; city officials from Twin Falls were informed that although "the great majority of cities in the West have ideas of what they are going to become," hard current numbers were the only way to justify a grant.[32]

"Hard current numbers," however, could be particularly difficult to determine even for the most honest Intermountain West applicants. Some communities, like Hermiston, Oregon, simply had *no* verifiable figures at all to report, for their application preceded their first census. Others could only show the figures of earliest settlement, though they had grown exponentially in the intervening years. Bertram inevitably reacted with incredulity to assertions of remarkable growth, telling a correspondent from

29 Bobinski, *Carnegie Libraries*, 203–4.

30 Ibid., 45–46.

31 Letter from J. W. Buchanan to James Bertram, Mar. 16, 1904, CCA.

32 Letter from James Bertram to W. Zenas Smith, Dec. 13, 1916, CCA.

Twin Falls that the 200 percent population increase claimed in one year was impossible.[33]

If a community was insistent and seemed able to make a reasonable case that a population explosion had happened between censuses, Bertram did allow alternate modes of documentation, most commonly tax valuations. But even these figures, if sloppily kept by novice city administrators, could be hard to come by. When Bertram demanded verifiable, exact figures from Ray Gundmunsen, the latter had to admit that they could not be retrieved. "For the past several years," he wrote, "the public records have not been kept in such shape as they can be readily referred to on such matters . . . The actual population of Burley is in no ones hands at this time, that is up to date."[34] In such cases Bertram refused to act, impelling communities to wait for the next census or to drop their applications.

Other communities were handicapped by the fact that censuses did not recognize the seasonal fluidity of western populations. Ranching centers like Steamboat Springs, Colorado, and mining centers like Lewiston and Wallace, Idaho, saw their populations grow substantially in the winter, when men came to town to rest and enjoy civilization until the weather again permitted work. While these seasonal transients were often the very people Carnegie application letters specifically targeted as needing the wholesome recreation a library would provide, they did not appear in the totals necessary to secure such an institution. Geography could also complicate population reporting in the interior West. While conducting the 1900 census, enumerators unfamiliar with the hilly, river-cut landscape of Spokane missed several neighborhoods, omitting eight thousand residents and qualifying the city for a Carnegie award $10,000 smaller than it should have received. Bertram at first refused to believe that a mistake had been made, protesting, "it is an extraordinary statement to make that the United States Government, in taking the census of a city, left out whole districts." But after a recount conducted by desperate city officials verified the higher number, Carnegie raised his award appropriately.[35]

Shifting legal geography was a more common cause of difficulty, for Intermountain West communities were characteristically engaged in the process of expanding their municipal boundaries during the first decades of

33 Letter from James Bertram to Stuart H. Taylor, Nov. 9, 1916, CCA.

34 Letter from Ray Gundmunsen to James Bertram, Feb. 19, 1916, CCA.

35 Letter from James Bertram to L. F. Boyd, Jan. 25, 1905, CCA and letter from L. F. Boyd to James Bertram, Feb. 1, 1905, CCA.

the twentieth century. Some had incorporated border neighborhoods since the last census and some were in the process of doing so, or planning to. Some, like Boise, were doing all three. It took a great deal of argument to convince skeptical Bertram that these areas constituted justifiable additions to a municipal total, even though the actual occupants of the districts took their status as city residents for granted.

Describing the state of current library facilities was an easier task, but one that had to be handled with diplomacy. Those that did not possess pre-Carnegie libraries held the advantage, for their need was clear. Those that did have a library faced a challenge. Demonstrating enthusiastic support of the extant institution would strengthen their case. But if they made that institution sound too solid, Carnegie might judge current facilities adequate. The typical solution was to emphasize an impressive number of books and to report lively circulation figures while presenting physical facilities in the most disparaging light possible. The inadequate size of rented or loaned rooms was often stressed, as on a "Schedule of Questions" from Ontario, Oregon, that reported a space of sixteen feet by thirty feet housing both its book collection and its reading area.[36] Free-standing buildings used as libraries were uniformly derided. A correspondent from The Dalles, Oregon, used the words "dilapidated" and "cramped" to describe that town's frame library and one from Union, Oregon, called that community's "little better than a shed."[37]

Such descriptions mirror those made by applicants from other regions of the country.[38] In some Intermountain West correspondence, however, the descriptions of extant facilities take on a distinctively Western flavor. Several correspondents, including those from The Dalles and Spokane, emphasized that current library collections were located in their frontier-style tenderloin districts, complete with prostitution and gambling. A writer from Wallace, Idaho, told Carnegie that his local library was housed "over the place where the horses are kept." As a result it presented "not a very agreeable smell" and was thus "not so inviting as the thirty saloons that we now have in Wallace, so you can see that it is of a constant struggle for us to combat these terrible downward tendencies."[39]

36 Schedule of Questions from Ontario, Oregon, CCA.

37 Letter from J. L. Kelly to James Bertram, Feb. 8, 1907, CCA.

38 Bobinski describes claims made about pre-Carnegie library buildings in *Carnegie Libraries*, 34.

39 Letter from Jasper Brower to Andrew Carnegie, Apr. 28, 1905, CCA.

Promise

If the "Schedule of Questions" demonstrated that a community met minimum requirements and needed a library, Carnegie then issued a conditional promise for a specific amount. This offer was phrased (using language reminiscent of the "on completion of requirements" formula familiar from academic graduations) in the form of a provisional contract letter. The letter Wenatchee received provides a clear example:

> Responding to yours of March 17th and other communications on behalf of Wenatchee,–if the City agrees by Resolution of Council to maintain a Free Public Library at the cost of not less than One Thousand Dollars a year, and provides a suitable site for Bilding [sic], Mr. Carnegie will be glad to give Ten Thousand Dollars to erect a Free Public Library Bilding for Wenatchee.[40]

Despite the terse phrasing and the strange simplified spelling (an enthusiasm of Carnegie's, stipulated to his employees), Intermountain West promise letters were commonly reprinted *verbatim* in local newspapers, as if Carnegie had effusively commended the town on its worthiness. Editorials congratulated the negotiators and proclaimed the community's validation and bright future. Some recipients even sent thank-you notes to Carnegie, like the note from Clarkston/Vineland, Washington, which informed Carnegie (with some understatement given the local hue and cry the offer inspired), "The people are very much pleased with your offer."[41]

Further Negotiation of Promise Amount

Gratitude did not prevent a large proportion of Intermountain West communities (like communities across the country) from attempting to bargain for more money. As suggested above, some communities complained about inaccurate census figures (Spokane) and/or predicted inevitable growth (Ontario). Others argued citizens' willingness to pay higher library taxes (Preston, Idaho) or contended that the amount of Carnegie's offer, while probably adequate elsewhere, would not be enough to cover particularly exorbitant local building costs (St. George, Utah). In most cases, these appeals came to naught.

40 Letter from James Bertram to Howard Thomas, Mar. 27, 1909, CCA.

41 Letter from W. E. Howard to James Bertram, Feb. 13, 1912, CCA.

A new census that reported population growth in mid-application was no assurance of an increased stipend, as Grand Junction, Colorado, discovered. "After Mr. Carnegie has made a gift," Bertram replied, "if towns were to come back again as their levy increases and ask for more money for extension of the building . . . Mr. Carnegie's work would never be done. Life would not be worth living."[42] Grand Junction was forced to build a library with funding based on ten-year-old statistics.

Now and then the amount was raised, sometimes based on strong evidence or the presence of an influential mediator, sometimes apparently by whim. North Yakima, Washington, saw its original promise of $10,000 raised to $15,000 based on 1905 valuation figures.[43] Phoenix's award expanded after local library proponents enlisted Charles Walcott, Director of the US Geological Survey and a man known personally to Carnegie, to testify to the city's inevitable growth. "With the completion of the Tonto reservoir on Salt River four years from now, the irrigable land and population in and about Phoenix will be more than doubled," Walcott wrote to Bertram,[44] a claim which turned out to be true. Evanston was similarly successful after city officials solicited letters from Senator Clarence Clark, who had consistently voted in ways favorable to Carnegie enterprises.[45]

Stubbornly continuing to insist on a larger grant in the absence of such advantages, however, was a dangerous course, one that could delay an application for years or cause it to fail. Those who attempted to play that game late in the program, in particular, courted disappointment, for the granting process was suspended when America entered World War I. Communities which had never formally signaled their acceptance of a conditional promise could find their offer suspended. Smithfield, Utah, nearly lost its Carnegie offer this way; Burley and Twin Falls did.

Maintenance Levy/Resolution of Support

Once a community had received a provisional offer it was willing to accept, the first step toward accessing funds was to impose a library support tax levy. Exactly who levied this tax and how the process worked varied depending

42 Letter from James Bertram to Mrs. A. N. Jay, Sept. 4, 1905, CCA.

43 Letter from James Bertram to Grace Barrett Robinson, Nov. 5, 1905, CCA

44 Letter from Charles Walcott to Andrew Carnegie, Nov. 17, 1905, CCA.

45 As chapter 8 notes, Clark selected stationery from the US Senate Committee on Railroads, of which he was a member, for his correspondence with Carnegie. See, for example, his letter of Mar. 27, 1902, CCA.

on state law. In some states, municipal governments or county commissioners could impose a levy on their own initiative and in others officials were required to hold referendums.

The first scenario proved the smoothest for library proponents. As noted in the previous chapter, those who championed Carnegie library grants in the Intermountain West were typically members of village elites. Sometimes these people themselves held local office; often officials were their friends, business associates, or family members, people of like mind. The Carnegie library proposal presented by the women's club of Hood River, Oregon to the city council passed so summarily that "the remainder of the evening was spent socially" since so many married couples were present.[46] Only in communities where local politicians inhabited a lower segment of the middle class than library proponents (as in Pocatello, Idaho) did such applications stall.[47]

If a referendum was required, library supporters faced the more complicated task of rallying public support for the levy. Many Carnegie library proponents enlisted newspaper editors to write in support of the projects and some wrote articles themselves. In Utah, Mormon Church leaders spoke during services or other church-related activities. Pro-library mass meetings were organized and door-to-door campaigns were orchestrated. Some library supporters collected donations for a library site and/or library books from project sympathizers as they campaigned for votes so that they could assure the rank-and-file that public expenses would not multiply.

In only a small proportion of Intermountain West communities did efforts to rally public support meet with significant opposition. Economically based dissent was most common in the interior West, as Robert Sidney Martin's *Carnegie Denied* suggests, it was nationwide. Indeed, *every one* of the seven unsuccessful Intermountain West Carnegie library building grant applications failed for economic reasons.[48]

46 *Hood River Glacier*, Nov. 14, 1912.

47 See chapter 6 for a discussion of this application and another from Caldwell, Idaho, which faced the same difficulties.

48 Ideological objections to accepting a Carnegie library did surface in one unsuccessful community with a history of labor violence, Coeur d'Alene, Idaho, but contemporary newspaper stories confirm that an economic downturn proved the decisive factor. While the project was awaiting city support, citizens were so outraged at municipal indebtedness and the outrageous charges of a local power company that they organized a mass meeting to call for tax relief and threatened to dismiss any official in favor of increasing taxes for any reason. See *Coeur d'Alene (ID) Press*, Nov. 18, 1913 and Sept. 19, 1913.

The labor-based opposition to which Martin's book alludes did occasionally make its voice heard in the interior West. As Martin explains, Carnegie had gained a "reputation as one of the most brutal employers in the history of capitalism" thanks to the violent Homestead strike of 1882, during which Pinkerton guards and strikers engaged in a twelve-hour battle near one of his steel mills. Some leftists and union men thus considered his money "tainted."[49] In Wenatchee "several prominent people" sounded exactly this theme when they complained that a library building grant constituted "blood money" wrung from Carnegie's employees. In Prosser, a left-leaning newspaper editor proclaimed, "We Should be Ashamed" to take "Hush Money" from "The Steal King." In Wallace "a prominent mining man" trumpeted self-reliance. "I don't know how or where Carnegie got his money, but the people of Wallace don't want any of it, and none of the strings attached to it." Such voices, however, were decidedly in the minority, and Wallace, Prosser, and Wenatchee went happily ahead with their grants.[50]

Once a library support levy was authorized by fiat or by referendum, Carnegie required community officials to pass a formulaically phrased resolution of support, even if taxes were already being collected to support an extant library. The resolution had to be phrased so that the levy was set at exactly 10 percent of Carnegie's pledge yearly, even if the community was currently raising a higher amount than that, for Bertram feared that higher amounts might be used as claims for additional Carnegie monies. The amount had also to be stated in dollar figures to protect the fixed amount against potential local property devaluation.

By 1914, so many municipalities had gone over-budget during construction—forcing Carnegie to issue a *de facto* grant increase to insure that their libraries would be operational—that stricter language than previously required was stipulated in the resolution. In the later years of the building grant program, officials were obliged to pledge that their building would not exceed the promise amount and would be "complete and redy[sic] to occupy" at that price.[51] Community officials careless with their diction, like those in Goldendale, Washington, could find their applications delayed by months with rewriting.

49 Martin, *Carnegie Denied*, 176–67. For an account of the Homestead strike, see Wall, *Andrew Carnegie*, 547–62.

50 Gellatly, *History of Wenatchee*, 210. The remark from Wallace was reported in the *New York World*, Nov. 6, 1909 (clipping bundled with Wenatchee materials in the CCA).

51 Bobinski, *Carnegie Libraries*, 43, 47.

Site

Carnegie also required communities to demonstrate that they held clear title to a building site. Fortunate municipalities such as The Dalles already owned appropriate and vacant properties.[52] This obstacle was also easily cleared where organizations simply donated sites. This happened often in rural Utah, where the Mormon Church offered land adjacent to its own buildings. Sympathetic landowners sometimes also had property to spare, like a prominent businessman in Mountain Home, Idaho, who offered two lots for "public purposes."[53]

The majority of Intermountain West communities, however, found themselves obliged to purchase building sites. Surprisingly, raising money seems rarely to have been a problem. On occasion the people lobbying for the projects donated it themselves (Hood River, Oregon) and in other places they collected it from their fellow citizens, as happened in Sunnyside, Washington, where the people were reportedly "very generous."[54]

The greatest difficulty in many interior West communities (as elsewhere) was agreeing on a site.[55] Self-interest most often formed the root of dissention. People in the Intermountain West quarreled because they wanted libraries in their own neighborhoods, not only for convenient access, but because they believed their property values and/or neighborhood prestige would thus rise. Such disagreement frequently occurred in communities that had expanded to incorporate new additions. Settlers of longer duration feared that Carnegie libraries would become pawns in campaigns to shift municipal cores. Where the additions were markedly more prosperous than old downtowns and/or had already garnered significant institutions, class rivalry fueled contention. Three such communities, Missoula, Montana, Klamath Falls, Oregon, and Alturas, California, are discussed in chapter 9.

Even where municipal footprints had remained relatively stable, severe infighting could break out among library board members who represented rival neighborhoods. In Idaho Falls, competition accelerated until rivals actually bought competing properties and proclaimed

52 Letter from J. L. Kelly to James Bertram, Feb. 8, 1907, CCA.

53 Hepworth, "Carnegie Libraries in Utah," 42 and Groefsema, *Elmore County*, 202.

54 *Sunnyside (WA) Sun*, Aug. 11, 1910.

55 Bobinski, *Carnegie Libraries*, 41.

donations, then even presumed to ask Bertram and Franks to back their respective claims.[56]

In no case, however, did Bertram choose a site for a community. "An effort should be made to reconcile all parties," he blandly wrote to a correspondent from Idaho Falls who had pleaded for his intervention.[57] Eventually that community chose a site from among the rivals, as did all but a few Intermountain West towns which faced such internal dissention. The bitterness that resulted, however, could be severe and long lasting, as it proved in Klamath Falls.

Architectural Plans

Communities which applied for Carnegie grants in the program's first decade were free to build as they saw fit after fulfilling preliminary requirements. By 1908, however, Carnegie and Bertram had become convinced that many of the library buildings subsidized by the program had not been well designed. Money had been regularly wasted, they complained, on ostentatious ornamentation, inefficient and pretentious layout, and inconvenient reading rooms. Thus a new requirement was added to the application process, a requirement that accounted for by far the majority of delays in the construction of Carnegie libraries in the interior West. Communities were now required to submit their plans to Bertram for approval (or to Franks, if Bertram was unavailable).

To guide applicants in library design, Carnegie, Bertram, and Franks consulted with authorities in library practice and architecture and developed template plans appropriate to various funding levels. Beginning in 1911, a leaflet containing these plans, entitled "Notes on the Construction of Library Bildings," was sent with every promise letter. Through six revisions, "Notes" advised applicants on best practices regarding such matters as allocation of space, arrangement of rooms, and basement use.[58] Carnegie library architecture became relatively standardized, though considerable variation

---

56 A particularly heated five-page letter came from the Idaho Falls Development Company (signature illegible), complaining about the fact that a rival group's proposed site occupied "one of the dustiest corners in our city," exposed to prevailing southwest winds and near a railroad switching yard. See letter to R. A. Franks, Apr. 2, 1913, CCA.

57 Letter from James Bertram to Adelia Scott, Nov. 5, 1913, CCA.

58 Bobinski, *Carnegie Libraries*, 52–63.

continued to exist, as several studies have documented.[59] Communities began by working with one of these templates or by hiring architects who fashioned themselves into regional experts in Carnegie library construction, like J. E. Tourtellote of Boise.[60] Still, the peculiarities of individual sites, the building materials available or unavailable in particular places, and the preferences of library supporters inevitably led to tweaking of the templates in "Notes." And there the problems began.

Today we'd say that Bertram "micro-managed" individual Carnegie library designs; at the time, he considered himself a righteous watchdog protecting his employer from bumbling novices or exploitative grafters.[61] He dictated specific changes in major construction elements like stairway placement and size of lecture and children's rooms. He demanded that features dear to applicants but deemed inessential in New York like kitchens and clubrooms be deleted. He critiqued minor details, including proposed carpeting.[62]

These dictates were not diplomatically delivered. When North Yakima, Washington, decided that it needed to enlarge its pre-"Notes" Carnegie library and submitted a blueprint at Bertram's request, the Confidential Secretary replied in no uncertain terms,

> Mr. Carnegie is not disposed to add to the amount allowd for North Yakima Bilding, becaus the money alredy given has not provided the library accommodation which mite hav been secured. Your entrance feature, portico, etc., outside of the front line of the bilding proper, represents a considerable expenditure for which there was no need and which givs no return in accommodation. There are two stairs to the basement vestibule, neither of which was necessary . . . The stack room has been very much reduced by frittering away the accommodation in toilet, etc . . . The basement space has been simply wasted.[63]

---

59 See Van Slyck, *Free to All*, and Jones, *Carnegie Libraries Across America*.

60 Some communities ignored "Notes" and surveyed standing Carnegie library architecture in their region instead, a strategy that could backfire if the buildings in question had been constructed before 1908. Clarkston-Vineland, Washington, found its library construction significantly delayed for this reason.

61 The communication process was further complicated by the fact that Bertram refused to correspond with architects, forcing correspondents to act as go-betweens even when they expressed confusion. See letter James Bertram to Adelia Scott, Nov.5, 1913, CCA.

62 Bobinski, *Carnegie Libraries*, 63–66.

63 Letter from James Bertram to H. P. James, Jan. 17, 1912, CCA.

Bertram was particularly impatient with applicants' appeals to aesthetics, denying, for example, Garland, Utah's request that it be allowed to build a grand-looking library because a bungalow design would not "harmonize well" with the English Gothic Mormon tabernacle nearby.[64] When a correspondent from beleaguered North Yakima suggested that libraries should "educate the public in architectural beauty," he was told,

> The purpose for which Mr. Carnegie provides a Library Bilding is to secure accommodation for the housing of books, and for their being red. You cannot get Greek temple features out of an appropriation of $10,000. . . A utilitarian bilding can be erected in such good taste as to improve the taste of the community. . . Mr. Carnegie is bilding working Libraries, not temples.[65]

Special pleading based on particular local circumstances was no more sympathetically received. When St. George, Utah, moved its Carnegie library entrance from the position illustrated in "Notes" to a spot that would be shaded from the area's hot afternoon sun, Bertram protested.[66] Sunnyside was ordered to put its lavatory on the first floor rather than in the basement, even though the city had as yet constructed no sewers and the proposed design would allow the facilities to drain directly into a septic tank.[67]

In the end, most communities capitulated and emended their plans.

Bids and Construction

After Bertram or Franks approved plans, the people directing community Carnegie library building grant applications were authorized to advertise for bids from construction companies. In the Intermoutain West, these bids frequently came in over promise amounts even when applicants worked in good faith. In some cases, suitable building materials weren't available locally (Yuma, Arizona), and shipping them in by rail inflated their cost dramatically.[68] Where communities lay at a distance from rail lines and

64 Letter from R. L. Bush to James Bertram, Dec. 1, 1913, CCA.

65 Letter from G. A. Fechter to James Bertram, Jan. 29, 1912, CCA and letter from James Bertram to G. A. Fechter, Feb. 5, 1912, CCA.

66 Letter from John Woodbury to James Bertram, May 12, 1913, CCA and letter from James Bertram to John Woodbury, Dec. 14, 1914, CCA.

67 Letter from Stephen E. Chaffee to R. A. Franks, Oct. 13, 1910, CCA.

68 Letter from Frank Stanley to James Bertram, June 16, 1914, CCA. Distances from supply points also caused construction delays, as in Tucson, Arizona, where builders

materials had to be transported overland, over-runs became even higher. Bertram remained immovable in the face of such circumstances, as he was when a correspondent from St. George, Utah, pleaded that "the long haul from the railroad, 65 miles, makes the cost of building materials very much higher than in more favored places." Residents of St. George ended up raising the necessary supplement locally.[69]

Bertram made no objection to St. George's addition to Carnegie funds after the community documented its expenses. In cases where communities supplemented promises in the service of grander designs or features he deemed unnecessary, however, his wrath flared. "Why giv a pledge only to ignore it?" he thundered when the county commissioners in Umatilla County, Oregon, added $10,000 for fireproofing to Carnegie's offer of $25,000. "It would surely be futile for us to attempt to proceed with this work if pledges presumably deliberately entered into were often to be ignored." His anger was compounded when he discovered that Carnegie funds for the branch library for Milton, Oregon, had also been bolstered by the same commissioners. Umatilla County Judge Charles Marsh assured Bertram that no deception had been intended ("It is hard for me," he wrote, "to realize the seriousness of what you consider a grave error but what we had thought a very commendable act, knowing as I do the motives and the entire innocence that a mistake was being made."), but Bertram was not mollified. Carnegie would never have promised the amounts he did in Umatilla County, Bertram wrote, if he had known that money was already available there.[70]

Once such disagreements were finally ironed out, communities could collect the first of the partial payments Franks dispersed. Ground-breaking and cornerstone-laying inspired formal ceremonies in many Intermountain West communities, as in Durango, Colorado, where a contingent of Masons set the cornerstone with a silver trowel, dignitaries placed a time capsule in the cornerstone, and musical numbers, speeches, and prayers were offered.[71]

Despite such enthusiastic beginnings, the extreme Intermountain West climate frequently delayed construction. A winter "more severe than

---

waited impatiently for two months for bricks to arrive from El Paso, see *Tucson (AZ) Star*, June 30, 1901.

69 Letter from John Woodbury to James Bertram, July 14, 1914 and Sept. 24, 1915, CCA.

70 Letter from James Bertram to Charles H. Marsh, Sept. 15, 1916, CCA and letter from Charles H. Marsh to James Bertram, Sept. 28, 1916, CCA.

71 Ayres,"History of the Durango Public Library," 6.

any known for many years" stalled excavation in Clarkston/Vineland, Washington, from December 1912 to March 1913.[72] Natural disasters also caused dramatic delays, suggesting just how tenuous life in the Intermountain West could be, despite citizens' claims of comfortable permanency. Caldwell, Idaho's Carnegie application was stalled for two years after a "disastrous flood" financially crippled the city.[73] A forest fire destroyed a third of all of the taxable property and three essential bridges in Wallace in the summer of 1910, as that community was readying library plans (ironically, Bertram had recently been objecting to city fathers' request for additional monies for fireproofing).[74] Fire also slowed Prescott's Carnegie library construction when a Fourth of July fire in 1900 destroyed the town's central blocks and eighty business establishments.[75]

Such catastrophes inspired little sympathy in Bertram. Although Wallace and Prescott requested additional funds (pointing out that the cost of community rebuilding would deplete tax reserves formerly dedicated to furnishing and stocking the library), he refused to increase their promise amounts, reminding them that the corporation provided monies based exclusively on population, not special need.[76] When he learned that Prescott had temporarily halted library construction to divert manpower to town rebuilding, he went so far as to suggest impropriety. "It was likewise expected, and practically promist [sic], by Mrs. Sara Winter Kellogg in letter of March 26, 1900," he complained, "that the library bilding would be erected immediately, altho it does not seem to hav been erected for several years after Mr. Carnegie had sent the money, which instead of being used immediately was placed in the bank and held there for a considerable time."[77]

Bertram's greatest wrath was reserved for communities that over-spent pledged amounts—a relatively common occurrence in the Intermountain West—then requested compensation. When Eureka, Utah exceeded its budget for library construction, Bertram first refused to compensate the town

72 Letter from W. E. Howard to James Bertram, Mar. 11, 1913, CCA.

73 Letter from Jennie Wood to Andrew Carnegie, Dec. 19, 1911, CCA.

74 Letter from L. H. Leighty to James Bertram, Aug. 25, 1910, CCA. The great northern Idaho fire that decimated Wallace is described in Stark, "Wallace . . . City of Old Timers . . . and Millionaires," *Spokesman-Review (Spokane, WA)* June 1, 1958.

75 Toney, *The Prescott, Arizona Story*, 12 and Weiner, *Prescott Yesterdays*, 37.

76 Letter from James Bertram to L. H. Leighty, July 4, 1911, CCA.

77 Letter from James Bertram to Ziba O. Brown, Apr. 6, 1916, CCA.

Photo courtesy of Sharlot Hall Museum Library and Archives, f 2122pa.

Prescott, Arizona, after the catastrophic fire that delayed Carnegie library construction.

even for a small portion of the $4,000 which it had spent out-of-pocket. "It is a hard matter for amateurs to make any closer estimate on a $15,000 institution than we did," protested the town's mayor.[78] Only after the community submitted a meticulously itemized list of expenses did Bertram grudgingly allow reimbursement.

Citizens who worked for Carnegie public library building grants thus often encountered frustrating delays as they negotiated grant amount, site choice, library design, and budget over-runs. Only a few communities (blessed with good weather, local accessibility and/or prompt delivery of materials, and capable labor) completed their libraries within a year after initial contact with Carnegie.[79] The regional average was about four years, and some projects became discouragingly protracted. Among the longest was Idaho Falls's nine-year epic, during which nearly everything that could go wrong did, including hard-headed negotiations with Bertram for a larger

78 Letter from J. D. Stack to James Bertram, Mar. 21, 1909, CCA.

79 As did Hamilton, Montana, in a record eight months, see *Ravelli (Hamilton, MT) Republican*, Dec. 24, 1915.

promise, controversy over the site, many revisions of plans, and trouble with contractors. No wonder that, as the opening date approached, a correspondent confessed to Bertram that "some say they will not believe it until the actual work is done."[80]

Dedication

When Carnegie libraries were finally completed, nearly every community in the Intermountain West, like communities nationwide, celebrated with enthusiasm. Local holidays were declared to allow the public to tour the building and attend elaborate opening ceremonies.[81] Schoolchildren were shepherded *en masse* to such events, as when Salt Lake City's Chapman Branch library opened.[82] Local officials chronicled the history of the library movement in the community and effusively praised participants. Eminent outsiders (including the head librarian of Seattle who attended The Dalles, Oregon's dedication, and the governor and state superintendent of schools who attended Eureka, Utah's) commented on the enhancement of the community's reputation. Refreshments were served. People sang, prayed, and juggled. Parties frequently followed, as in Beaver, Utah, where the commercial club's annual "grand ball" was coordinated with opening of the town's new Carnegie public library.[83]

Intermountain West communities even occasionally invited Carnegie to share their joy by attending such festivities, but he always declined.[84] Instead, he sent personal congratulations, as when he thanked Ephraim, Utah, for its "kind message" and offered his formal "best wishes for the success of the Library and the happiness of the people in your community."[85] Some communities, including Spokane and Cedar City, Utah, settled for

80 Letter from Adelia Scott to James Bertram, May 14, 1914, CCA.

81 See, for example, the description of Prosser, Washington's celebration which opens this book. Ring has termed such events "a symbol of social bonding . . . one way of articulating a sense of community, " see,"Carnegie Libraries as Symbols for an Age," 13.

82 *Deseret News (Salt Lake City, UT)*, May 28, 1918.

83 *The Dalles (OR) Weekly Chronicle*, Sept. 23, 1910; *Eureka (UT) Reporter*, Oct. 15, 1909; *Prosser (WA) Record*, July 29, 1910; *Beaver (UT) Weekly Press*, Jan. 29, 1915.

84 As he never did for any community with which he was not personally acquainted, see Wall, *Andrew Carnegie*, 819.

85 Letter from James Bertram to P. D. Jensen, Mar. 21, 1915, CCA.

busts or portraits of Carnegie as library decorations, obtaining them with Bertram's guidance.[86]

As Carnegie library proponents regarded the completed buildings that their labors had secured for their communities, they could take pride in the having negotiated a rigorous, exacting process complicated by an irascible bureaucrat. They had also accomplished the arguably even more daunting process of mustering grassroots support for the projects—of convincing their fellow citizens that "culture" deserved tangible public support, even in inauspicious conditions and tough economic times. The remaining chapters of this book describe the various ways in which that feat was accomplished.

86 Bobinski notes that communities across the country made such requests in *Carnegie Libraries*, 52.

3

Boom Towns: Carnegie Libraries and Boosterism

"A distinct acquisition and credit to the city"

ONE POPULAR MYTH OF THE AMERICAN WEST HOLDS that the region once witnessed a golden age of idealistic support for books and reading. In the early days of settlement, as the story goes, pioneers who believed that life without literature was not worth living struggled to ensure that their new homes would have books, laboriously transporting volumes to the West and sacrificing to buy books once they arrived. According to this "books-in-every-wagon" narrative, the pure desire for reading material was so intense that Westerners who could find no other printed volumes read the dictionary, and even sheepherders customarily built bookshelves into their wagons.[1]

Certainly many early Intermountain West citizens did value books for the sheer pleasure of reading, just as many residents do today. Unfortunately for commentators who take satisfaction in proclaiming the steady decline of the human race, however, the region's Carnegie library applications suggest that less idealistic notions more often inspired support for institutions that provided the printed word a hundred years ago.

One particularly philistine—and common—theme in pro-Carnegie library rhetoric held that a Carnegie library would enhance a community's bottom line.[2] In about a quarter of Intermountain West building grant

1 Bobbie Magee Hepworth, 28 and William Targ, *The American West*, 485.

2 See Van Slyck, *Free to All*, 136; Ring, "Carnegie Libraries as Symbols for an Age"; and Swetnam, "Pro-Carnegie Library Arguments," 64–65 for discussions of economic motives in Carnegie library development.

applications, it did not occur to the men who shaped public discourse to speak idealistically about the power of books to enrich the lives of their fellow citizens or their children; they did not suggest that books could help promote democracy or bootstrap self-education. Nor did they plead their desire for personal intellectual enrichment. Instead they evoked a more literal kind of profit: the power of Carnegie libraries to provide economic advantage in the battle for municipal regional dominance. To read their words is to enter a West driven by self-interest and aggressively on the make, a reality nothing like the idealistic Jeffersonian polis of legend. If these men had carried books in their wagons, they would not have been reading them but flourishing them proudly, taunting their fellow travelers with this evidence of their own inevitable success.

So direct were the commercial metaphors these men used in conjunction with Carnegie library applications that their words seem crass. Supporters in Prosser, Washington, for example, promoted a new Carnegie library as "an investment that would repay itself many times over." Beaver, Utah's, Carnegie building was touted as "a distinct acquisition and credit to the city." In Milton, Oregon, a newspaper editor concluded, "All things equal, the merchants will receive a direct gain in dollars and cents" from the proposed Carnegie library. The structure, he explained, would encourage rural trade, drawing outlanders to Milton rather than to rival business centers because it would offer a place "where the farmer who comes to town to do his week's trading can take 'mother and the girls' to rest and refresh themselves before they begin their shopping tour of the town."[3]

The men themselves, however, would have been surprised—and hurt—by suggestions that their arguments were philistine, for to them "booster" was not a slur but a term of commendation for a most worthy vocation. By the time the Intermountain West was beginning to be settled, boosterism had been widespread in the American West for many decades, as Daniel J. Boorstin has noted, and many of these men would have grown up in communities where boosters were respected as men who worked for community stability and progress.[4] These energetic turn-of-the-twentieth-century citizens, as David Wrobel has written, possessed "psychological attachment" to their towns; they were men with "deep personal investment in lauding the

3 *Prosser (WA) Record*, Jan. 11, 1907; *Beaver (UT) Weekly Press*, Jan. 1, 1915; *Milton (OR) Eagle*, Mar. 19, 1908.

4 Boorstin, *The Americans*, 113–68.

new areas they called home because the very survival of those places, and consequently their own well-being, depended on others viewing their . . . town as a promised land and moving to it."[5] Many were merchants and/or provided services, including real estate, loan, and insurance salesman W. E. Howard of Clarkston-Vineland, Washington. Others made their livings as small-scale developers (C. Thompkins of the Prosser Falls Land and Power Company in Washington), or as bankers (C. M. Scott of Sunnyside, Washington), or as irrigation engineers (R. L. Bush of Garland, Utah). Some practiced medicine or law (Daniel Boyd of Enterprise, Oregon). Proudly self-identified as businessmen, they often chose professional letterhead for their correspondence with Carnegie ("Smith Candy Company," "Emmett Callahan, Attorney," and "Interstate Land Company: Improved Ranches and Dwellings in the City") even if they were also members of library boards or elected officials. Alternately, they used the stationery of the commercial clubs in which they associated. Today it may be hard to imagine developers as enthusiastic proponents of culture. But Intermountain West Carnegie library history admits no doubt of such participation a hundred years ago.

The following economically driven cluster of Carnegie applications is the largest this book will discuss. It is also the one with the highest failure rate in the region. Economically motivated Carnegie library building grant campaigns did succeed in fourteen communities: Baker City, Enterprise, Hermiston, La Grande, and Milton, Oregon; Beaver City and Garland, Utah; Clarkston-Vineland, Pasco, Prosser, Sunnyside, Walla Walla, and Wenatchee, Washington; and Kalispell, Montana. Unfortunately, in five other places businessmen failed to complete their libraries. In Steamboat Springs, Colorado; Burley and Twin Falls, Idaho; Palouse, Washington; and Goldfield, Nevada, businessmen received Carnegie promises, but never saw their libraries materialize. While the desire for profit could be a powerful spur to library development in this newly settled country, it could also be a risky one.[6]

5 Wrobel, *Promised Land*, 6–7.

6 While the other two failed applications—Coeur d'Alene, Idaho and Bountiful, Utah—were not primarily directed by profit-minded businessmen, economic downturns also spoiled these two applications. These conclusions about reasons for failure are mine; Martin's *Carnegie Denied* does not include any Intermountain West applications in its sample. For a comprehensive list of failed applications, see Bobinski, *Carnegie Libraries*, 116–33.

The Local Context of Economically Motivated Carnegie Applications

The men who set priorities in these nineteen communities had never seriously imagined incurring significant debt for enhanced library service until particular circumstances sparked their interest. Women's clubs had established pre-Carnegie public libraries in about half of these communities, and in a few places community leaders had even been persuaded to grant modest municipal support for these institutions, but where the women had attempted to interest their community's opinion leaders in a Carnegie application—as did the women of Baker City's Alpha Club in 1902—their efforts had come to naught.

It took a particular local Zeitgeist to interest these men in library development, a point in history where phenomenal growth occurred or was anticipated. Such a mood overtook Baker City in 1905, when a building boom anticipating a "stampede" of new immigrants began. Just three years after municipal officials ignored the Alpha Club's request, Baker City leaders themselves became energetic proponents of a Carnegie library.[7] Beaver City was in the process of expanding from a "sleeping hamlet" to "a progressive city of nearly 3,000 inhabitants" when its business leaders began an application in 1913. Enterprise's population more than doubled between the initiation of its application (1,242) and its library's completion (2,700).[8] Sunnyside nearly doubled during the *single* year that saw its Carnegie application, 1909, as did Kalispell in the year before its application (2,500 people in 1900 to 4,000 in 1901).[9] Library proponents in Goldfield, platted just four years before its application, found themselves mustering support from people who lived in tents because houses could not be built quickly enough to accommodate them.[10]

Irrigation project development was a common spur to such extraordinary growth. Wenatchee's initial inquiry came as its High Line Canal

7 Letter from E. Callahan to Andrew Carnegie, Jan. 29, 1902, CCA.

8 *Baker City Morning Democrat,* March 21, 1907; Author, *The History of Wallowa County,* 20; *Beaver City Weekly Press,* Jan. 3, 1913.

9 Sheller, *Sunnyside at Sixty,* 10–14 and letter from J. K. Edwards to Andrew Carnegie, Nov. 29, 1901, CCA.

10 Paker, *Goldfield: Boom Town,* 5 and Zanjani, *Goldfield, The Last Gold Rush,* 80.

was being built.[11] The North Side/South Side and Minidoka Projects were opening vast tracts of land around Twin Falls.[12] Pasco's initial inquiry letter was written *within a week* of news that development of long-desired irrigation would soon begin in its neighborhood.[13] These were all new communities, but even places that had been quietly subsisting for decades found themselves transformed under such stimulus. A 1903 newspaper editorial in forty-year-old Walla Walla proclaimed "the almost instantaneous quadrupling of the population with a greater increase still to come" thanks to the Big Bend irrigation project. Encouraged to dream big by a proclaimed "disposition to look for the heaviest colonization the [W]est has ever had within the next few years," Walla Walla soon submitted a Carnegie application.[14]

Other Carnegie library building grant applications in this group coincided with railroad development. Representatives from Sunnyside wrote to Carnegie when a Northern Pacific branch line reached town, promising transportation for the area's fruit. Clarkston-Vineland (another fruit-growing district) made its initial inquiry in 1911 as Harriman representatives were conducting a final survey and the connections the community had so long desired seemed certain.[15]

In other communities significant industrial development correlates with Carnegie library applications. Garland was benefitting from recent construction of an Idaho-Utah Sugar Company beet sugar plant when it applied for its Carnegie library and Kalispell had recently acquired a Northern Pacific mill and railroad tie works. Mining strikes often served as catalysts, as in Goldfield, where the community's Carnegie application occurred in the midst of the much-celebrated 1907 discoveries. Beaver City, founded as a Mormon agricultural settlement in the 1850s, did not apply for a Carnegie library until gold was discovered nearby in 1913. The 1905 boom that sparked Baker City's Carnegie application was also driven by

11 Gellatly, *History of Wenatchee*, 55, 60. Wenatchee was forced to wait to pursue its application, however, until Washington state library law was emended in 1909 to allow library taxes in cities smaller than first class.

12 Gentry, *In the Middle and On the Edge*, 152–82.

13 *Pasco (WA) Express*, Sept. 2, 1909 and letter from B. B. Horrigan to Andrew Carnegie, Sept. 8, 1909, CCA.

14 Orr, "Development of the Walla Walla Public Library," 3–5 and *Walla Walla (WA) Union*, Oct. 31, 1903 and July 9, 1903.

15 Sheller, *Sunnyside at Sixty*, 10–14 and letter from W. E. Howard to Andrew Carnegie, Nov. 28, 1911, CCA.

U & I Sugar Factory, Garland, Utah.

anticipated riches from extractive industry, in this case copper. "Expert engineers declare that this will be the greatest copper camp the west has ever known," declared the *Morning Democrat* during the period when the city was pursuing its Carnegie application.[16]

Dreams of local prosperity dominated civic thinking when citizens in these nineteen communities applied for Carnegie libraries. Welcoming or anticipating waves of new settlers, residents began to imagine that their towns could become regional market centers with soaring property values. The sense of a new era dawning is explicit in their newspapers, which offer striking examples of the extravagant optimism and active dedication to town-building that historian Daniel Boorstin has discussed as characteristic of the "booster press."[17] "Beaver City has taken on new life during the year," its *Weekly Press* proclaimed. "The long-looked for boom is on, and what's most important, it is on to stay . . . Beaver County in the next four or five years will be transformed into one of the most populous counties in the state."[18] A writer from Prosser declared, "We are about to take our proper place as a progressive community among the many such to be found in the state of Washington." Garland's citizens were told that the town was "destined to become one of the

16 Beal, "History of Garland, Utah"; Letter from J. K. Edwards to Andrew Carnegie, Nov 29, 1910, CCA; Paker, *Goldfield: Boom Town*, 11; *Beaver City (UT) Weekly Press*, Jan. 3, 1913; *Baker City (OR) Morning Democrat*, Mar. 21, 1907.

17 Boorstin, *The National Experience*, 124–34.

18 *Beaver City (UT) Weekly Press*, Jan. 3, 1913 and May 2, 1913.

great cities of the state."[19] Baker City's newspaper declared, "Let the watchword . . . be, 'Boost Baker'," predicting the community's future as a "Denver of Oregon" and "Queen City of the Inland Empire."[20]

Despite such optimism, citizens did recognize that their towns were not quite Denvers yet.[21] To attract "the higher class of settlers," wealthy people who expected "the broader and better elements of life," they needed the kinds of amenities that would define their communities as civilized places.[22] Other public works were consequently blossoming at exactly the same time as Carnegie applications in these communities. Kalispell tapped water power for its first electrical plant immediately before its Carnegie application; Beaver City was improving its lighting and water system and ordering new firefighting equipment; Walla Walla was paving streets for the first time and building a modern waterworks system.[23] Additionally, Garland was planning a sewer system and Prosser was developing a trolley said to ensure "the supremacy of Prosser as a commercial center of this part of the valley for years to come."[24] State governments were being lobbied for grand improvements beyond municipal funding capacities. Beaver City was prompting a highway through the mountains behind town and Wenatchee was arguing for a bridge over the Columbia River.[25] In some cases the juxtaposition of Carnegie applications and other projects is startling in its immediacy, as in Baker City, where the mayor wrote his initial inquiry letter to Carnegie on *the very day* after a street paving bond was approved by voters. It seems plausible to imagine that he had just checked off one item on a prioritized wish list of projects and was moving systematically to the next.[26]

---

19 *Prosser (WA) Record*, Jan. 7, 1909 and *Garland (UT) Globe*, Oct. 10, 1914.

20 *Baker City (OR) Morning Democrat*, Feb. 7 and 9, 1908 and Baker County Historical Society, *The History of Baker City*, 22.

21 Even the over-wrought *Baker City (OR) Morning Democrat* had to admit that "those who are accustomed to the comforts of civilization and are leaving little cities in the east . . . are not easily persuaded to build a home in a quag mire [sic] . . . no matter how prosperous it is," Mar. 22, 1907.

22 *Pasco (WA) Express*, Aug. 12, 1909. Wrobel discusses promoters' recognition that they needed to reassure potential immigrants that "the hardships of pioneering" were past in *Promised Lands*, 59–60.

23 Letter from J. K. Edwards to Andrew Carnegie, Nov. 29, 1901, CCA; *Beaver City (UT) Weekly Press*, Jan. 3, 1913; *Walla Walla (WA) Union*, Apr. 16, 1904.

24 Letter from B. Smith to Andrew Carnegie, Jan. 31, 1908, CCA and *Prosser (WA) Record*, Nov. 9, 1906.

25 *Beaver City (UT) Weekly Press*, Oct. 16, 1914 and Gellatly, *History of Wenatchee*, 218.

26 *Baker City (OR) Morning Democrat*, Mar. 25, 1917.

Oregon Historical Society Research Library, image #ORHi: 9931.

"Let the Watchword Be 'Boost Baker!'" Parade in Baker City, Oregon.

Commercial Clubs and Booster Campaigns

The men who directed Carnegie public library building grants in these nineteen communities were inevitably members of local commercial clubs. Forerunners of today's chambers of commerce, these businessmen's associations were common in turn-of-the-twentieth-century Intermountain West communities, but they assumed a particularly high profile in this cluster of communities around the time of local Carnegie applications. Compared to such clubs elsewhere in the region, these nineteen were particularly large, with Prosser's club boasting 141 members. Some were brand-new and

Idaho State Historical Society, photo #73.221.144.

Commercial club luncheon, Twin Falls, Idaho.

determined to prove themselves, including Sunnyside's and Beaver City's. Others, longer-standing but newly revitalized by prosperity, were conducting high-profile membership drives (La Grande and Walla Walla). A few clubs could even boast concrete achievements, including Enterprise's, which had been instrumental in establishing the new Wallowa County and fixing their town as its seat.[27]

While occasional reports of commercial club activity appear in the newspapers of other Intermountain West Carnegie library communities, these men regularly received front-page coverage in the local press. Often the editor was a club member and sometimes other men contributed editorials and promotionally tinged "news" stories. Coverage was systematic and extensive. In Wenatchee, the names of new recruits were published on the front page of each issue of the local newspaper and in La Grande, the commercial club contributed a monthly "development section" providing highly favorable "authentic statistics and general information" about the town. Not

27 *Prosser (WA) Record*, Feb. 8, 1909; Sheller, *Sunnyside at Sixty*, 10; *Beaver City (UT) Weekly Press*, Jan. 17, 1913; *La Grande (OR) Weekly Observer*, Oct. 13, 1911; Wallowa County Museum Board, *The History of Wallowa County, Oregon*, 19.

content to spread the good news to neighbors, the latter club funded the printing of five thousand extra copies of these issues to be mailed to other parts of the country.[28] Several other clubs, including Sunnyside's and Walla Walla's, published their own promotional booklets.[29]

Prosser's club was a bit extreme in blazoning "Boost for Prosser" on its stationery, but its enthusiasm differed only in degree, not in kind, from the mood in other communities in this cluster at the time of their Carnegie applications. "Work for Walla Walla" proclaimed the *Walla Walla Union*'s headline on November 20, 1903, less than two weeks after that community had received a promise from Carnegie. "There comes a time in the affairs of every community," the editor remarked, "when a concerted action on the part of its businessmen and commercial interests can mark an epoch in its history. It would seem that the time has arrived in Walla Walla. . . . With the [newly irrigated land] opening of this coming spring there will doubtless be another move of emigration from the Eastern States, seeking new homes. . . . To get its fair share of these people and enterprises, a community must get in and hustle."[30] "We will not let the sun set on our optimism or our faith in the coming greatness of Beaver County," city fathers of that municipality announced in a formal resolution.[31] Milton's *Eagle* rhapsodized in 1905, "Happy Milton, beautiful for situation! Where boast is of her fertile soil, her oceans of flowers, fruit, and grain, her mild and balmy climate, her delightful and hospitable homes, her moral and churchgoing people, and her well-attended and up-to-date schools."[32] In a more rhetorically restrained but no less enthusiastic vein, Enterprise's residents were assured that "signs of prosperity" were everywhere in the region, testifying to "a prosperous country, and a prosperous set of businessmen."[33]

---

28 *Wenatchee (WA) World*, March 9, 1909 and *La Grande (OR) Weekly Observer*, Oct. 13, 1911.

29 Sheller, *Sunnyside at Sixty*, 11 and *Walla Walla (WA) Union*, Nov. 10, 1903.

30 *Walla Walla (WA) Union*, Nov. 22, 1903.

31 *Beaver City (UT) Weekly Press*, Jan. 2, 1914.

32 *Milton (OR) Eagle*, Feb. 20, 1905.

33 *Enterprise (OR) Record-Chieftain*, July 13, 1911. Considerable pressure existed to join the cheerleading, with anyone who voiced reservations or even cautious optimism chided in the press. The *Pasco (WA) Express* termed citizens who were skeptical about a proposed irrigation project "assassins of progress" (July 22, 1909 and Aug. 12, 1909), and the *Twin Falls (ID) Times* thundered at cynics and slackers, "You have no right to stand on the street corner and criticize the efforts of the loyal booster who may be in the parade doing his part to make it a success . . . Above all just get the idea that you

Now and then promotional efforts involved more than words. Several commercial clubs among these nineteen organized elaborate junkets to show off their towns to influential outsiders, including Goldfield, where the chamber of commerce paid the expenses of 150 state legislators and their wives who traveled by train to tour the community. In a rare show of cooperation, Wenatchee's commercial club organized a conference, inviting brother club representatives from the Okanagan Valley to help coordinate a regional promotion campaign.[34]

Characteristically, however, these men considered all nearby communities as deadly rivals, an attitude reflected in community newspapers. Bragging stories favorably compared the home community to others. "It is one thing for a city to make big claims," proclaimed the *La Grande Weekly Observer*, "and it quite another for those claims to be substantiated by fact. To claim enormous business activity in public and extensive improvement without proof is a mere waste of time . . . Where can you find another city that is doing the real improvement that La Grande is doing in the northwest?"[35] Alarmist rhetoric warned citizens about potential competition from neighbors. An editor in Baker City cautioned readers that "It would be well for us to get busy locally if we want to keep in the lead of the procession of Eastern Oregon towns, for Hermiston is pretty swift for a yearling." Boise, Pendleton and Walla Walla, he suggested, were also potential rivals to Baker City.[36]

A less savory tactic involved smearing neighbors.[37] La Grande's *Weekly Observer*, a particularly energetic example of such journalism, routinely published front-page reports impugning the politics, the morals, and the general get-up-and-go of nearby communities. "Baker Negro assaults Lady," it trumpeted on October 27, 1911, and "Wallowa folks accused of house of ill fame, selling liquor" just a few days later. Milton slurred its rivals (reporting, for example, that the river-valley rival community of Pendleton was "in a hole, and she cannot get out. That's the pity") while they simultaneously

---

have some responsibility for the success of every public undertaking in this town." (Sept. 12, 1913).

34 Letter from Howard Thomas to James Bertram, Mar. 17, 1909, CCA and *Wenatchee (WA) World*, Mar. 9, 1909.

35 *La Grande (OR) Weekly Obeserver*, Nov. 10, 1911 and May 31, 1912

36 *Baker City (OR) Morning Democrat*, Mar. 23, 1907.

37 Boorstin, *The National Experience*, 161–68, notes that competition was common among "upstart" communities. See Wrobel, *Promised Lands*, 36–38,for a discussion of smear tactics.

slurred her. No one wanted to file for land in Milton, the *Walla Walla Union* assured its readers, so the former community's business was consequently "badly up in the air."[38]

The Rhetoric and Orchestration of Economically Motivated Carnegie Library Campaigns

David M. Wrobel has noted that boosters across the West engaged in "hyping . . . cultural amenities" to assure prospective settlers that they would not be coming to raw, uncivilized places,[39] and in these nineteen communities Carnegie libraries were promoted along with educational institutions as attractions that could help a community stand out from its neighbors. Pasco's editor argued directly that "with the new school house and a suitable library, Pasco would have some practical inducements to offer" cultivated potential citizens.[40] Such words fell on ready ears, and once commercial club members became obsessed with drawing "eastern homeseekers and capitalists," they enthusiastically pursued Carnegie grants. Wenatchee's commercial club (which had never expressed any interest in a public library previously) held such a "rouser" of a meeting about the issue in 1909 that a member was deputized to write an initial inquiry letter to Carnegie the very next day.[41]

"A public library is a necessity, not a luxury," wrote the editor of the *La Grande Weekly Observer*, himself a commercial club member. "Every community which realizes this and establishes a library, proclaims itself an intelligent progressive town and one worth living in." A Carnegie library, he suggested, would help the community hold its own against its arch-rival Baker City, which had unfortunately anticipated La Grande in applying. "Such improvements would be considered out of the question in most places the size," he noted proudly, reassuring readers that "the site, the size of the building, and the liberal maintenance will give La Grande a library exactly equal to that of Baker."[42] Beaver City's citizens were reminded that, "Every town of importance in the State is working hard to get a Carnegie library."

---

38 *La Grande(OR) Weekly Observer*, Nov. 10, 1911 and May 31, 1912; *Milton (OR) Eagle*, April 30, 1908; *Walla Walla (OR) Union*, Feb. 5, 1904.

39 Wrobel, *Promised Lands*, 39–40.

40 *Pasco (WA) Express*, Aug. 12, 1909.

41 Letter from Howard Thomas to James Bertram, Mar. 17, 1909, CCA and *Wenatchee (WA) World*, Mar. 9, 1909.

42 *La Grande (OR) Weekly Observer*, Dec. 15, 1911.

"If Cedar [Cedar City, a nearby town] can afford $10,000 for a library building, surely Beaver is able and just as deserving."[43] In a blatant visual representation of the library-as-economic-stimulus theme, the Garland's *Globe* (which had directed citizens to "Boost for the Carnegie Library") featured on the cover of a special promotional edition juxtaposed images of a sugar beet (representative of the new Utah-Idaho Sugar Company factory) and the town's planned Carnegie library.[44]

Conceiving the library building grant applications as components of booster campaigns, commercial club members naturally took charge of them in these nineteen places. Beaver City's Carnegie application was presented as "a golden opportunity for the Beaver Commercial Club to get busy and give the people a sample of that keen business acumen for which Beaver businessmen are justly noted." Even a powerful man like Colonel Prosser, founder of the Washington town which bears his name, passed the project along to local businessmen after he initially contacted Carnegie.[45]

In these communities, the women who had established pre-Carnegie libraries seem to have been contented to hand the work of pursuing a building grant over to businessmen, even if they were the ones who had written the initial inquiry letters and received the "Schedule of Questions," as happened in Sunnyside, Milton, and Union. Women's names only occasionally appear on Carnegie correspondence from these booster towns, and women rarely served on building committees.[46] Instead, they accepted more stereotypically domestic roles, choosing interior decorations or providing food for dedication ceremonies.[47] When they did (rarely) disagree with the way

43 *Beaver City (UT) Weekly Press*, Feb. 14, 1913.

44 *Garland (UT) Globe*, Jan. 24, 1914.

45 *Beaver City (UT) Weekly Press*, Feb. 14, 1913 and letter from H. W. Carnahan to James Bertram, Apr. 13, 1909, CCA.

46 The extent to which Carnegie library grants were associated with business-driven values in these communities is underlined by the fact that one woman who did write to Carnegie chose her husband's business stationery (headed "Shields Fruit Company, Strawberries, Blackberries, Raspberries, Dewberries, Cherries, Peaches/Prunes, Apples/pears, Grapes, Etc.") even though she was an officer of the community's women's club (Letter from Mrs. C. M. Shields to Andrew Carnegie, Nov. 12, 1908, CCA).

47 The women of Sunnyside organized refreshments, entertainment, and decoration for the library's dedication ceremony, see, *Sunnyside (WA) Sun*, May 4, 1911 and May 11, 1911. The women of Wenatchee were invited to help the exclusively male Carnegie library choose furniture and books, components in which their feminine sensibilities were apparently believed to be desirable, see, "Washington (State) Wenatchee Public Library," 3–4.

the applications were being handled, it was most often in conjunction with the library's location.[48] One can detect lasting bitterness over such a decision in a retrospective history of the Baker City Carnegie library written by a women's club member. "The library site," she writes, "was selected primarily for its economic features, and with no thought to civic beauty. Consequently the beautiful building given by Mr. Carnegie was placed in a regrettable location."[49] It is a testimony to the immense power of local symbolism, however, that this is the *only* instance of gender-based fracture this researcher was able to find for any of these twenty communities.

Placing Carnegie library business on their agendas along with such other pressing matters as "Apple Days" celebrations,[50] commercial club members kept their own hands firmly on the Carnegie application reins. La Grande's S. M. Slough, commercial club publicity manager, did all the negotiating with Bertram about grant amount and library design; he even helped city officials correctly phrase the support resolution when they proved unequal to the task. The secretary of the board of trade in Kalispell did the same. In Twin Falls, citizens convened in commercial club rooms—not city council chambers—to discuss competing library sites.[51] Wenatchee's library board meetings were similarly held in the commercial club's new quarters—as well they might have been, for the town's new library board had been constituted as a subcommittee of the commercial club.[52]

Riding high on their own enthusiasm, selling a vision of community which seemed desirable and viable, the men who directed these nineteen Carnegie applications orchestrated some the most trouble-free campaigns in the Intermountain West. In Garland a "large and enthusiastic crowd" held what was essentially a library pep rally, inspiring a decisive support

48 Van Slyck notes that women nationwide similarly deferred without protest, but that site selection could engage the competing priorities of men and women relative to public library service in *Free to All*, 134–35, 137–38.

49 Baker City Historical Society, *History of Baker City*, 66–67.

50 The frequent reports of commercial club business that appeared in the *Wenatchee (WA) World* from January-March 1909 reveal that during the period of Carnegie library negotiations the club was simultaneously collecting money for a clubhouse, hosting its regional conference of brother clubs, lobbying for sewers, and planning for the yearly celebration of the town's most famous product, apples.

51 Library Board Minutes, Twin Falls, Idaho, June 11, 1915 and July 26, 1915.

52 Wenatchee's commercial club was unknowingly doing itself a favor in working so hard for a Carnegie building: at this writing, the structure houses the community's chamber of commerce.

referendum.[53] Where plebiscites were not necessary, town councils dutifully signed levies—a process expedited where commercial club members themselves numbered among the council's roster.[54] An embarrassment of library sites were proffered by prominent citizens (Milton), by businesses (Clarkston-Vineland), or by commercial clubs themselves (Prosser).[55] Where no free sites were available, boosters held fundraising campaigns to purchase prime locations (Sunnyside).[56] Supervised by self-proclaimed "men of business" with connections to suppliers and contractors, few of these buildings encountered construction delays. Kalispell opened its completed building only eight months after laying the cornerstone, despite the challenges of building in a far-northern region with very short summers. Additionally, Beaver City, Prosser, and Sunnyside completed the entire process, from initial inquiry to dedication, in less than two years.

Once completed, these Carnegie libraries inspired orgies of self-congratulation. The *Kalispell Bee* reported with satisfaction that "the value of every dollar spent in the construction is plainly apparent and no better building for the price has ever been constructed anywhere."[57] Smug competitive advantage was also invoked in Baker City, where the new library was termed "one of the handsomest structures in the northwest."[58] "Something about every concerted effort made in Wallowa County causes success to be achieved, which reflects splendid credit to the people who live in that little empire," the *Enterprise Record-Chieftain* noted in reference to its own "tasty and very substantial" Carnegie library.[59]

53 *Garland (UT) Globe*, Nov. 2 and 9, 1907.

54 As was the case in Enterprise, Oregon, where Daniel Boyd and C. T. Hackett, both Carnegie correspondents, were also members of the town council, see, *Enterprise (OR) Record-Chieftain*, Feb. 27, 1913 and July 26, 1913.

55 Occasionally dissention arose among commercial club members who offered competing sites, convinced that the libraries would attract consumers to their personal businesses. Letter from Robert Foster to Andrew Carnegie, May 29, 1912; *Prosser (WA) Record*, July 9,1909; *Enterprise (OR) Record Chieftain*, July 10, 1913.

56 *Sunnyside (WA) Sun*, June 9, 1910.

57 *Kalispell (MT) Bee*, Jan. 15, 1904.

58 *Baker City (OR) Herald*, Jan. 21, 1909.

59 *Enterprise (OR) Record-Cheiftain*, Jan. 2, 1913. Some Carnegie libraries remained symbols of local competitive superiority for many years. In 1928, fourteen years after the Garland Carnegie library's dedication, a child of the town's mayor noted in a master's thesis that "the generally progressive and enterprising attitude of the citizens is evidenced by the Garland Carnegie library and the Stake Tabernacle. Both of these buildings should reflect credit on larger and wealthier communities," see, Beal, "History of Garland, Utah," 11.

Economically Motivated Carnegie Library Campaigns Which Failed

Failure Because of Economic Downturn

Although desire for economic prosperity could be a compelling motive for public library support, it did not guarantee success. In the boom-and-bust economies of the Intermountain West, basic solvency (much less booming prosperity) could quickly evaporate, and libraries that were linked in the public mind to development could lose their perceived relevance. Three communities of the nineteen in this cluster saw their applications flounder on just these grounds.

Steamboat Springs's story, one of hopes raised and then dashed by the Moffat Road, has been told in chapter one. The history of Carnegie application failure in the second town, Goldfield, recalls the events in Steamboat Springs, though at the frantically accelerated pace appropriate to a western mining town. Although Goldfield was platted in 1903 on previously empty ground, it did not have to wait long for its rail connection to the outside world. Within two years, its gold strikes had proved so rich that a spur line was constructed specifically for this town. In 1906 alone, the community's population grew from fifteen to twenty-five thousand. Houses could not be constructed quickly enough to accommodate the influx, and, as noted above, some residents slept in tents.[60]

Full of optimism, in 1907 Goldfield's commercial club began a promotional campaign, partnering with the town's exclusive Montezuma Club, which boasted 750 members and a three-story clubhouse.[61] As in so many communities in this economically motivated cluster, a Carnegie library was among early projects these men pursued. "This town of GOLDFIELD, in the State of Nevada has grown from nothing to at least 20,000 persons in the short period of 3 years," the initial inquiry letter claimed to Bertram in mid-1907. "It continues to grow rapidly, and it is estimated that there will be 50,000 people here two years hence."[62] Milton Detch, a member of both clubs and "the greatest booster that the district ever had," assumed management of the application.[63]

---

60 Paker, *Goldfield: Boom Town*, 2–5 and Zanjani, *Goldfield: The Last Gold Rush*, 80.

61 Shamberger, *Historic Mining Camps*, 107 and Zanjani, *Goldfield: The Last Gold Rush*, 147.

62 Letter from A. A. Codd to Andrew Carnegie, June 1, 1907, CCA.

63 *Reno (NV) Evening Gazette*, Mar. 2, 1921.

The boom before the bust in Goldfield, Nevada.

Despite his civic optimism, Detch found himself struggling to convince Bertram that Goldfield really would be a good Carnegie investment. Documenting even the current population proved a serious problem. Goldfield had not existed in 1900, so there were no census numbers. Speculation puffed valuation figures one day, then dropped them the next, so those figures were also unreliable. Two years and many letters after the initial inquiry, the community had not yet obtained even a promise.

This delay proved fatal to Goldfield's Carnegie library hopes, for things began to fall apart in 1908. A violent strike paralyzed mining operations. Federal troops occupied the town, decidedly lowering its appeal to aspiring capitalists. Dissention split the Montezuma club, as the mine owners among its members quarreled with the union sympathizers and wealthy miners. Somehow $200,000 disappeared from county funds. When officials attempted to raise taxes to keep already approved municipal projects going, citizens staged a tax rebellion.[64]

Finally, in early February, 1909, Goldfield did receive a promise from Carnegie. But by then the community was in a very different mood than it had been in 1907. The Montezuma Club, distracted by internal rancor, had lost interest in promotion. Many of the businessmen in the commercial club had fled or were looking to flee. Citizens had already registered to officials that they would tolerate no new taxes. The promise was barely announced, the issue of a support levy was never raised. After conditions stabilized a

64 Zanjani, *Goldfield: The Last Gold Rush*, 217, 221, 232.

few years later, what members were left of the commercial club did half-heartedly talk about re-starting the application, but the matter soon dropped. Goldfield's "inexhaustible" mineral wealth proved exhaustible. Its Carnegie library building grant promise lapsed as the city shrank to "a small and quiet" town, where all significant mining ended in 1919 and the population dwindled to 1600 by 1921.[65] Though this number was still large enough to qualify for a Carnegie grant—indeed, several Utah towns of this size eagerly supported grants—with the dreams of prosperity that had been its *raison d'etre* faded, Goldfield's application apparently seemed irrelevant.

Palouse's failed Carnegie library application presents a poignant variation on this theme. It also offers striking evidence of just how deeply these businessmen believed in the power of Carnegie libraries to stimulate local economies, for Palouse pursued its grant during what was clearly the back-end of a wave of prosperity, rather than during its rise.[66]

A forest-industry town in a remote section of eastern Washington, Palouse found itself at a new "high point of expectations" in 1904–5, a few years before its Carnegie application began in 1909. A mill had existed in Palouse for years, but by 1904 the ever-critical railroad spur had reached town. No longer would Palouse have to rely on local logging efforts; now it could process rich stands of timber from across the Idaho border. Residents anticipated that Palouse's population would soon number ten thousand. Citizens anticipated and sought to foster such growth by investing in multiple municipal improvements, including paved streets, a new hospital, and a new school.[67]

By the time the city's mayor inquired about a Carnegie library, however, abundant signs suggested that Palouse's expectations had been premature. The population had not grown as expected, nor was business booming. Still, city leaders doggedly pursued the application, receiving a promise in

65 Ibid., 95, 232.

66 Hamilton, Montana's Carnegie library application—a hybrid application co-directed by that city's women's club and its businessmen—also came at what a local historian admits was the "tail end" of "The Big Ditch Boom" and subsequent "Apple Boom," but these Montana library proponents were more fortunate than those in Palouse, for their community's Carnegie library was dedicated just before a Chicago bank foreclosed on the local irrigation company and a sawmill went out of business. (Michels, "Hamilton Development," 61–78). With a more diversified economy than Palouse, Hamilton managed to regain its feet, though, confirming that proponents' confidence in their community had been well founded.

67 The story of Palouse's decline is told in Rodewald, "Palouse," 20–35.

the spring of 1910.[68] Unfortunately that was also the spring when a rumor circulated that the Potlatch Mill—Palouse's major employer—would close as operations moved to another company towns. Out-migration began, and houses stood empty. Local business of another sort suffered its own setback when touring temperance advocate Carrie Nation inspired the town to go dry—a decision that hurt not only the saloonkeepers themselves, but also city coffers, thanks to lost license fees. Faced with a budget shortfall, city fathers stopped illuminating half of the community's streetlights at night, giving literal embodiment to the community's darkening fortunes.

By 1911 Palouse's boomer optimism had dissipated. Several bonds for civic improvements failed and progress toward a Carnegie library stalled as stressed citizens quarreled over alternate sites.[69] Correspondence between the mayor and Bertram broke off. A year later the town's worst fears were realized when the Potlatch Corporation announced that the Palouse mill would be closing. The very railroad once believed to be bringing prosperity began transporting mill machinery away to Montana. Eleven businesses closed or changed hands in 1913 as the population shrank. The people who remained had neither the financial resources nor the motivation to take advantage of Carnegie's promise, and they never constructed Palouse's library.

Failure Because of Over-Reaching

The other paradigm of failed Carnegie libraries in this cluster involves not objectively changing fortunes, but vainglory. In both Burley and Twin Falls, boosters simply dreamed too big, stubbornly holding to their own contentions even when it became clear that Bertram refused to believe them.

Burley's Carnegie library champions appear to have been running totally on the fumes of wishful thinking. On the surface, the community had much in common with other Carey Act towns that really did prosper: it arose in consequence of the construction of a dam crucial to the major Northside/Southside irrigation project and it possessed a connection to the outside world via the Oregon Short Line Railroad.[70] Those who platted

---

68 Letter from George Lamphere to Andrew Carnegie, Jan. 18, 1910, CCA; resolution signed by George Lamphere and others, Feb. 15, 1910, CCA; letter from James Bertram to George Lamphere, March (ill.), 1910, CCA.

69 Letter from George Lamphere to Andrew Carnegie, June 18, 1910, CCA.

70 Two locally written resources held in the Burley Public Library provide the most detail available on Burley's history, see, Author, *The History of Cassia County and Burley*, and Author, "Know Your Town."

the town originally named it "Commerce," but, reasoning that they might benefit by complimenting a local developer, they changed the name to his. Businessmen systematically promoted the community, even chartering excursion trains to bring potential settlers from Salt Lake City and other parts of Idaho. The panic of 1907 and a four-year delay in delivering irrigation water broke some investors, but by 1912 Burley was in a growth-oriented mood thanks to a new sugar beet factory. Citizens predicted the immanent in-migration of 10,000 people.

But Burley had not in fact actually prospered—at least not to the extent boosters had claimed it would—by 1915, when its Carnegie application began. The city still lacked the basic services many of its neighbors had established. Its municipal government appears to have been sloppily run (this was the home of county recorder Ray Gundmunsen, quoted in earlier chapters). Its growth had stalled. Though city officials claimed 2,700 people and a million-dollar valuation, Gundmunsen was unable to document these numbers. Six months later the mayor had retreated to 1,470.[71] Correspondents, though, kept attempting to inflate Carnegie's offer, arguing inevitable growth. By the time the community finally accepted a $10,000 promise, World War I had inflated building costs, and "financial stringency" gripped labor-depleted Cassia County. "We do not see any way whereby we can carry to completion the building that would meet the requirements," city clerk Edward Davis confessed to Carnegie.[72] Burley, which had attempted to insist on a grander Carnegie library than it really deserved, never built any Carnegie library at all.

Though Twin Falls was truly in the midst of astounding growth when it applied for its Carnegie library, it suffered a similar fate. Platted in 1905 as a result of the same irrigation development that fostered Burley, Twin Falls was blessed with a better location, more effective promoters, and a more efficient bureaucracy. As Twin Falls's Carnegie library application began in 1913, the city had completed a sewer system and paved sidewalks and a county courthouse was planned. According to the local chamber of commerce, Twin Falls had become the third largest city in Idaho and the second largest shipping point in less than ten years of existence.[73]

---

71 Letter from Edward Davis to James Bertram, Oct. 28, 1915 and letter from Roy Gundmunsen to James Bertram, Feb. 19, 1916.

72 Letter from E. C. Davis to Carnegie Corporation of New York, Dec. 10, 1920, CCA.

73 Twin Falls Historical Society, *The First Hundred Years*, 11–33. The remark cited appears in a letter from Stuart Taylor to James Bertram, Oct. 17, 1916, CCA.

Idaho State Historical Society, photo #78.32.2.

Land allotment, Twin Falls, Idaho.

In this atmosphere of expanding possibilities, commercial club members W. Zenas Smith (baker and candymaker), W. H. Eldridge (banker), and Stuart H. Taylor (attorney) approached Carnegie. In August 1913 they received a promise for a $15,000 building. This level of funding, however, did not satisfy them, for it was based on Twin Falls's population in 1910, not on the ten thousand residents they now claimed. Given the city's 200% growth in seven years, they argued, it was reasonable to assume it would soon be home to twenty thousand, and they needed a library sized to anticipate such a population. Enlisting Idaho's governor and a senator to write support letters, they began pressuring Bertram and released an announcement to the *Twin Falls Times* that the city was "virtually certain of having a beautiful twenty-thousand dollar library."[74]

Bertram was not so easily swayed. "The great majority of citizens in the west hav ideas of what they ar going to become and seek to hav us consider their library applications on that basis," he replied, refusing their request outright. His skepticism was actually well taken, for even the *Times* had to admit that the town's assessed value in 1915 was "About the same as last year."[75] Twin Falls's library boosters then committed the serious error of

74 Letter from Stuart H. Taylor to James Bertram, Oct. 17, 1916, CCA; letter from A. Smith to The Carnegie Corporation, Dec. 8, 1916, CCA; *Twin Falls (ID) Times*, Aug 13, 1915.

75 Letter from James Bertram to Zenas Smith, Dec. 13, 1916, CCA and *Twin Falls (ID) Times*, Aug. 13, 1915.

trying to deceive Bertram. Apparently assuming the secretary would cover over-runs, they approved a library plan so grand that no one could have believed it might have been constructed for $15,000—indeed, the lowest bid came in just under $32,000. When Bertram learned of this figure, he refused to release any funds, demanding a scaled-down version. Correspondents, just as stubborn, continued to insist on the original plans.[76] Though they won a grudging increase to $20,000, that number failed to satisfy them, and the battle continued.

"To[o] few library projects hav we had to give the attention which has been bestowed on Twin Falls," Bertram wrote in frustration. He issued an ultimatum: if Twin Falls did not immediately agree to $20,000, Carnegie would cancel the offer. City officials, however, continued to lobby for higher amounts. While they wheedled, World War I began and communities that had not yet received promises found their applications abruptly suspended. Twin Falls remained without a purpose-built public library until 1938, when citizens voted to match Public Works Administration funding of $22,500 with $27,500 in municipal bonds for library construction.[77]

Taken as a whole, economically motivated Carnegie library building grant applications reveal an interior West far edgier and more self-serving than popular accounts of frontier cooperation might suggest. Whether the men who directed this cluster of nineteen applications succeeded or failed, they could afford to be blunt about their pragmatic motives, for most of their fellow citizens shared the same dreams. Epochs marked by big aspirations, high energy, and lots of bluster, these projects testify, could be a good time to sell anything—including culture—in the interior West.

76 Stuart H. Taylor, for example, insisted to Bertram that the town would "prefer" a terra cotta finish on the library to harmonize with the buildings around it, rather than the simple finish that Bertram suggested (letter from Stuart H. Taylor to James Bertram, Sept. 28, 1917, CCA). Library bids are discussed in a letter from James Bertram to Stuart H. Taylor, Mar. 23, 1917, CCA.

77 Letter from James Bertram to W. H. Eldridge, Dec. 6, 1917, CCA; letter from James Bertram to "His Honor, the Mayor," Dec. 3, 1918, CCA; Gentry, *In the Middle and on the Edge*, 285–86.

4

Small Mormon Towns: Carnegie Libraries to Protect Youth

"The cohesive force of love"

ANDREW CARNEGIE'S OFFER OF BUILDING GRANTS FOR FREE public libraries was greeted with particular enthusiasm in Utah. Twenty-four communities—the largest number of any state in the Intermountain West—applied for Carnegie funds, and twenty-three completed their libraries.[1]

Utah is not only distinguished among Intermountain West states for the number of its applications, however, for its inhabitants also offered the most diverse pro-library rhetoric used in any one state. The local signification assigned to Carnegie libraries in Utah, indeed, differs so sharply between clusters of applications that it's sometimes difficult to believe these people were talking about the same institutions.

This chapter begins with the largest cluster, fifteen rural Utah communities with largely Mormon populations that applied for Carnegie library building grants. Though all of these communities followed exactly the same procedures as economically motivated communities, and though several of these fifteen are located near the two Utah communities discussed in the previous chapter (Garland and Beaver City), the local logistics of their applications could hardly be more different in terms of the timing of their efforts relative to community history, their current socio-economic circumstances, the demographics of their application leadership, or their

1 Two university papers provide the most comprehensive overviews of Utah Carnegie library history: Evans's "A History of the Public Library Movement in Utah," and Hepworth's "Carnegie Libraries in Utah."

rhetoric. Most striking, perhaps, is their contrasting vision of what a library was *for*. When rural Mormon Utahans applied for Carnegie libraries, they did not dream of becoming Queen Cities in an earthly sense. Instead, they understood themselves as doing nothing less than building God's kingdom on earth.

The Culture of Mormon Agricultural Settlements in Utah

Religious faith shaped every aspect of community life in American Fork, Brigham City, Cedar City, Ephraim, Lehi, Manti City, Murray City, Panguitch, Parowan, Richfield, Richmond, Smithfield, St. George, and Tooele City (Utah) and Preston (Idaho)[2] at the turn of the twentieth century. All fifteen of these towns owed their very existence to the Mormon Church. Under Brigham Young's leadership, Latter-day Saints had migrated to Utah in 1847 after suffering persecution in the Midwest. When they arrived, the high desert land around the Great Salt Lake was nearly empty of European American presence, but Young anticipated that "gentiles" (as he described non-Mormons) would soon follow to harass and/or colonize, a prediction that proved correct. Establishing Mormon colonies on the outskirts of "Deseret," he reasoned, would give Latter-day Saints a claim to an expanded territory, not only establishing a buffer zone around the Salt Lake Valley but providing land where the waves of immigrants drawn by missionary efforts could settle. More particularly, colonists were directed to regions that held valuable resources, staking an LDS claim on the region's iron and coal, and establishing a presence in warm climate zones appropriate to the cultivation of specialized crops like cotton.

This expansion took the form of a very orderly and deliberate process. Rather than simply allowing people to choose where they wanted to live (though this happened too), church leaders "called" suitable families or specific groups of families to colonize specific regions. Obedience was a given, for the call was understood as a religious obligation.[3]

2 Just over the Utah/Idaho border, Preston belonged to Utah in spirit. Settled by Mormons directed to colonize the area, it was physically organized like a Mormon agricultural village and culturally shaped by Mormon beliefs. Brenchley, writing in 1968, argued that the town was "religiously, culturally, and economically . . . oriented toward Utah rather than Idaho . . . Preston is part of the greater Mormon community radiating from Salt Lake City," in "Preston, Idaho," 2.

3 The history of Mormon settlement in the West is discussed in Arrington, *Great Basin Kingdom*, Anderson, *Desert Saints*, and Campbell, "Early Colonization Patterns."

Cedar City, Utah, ca. 1910.

The fifteen rural Mormon communities which obtained Carnegie libraries were established as a result of such direction, spreading LDS settlement to the four compass points. To the north of Salt Lake City, Brigham City was settled in 1853, Richmond in 1859, Smithfield in 1860, and Preston in the 1880s. Tooele City, to the west of Salt Lake City, and Murray City, to its south, were both founded in 1849. Central Utah pioneers arrived in Manti and Ephraim Cities in Sanpete County in 1849 and 1853; they reached American Fork and Lehi in 1850, Parowan in 1851, and Richfield and Panguitch in 1864. In southern Utah, Mormon settlers were called from Parowan to Cedar City in 1854, and they established St. George in 1861.[4]

These communities were among the oldest European American settlements in the Intermountain West, and they assumed an equally distinctive physical and governmental shape. All were initially laid out on the "Mormon Village" plan, a design the Latter-day Saints brought with them from Ohio.[5] Rather than living on scattered farms, Mormons consolidated their houses and barns in towns and traveled daily into the countryside to work their allotted land. In their orderly villages, wide streets ran on a grid north-south

4 Capsule histories of all these towns, including dates and circumstances of settlement, can be found in Powell, *Utah History Encyclopedia*.

5 Nelson, *The Mormon Village*, 25–26.

and east-west, and central blocks were reserved for public buildings. This arrangement, historian Lowry Nelson argues, was influenced by Mormons' belief that they must gather in a sort of utopian "Christian communism" to await the imminent coming of the Savior.[6]

Such community structure encouraged social solidarity, and from the beginning the municipal governments in these communities presumed homogeneous values. These fifteen towns were organized as "theodemocracies," places where church authorities were assumed to have "the right and duty to govern as [God's] representatives on earth." The earliest local leaders, honored as the men who had been selected by the highest Mormon authorities to positions of trust,[7] allocated town plats and farmland to citizens and organized neighborhoods as "wards" (parishes of the Mormon Church). They supervised cooperative irrigation works and arbitrated disputes in courts which were at once religious and secular. A citizen could be excommunicated as punishment for a secular offense.[8]

Even after statehood in 1896—with its mandates for change—life in these villages retained the flavor of Mormon pioneer culture. "It would not have occurred" to citizens, one historian writes, "to distinguish between church and state."[9] Church leaders remained civic officials, as in Preston, where J. N. Larsen served as mayor, stake president, bishop, and first councilor.[10] Religious and secular organization blurred. When American Fork's city council decided to "properly recognize the boys" enlisted in the army in 1918–19, committees were constituted by ward, and the Mormon first ward in Murray and its board of education jointly owned land.[11] Religious and secular education was similarly conflated. Mormon seminaries were constructed beside or very near schoolhouses, and children were

---

6 Ibid., 35, 40.

7 Campbell, "Governmental Beginnings," 134. Technically the people had the right to challenge these men through the principle of "common consent," but this privilege was seldom evoked in practice.

8 Campbell and Campbell, "Pioneer Society," 285.

9 Said about Latter-day Saint historian Juanita Brooks and her fellow townspeople in Bunkerville, Nevada (Peterson, *Juanita Brooks*, 16). Gentile presence remained negligible in these towns for a long time. Preston was estimated to be 95% Mormon in 1900, when it incorporated (Judy, "History of Preston," 57). Richmond was said to have only ten gentiles among 1,300 residents in 1890 (Olsen, "Richmond," 1).

10 *Progressive Men of Southern Idaho*, 286–87.

11 Shelley, *Early History of American Fork*, 58 and Murray City Corporation,"Murray City Library," 40.

shepherded *en masse* to religious instruction immediately after school or even during the school day itself.[12]

As might be expected in a culture where "the saints drew no lines between religious and other activities," social life was structured around church activities.[13] Lowry Nelson has remarked on the plenitude of such activities, commenting that the person who attended all of them would hardly have had time for anything else. Besides attending long religious services, Mormons met weekly in groups relevant to their ages and genders: the Primary (for small children), the Young Men's or Young Women's Mutual Improvement Association (for adolescents), the Relief Society (for adult women), and the Priesthood (for adult men). While these groups studied religion and performed service, they also assumed "the responsibility for initiating, directing, and regulating the recreational activities of the community." Plays, concerts, debates, and athletic events were thus constituted as church projects.[14]

Turn-of-the-twentieth-century newspapers suggest how completely the citizens of these fifteen towns identified themselves as Latter-day Saints, for front-page news was regularly dominated by LDS stories. Even the most mundane doings of the Relief Society and the Mutual Improvement Associations were duly recorded for citizens' perusal. The events at semi-annual Mormon General Conferences in Salt Lake were reported in painstaking detail. General phrasing supposed a hegemonic worldview. Preston's newspaper regularly identified citizens as "Bishop" this and "Sister" that while Cedar City's endorsed a candidate for local office by praising his "sobriety and industry" and reassuring readers that the man was "morally . . . clean." Panguitch's newspaper was regularly sent to all Mormon missionaries and Richfield's was owned by the local Mormon Church between 1910 and 1915.[15]

These fifteen rural Utah Mormon communities were not only more homogeneous in their values than most in the Intermountain West, they were also much quieter. While they had welcomed modest influxes of settlers in their early years, their populations had long been stable by the turn of the

12 Campbell and Campbell, "Pioneer Society," 301.

13 Lyon and Leonard, "The Churches in the Territory," 318.

14 Nelson, *The Mormon Village*, 103.

15 *Iron County (Cedar City, UT) Record*, May 10, 1912; *Panguitch (UT) Progress*, Mar. 5, 1915; Sturgis, "The Mormon Village in Transition," 27.

twentieth century. And those populations were small. Parowan claimed just 1,100 people when it applied for its Carnegie library in 1913 and Panguitch just 1300 in 1915. Richmond's population actually declined slightly during the first two decades of the twentieth century, from 1400 in 1900 to 1200 in 1920.[16] In contrast to the communities discussed in the previous chapter, most of these places remained geographically isolated. When Parowan applied for its Carnegie library, the nearest railroad station was fifty-five miles away. Preston's economy was so insular that every business in town used scrip until just a few years before that town's Carnegie application.[17]

Agriculture dominated local economies. The Cache Valley towns of Richmond and Smithfield were dairy centers, and extensive orchards provided income and employment for Brigham City. Residents of American Fork, Panguitch, Preston, Richfield, and St. George raised livestock and farmed.[18] While factories did exist to process milk, cheese, wheat, or beef, those were long-standing and modest concerns, typically local cooperatives.[19]

Lacking changes that might ignite fantasies of explosive growth, these communities also lacked the aggressive culture of material progress described in the previous chapter. In turn-of-the-twentieth-century rural Utah, Mormon Church work demanded men's leisure-time energy, not community promotion. The few commercial clubs that did exist in these towns were new and low profile. Panguitch's club was just a year old when that community applied for its Carnegie library and Manti was "just

16 For a table of populations of Utah towns by decade, see Powell, *Utah History Encyclopedia*, 433–38.

17 Garfield County Chapter, Daughters of Utah Pioneers, *Golden Nuggets of Pioneer Days*, 30 and Brenchley, "Preston, Idaho," 31.

18 Several of these towns fell back to agriculture after brief mining booms played out. Cedar City, for example, turned to cattle and sheep ranching when iron manufacturing proved unworkable in Southern Utah, see, *Iron County (Cedar City, UT) Record*, June 7, 1912 and Johnson, *Cedar City*. While Tooele and Murray did support smelters, gentiles largely staffed such operations, with Mormon residents making their livings from producing livestock, dairy products, grain, corn, and fruit (for descriptions of the economies of these communities, see Mercer, *History of Tooele County* and Murray City Corporation, *History of Murray City*).

19 Richmond's creameries were built in 1892 and 1893 and its condensed milk plant began operations in 1903, all well before its Carnegie application in 1912 (Olsen, "Richmond," 5–6). Smithfield's creamery was built in 1894 and its condensed milk plant in 1912, the latter five years before its Carnegie application began (Harwood, "The Economic History of Smithfield," 17–20). Lehi's first sugar beet factory was constructed in 1890, twenty-seven years before it applied for a Carnegie library (Van Wagoner, *Lehi*).

beginning to realize the inestimable value of a live working commercial club." In Richfield, the newspaper editor was only beginning to urge that a club be considered.[20]

Municipal improvements lagged in these quiet places. Richfield did not construct cement sidewalks or install electric streetlights until 1925, more than a decade after its Carnegie library was built. Ephraim's first modern water system also post-dates its Carnegie library application. Several of these communities even lacked community newspapers at the time citizens wrote initial inquiry letters, including Parowan and Tooele.[21]

The Utah Library-Gymnasium Association

Carnegie library applications from these fifteen rural Utah communities were distinctively organized and coordinated. In contrast to the jealous independence of the Carnegie library boosters described in the previous chapter, rural Utahans gratefully shared a resource: a state agency proselytizing for Carnegie public library building grants, one happy to provide information and hands-on guidance.

This agency was the Utah Library-Gymnasium Commission, and while it assumed other duties besides promoting Carnegie grants, the Carnegie program helped inspire its foundation. Very early in the twentieth century, the first Utah citizens who attempted to secure Carnegie grants discovered that state legislation forbade communities other than first-class cities from levying a library tax sufficient to meet Carnegie's demands; the legislation that corrected that problem also formed the Commission.[22]

---

20 *Panguitch (UT) Progress*, July 9, 1915; *Manti (UT) Messenger*, Jan. 21, 1910; Sturgis,"The Mormon Village in Transition," 43. The few commercial clubs that existed in these fifteen communities invariably played supporting roles, if any, in Carnegie library applications. Richmond's new Industrial Club produced the initial inquiry letter, but as soon as Bertram requested "the proper authorities" become involved, club members deferred to local Mormon Church leaders, who assumed direction of the application (Letter from the Richmond City Public Library Board to the Carnegie Corporation, Aug. 14, 1912, CCA).

21 Centennial Book Committee, *Ephraim's First 100 Years*, 20; Sturgis,"The Mormon Village in Transition," 67–68; Garfield County Chapter, Daughters of Utah Pioneers, *A History of Garfield County*; Judy, "A History of Preston," 57–58.

22 The revision of Utah's library support law is described in the discussion of Provo's Carnegie application in chapter 9, following. The subject is mentioned in Hepworth, "Carnegie Libraries in Utah," 33 and Evans, "A History of the Public Library Movement in Utah," 51.

Nominally a secular institution under the jurisdiction of the Utah Department of Public Instruction, the Utah Library-Gymnasium Commission functioned as a quasi-Mormon entity because of the nature of its leadership, its assumption that church culture was general culture, and the rhetoric that it used to promote library development. Prominent Utah educator Howard Driggs was named its first director (or "secretary"), charged with spreading the library gospel in general and the Carnegie library gospel in particular.[23] Born in Pleasant Grove, Utah, in 1873, Driggs earned BA and MA degrees from the University of Utah, working first as a teacher and assistant principal in Cedar City from 1904–06. After attending the University of Chicago, he became supervisor of the English faculty at the University of Utah and principal of the institution's secondary training school there, positions which he held simultaneously with his appointment to the Library-Gymnasium Commission. His credentials in Latter-day Saint education included service on the Sunday School General Board for thirty-nine years and authorship of the standard church training manual for teachers.[24]

Driggs was assisted in his work first by Mrs. Karen M. Jacobsen and then in 1914 by Mary Elizabeth Downey, a nationally known librarian whose administrative responsibilities had included service as Ohio State Library Organizer. As a leader in the movement to professionalize librarianship, Downey directed a summer school Chatauqua for librarians for thirty years. Although she was not herself Mormon, Downey's philosophy

---

23 In addition to helping expedite Carnegie library building grants in Utah, the Commission's staff also did general work in support of public libraries in Utah. Driggs organized a meeting in Salt Lake City in 1912 where the Utah Library Association was established to promote American Library Association standards of professionalism; his assistants catalogued the collections of all libraries in the state and organized the state's county library system, see, Evans, "A History of the Public Library Movement in Utah," 55. The one major mistake the Commission made was suggesting to Utah communities that it would be a good idea to construct single structures housing both libraries and gymnasiums. Physical education was not a cause that interested Carnegie, and when Utah towns repeatedly asked for library-gymnasiums they irritated Bertram. "Mr. Carnegie does not include gymnasiums in his work—only Free Public Libraries pure and simple," he stormed in one reply, see, letter from James Bertram to J. D. Stack, Dec. 6, 1907, CCA.

24 Biographical details about Driggs are taken from his obituary, which appeared in the *Deseret News (Salt Lake City, UT)* on Feb. 18, 1963. Driggs's career took a new direction after his Commission work ended in 1923, he earned a PhD and taught at New York University.

Howard Driggs, head of the Utah Library-Gymnasium Commission.

fit well with the church's ethos. She emphasized the moral influence of books and she spoke a good deal about children. While working as a library administrator in Iowa, she had established the Children's Library League with the motto "Clean hearts, clean hands, and clean books." Her attitude toward her Mormon constituency, her biographer has suggested, was "benevolently patronizing," and she did not hesitate to speak from the Mormon pulpits.[25]

To call these three "energetic propagandists for the movement," as a thesis about Utah library history does,[26] seems an understatement, since all three logged thousands of miles across the state annually in the cause of bringing Carnegie public library building grants to Utah.[27] They held public meetings to inform citizens about grant availability, they distributed copies of Carnegie forms, and they spoke to committees about procedures. Ultimately, they essentially held the hands of applicants during the application process, offering advice about the best way to deal with Bertram's queries and writing their own support letters on occasion.

25 Evans, "A History of the Public Library Movement in Utah," 52–53 and Stauffer, "She Speaks," 38–62.

26 Evans, 50.

27 Stauffer, "She Speaks," 44.

Nearly all of their onsite meetings were held in Mormon churches.[28] Although this choice might have been practically motivated—Mormon churches were often the only large buildings in rural Utah towns—it functioned to connect their work and church concerns in citizens' minds. That connection was reinforced as Library-Gymnasium staff members worked within the Mormon infrastructure, presenting talks to priesthood groups and parenting classes.[29]

This blurring of library mission and church mission would have seemed natural to the residents of these fifteen towns, for what small pre-Carnegie book collections they possessed had been established in conjunction with the local church, heeding Mormon Church leaders' advice to "seek wisdom from the best books."[30] Local branches of the Young Men's Mutual Improvement Association had established initial community libraries in Lehi, American Fork, Tooele, and Ephraim. In the latter, the young men built a lime kiln to fund the project.[31] St. George's library was established to support the local Mormon Stake Academy and Smithfield's initial book collection was gathered at the request of Sunday school teachers, then a tax-supported municipal library was established when the local Daughters of Utah Pioneers chapter (a Mormon women's organization devoted to preserving pioneer history), explained that they needed a place to store relics.[32]

Such libraries were overseen by the Mormon Church. Tooele's library was supervised by the ward Ecclesiastical Board, and Parowan's hours were assigned to coordinate with Mormon services, with the building opening immediately after dismissal on Sunday afternoon for a children's story hour. Parowan's library rented space from the Relief Society, Smithfield's book collection was housed in the second ward tithing office, and St. George's occupied space in the Mormon stake academy building.[33] Library service was equated with church labor. Brigham City's librarian was paid initially from funds designated for the Young People's Improvement Association.

---

28 See, for instance, the account of Driggs's meeting with the general public in Brigham City in the town's Mormon tabernacle in *Box Elder (Brigham City, UT) News*, May 30, 1912.

29 *Iron County (Cedar City, UT) Record*, Mar. 29, 1912.

30 *Doctrine and Covenants*, section 93, verse 36.

31 Gardner, *History of Lehi*, 312; Shelley, *Early History of American Fork*, 84; Lindell, "Libraries," 103; Centennial Book Committee, *Ephraim's First 100 Years*, 106.

32 Miller, *The Immortal* Pioneers, 53 and *History of Smithfield*, 58–59.

33 Parowan, Utah, *Library Board Minutes*, May, 1913.

After those funds lapsed and the library temporarily closed, a local bishop "called" Miss Ida Young "to open up the library again and make it her mission," using the terminology of religious appointment.[34]

Though a LDS leader proclaimed that "the Glory of God is Education," these rural Mormon libraries promoted a very specific kind of education. Holdings were heavily weighted toward doctrinal works, church histories, and the periodicals published by church organizations. They also included the kind of useful nonfiction favored by Brigham Young, along with Shakespeare and some novelists whose works had been carefully vetted.[35]

Such blurring of church and state would have appalled Carnegie. Taking after his mother—who had no use for organized religion—Carnegie proclaimed himself a skeptic and did not attend church. "The whole scheme of Christian Salvation is diabolical as revealed by the creeds," he wrote to a friend in 1905. Had he imagined the proto-religious signification of the word "library" in these fifteen communities, Utah's success rate might not have been quite so high.[36]

Pro-Carnegie Library Rhetoric in Rural Mormon Utah

Given libraries' prior association with the local church and residents' embrace of Mormonism as "the entire way of life,"[37] the Utah Library-Gymnasium Commission staff chose what seems a very appropriate rhetorical strategy

34 Peters, "History of the Brigham City (Utah) Library," 3–10. In Cedar City during the spring of 1912, when initial correspondence with Carnegie was being conducted, the librarian of the town's long-standing public library similarly associated the institution with church work when she urged all LDS organizations to donate their magazines to the library, arguing that the gesture "would be a beautiful missionary labor," see, *Iron County (Cedar City, UT) Record*, Mar. 8, 1912. Sometimes administrative links between the local Mormon ecclesiastical structure and the community public library continued even after Carnegie buildings were erected. Part of the St. George Carnegie librarian's salary, for example, was paid by the St. George Stake Academy in early years, see, Hepworth, "Carnegie Libraries in Utah," 61.

35 At the time of Brigham City's Carnegie application, for example, it was said that "churchworks outnumbered other volumes" by a large margin, see, Peters, "History of the Brigham City (Utah) Library," 6.

36 Wall, *Andrew Carnegie*, 369, 1009. As Wall notes, Carnegie did intend patrons of the libraries he donated to read "improving" books—but he had another, more practical sort of improvement in mind.

37 Brenchley, Preston, Idaho, 2.

"Train Up Your Children in the Way They Should Go": Richfield School, Utah.

to promote Carnegie applications, one guaranteed to touch listeners. Carnegie libraries, they argued, would promote the moral development of youth.

Appropriate rearing of children was—and continues to be—a core value in the family-centric Mormon Church, a value grounded in Latter-day Saint theology. These turn-of-the-twentieth-century Mormons understood their children as souls released specifically into their care, "pearls of Great Price." "We have become the fathers and mothers of lives, and the Gods of the Holy Priesthood in the eternal world have been watching us and our movements in relation to these things," church president John Taylor declared. Therefore it was essential to "train up . . . children in the way they should go."[38] If parents succeeded and family members behaved rightly, they would realize joyful togetherness in the afterlife. Even during inevitably sorrowful mortal existence, parents held the power to make their family life "a little heaven on earth" by following exhortations to raise their children to be "good Latter-day Saints."[39]

As suggested above, the salutary effects of libraries on children had long been a theme of Mary Downey's, and she toured Utah giving talks with titles like, "The Child and the Book." Howard Driggs not only echoed this theme

38 Taylor, "Discourse," 19: 246 and 20:60.

39 Nelson, *The Mormon Village*, 101.

but added an alarmist spin. Young people in the current era, he emphasized in rural town after rural town, faced many temptations as boys in particular were being lured to mischief and wasting time by the unsavory influences proliferating in Utah. "Something must be done," he advised, "to substitute the saloon and billiard hall." Children with time on their hands would be tempted to become the sort of idle "street boys" who inevitably fell into pranks and advanced to crime.

The remedy which would "correct this evil," according to Driggs, was "a well-stocked library"—specifically a Carnegie library, a comfortable, modern space offering "refining pleasure" and "valuable information" in its carefully chosen selection of books.[40] In addition to spreading this library gospel orally, Driggs contributed an article in 1909 to *The Improvement Era*, a widely circulated Mormon publication. Two contrasting sets of photos illustrated this piece, which was titled "The Utah Library-Gymnasium Movement": one depicted solid-looking (even church-like) Carnegie libraries recently erected in Utah; the other presented ponderously captioned images of boys in iffy situations ("Little Boys on Street Corner. A Bad Place for Boys" and "Boys Playing Cards at Haystack. Bad for Character").[41]

In arguing the efficacy of appropriate literature in shaping character (and decrying the influence of "lurid literature," as this article also did), Driggs was sounding a theme that had been central to the profession of American librarianship from its beginnings. Wayne A. Wiegand writes that librarians in the United States have always subscribed to an "ideology of reading," being convinced that "good reading led to good social behavior, bad reading to bad social behavior." To decide what books fell into the former category, Wiegand explains, librarians deferred to "experts located outside librarianship," members of a conservative elite who endorsed a traditional canon.[42] In Driggs's case, though, the definition of what constituted "good reading" was more particular than the typical canon of books, influenced specifically by Latter-day Saint beliefs about what was appropriate. The particular subset of the population whose "good behavior" was emphasized was also different than the working class whose acculturation Wiegand describes as a

40 See, for example, the account of Driggs's address in Brigham City, *Box Elder (Brigham City, UT) News*, May 30, 1912. Evans also describes Driggs's rhetoric in "A History of the Public Library Movement in Utah," 50.

41 Driggs,"The Utah Library-Gymnasium Movement," 510–16.

42 Wiegand, "The Development of Librarianship in the United States," 100–2.

typical goal of library service. In focusing on children, Driggs was not simply evoking a characteristically LDS concern, but also a topical one.

For around the turn of the twentieth century these rural Latter-day Saints would have been particularly concerned about their children. The Mormon Church had denounced the practice of polygamy by its members after 1890 in order to obtain statehood, and once that status was granted in 1896 theocratic government became illegal also. Though only a minority of Mormons had ever practiced polygamy, its cultural roots were deep, for it had been established by Joseph Smith, the sect's beloved martyred founder. Federal anti-polygamy persecutions in the late-nineteenth century (during which polygamists were hunted down and imprisoned) had made polygamy into a symbol of Mormon self-determination. Now Utah's own political leaders were required to help eradicate polygamy's last vestiges.[43] Even worse, Mormonism's sacred control over its own children was compromised by federally imposed regulation, which forbade public schools to teach Mormon doctrine.

Utah's demographics as well as its culture were visibly changing. As Eastern capital expanded railroads, enlarged mining districts, and funded new industry, members of ethnic minorities came to Utah in ever-increasing numbers. Italians, Greeks, and Eastern Europeans argued for unions and they struck with highly publicized violence. With no interest in assimilating with Utah's dominant Mormon culture, they retained their old-country customs and their religions.[44]

As consequence of these changes, Mormons feared that the state's moral climate was being dangerously compromised. Though Utah had always suffered from "vice"—saloons, prostitutes, billiard halls—statehood seemed to encourage the proliferation of such secular influences. Mormon newspapers regularly featured scare stories about gentile city and state administrations that loosened regulations and ignored blatantly illegal activities. The election of the overtly anti-Mormon American Party to control of Salt Lake City's government in 1904 sparked particular apprehension.[45]

In 1907–08, those who feared that Utah was becoming completely corrupted responded with horror when that city government implemented

43 For an account of anti-polygamy crusades in Utah and nearby states, see Van Wagoner, *Mormon Polygamy*, 105–52.

44 Papanikolas, "The New Immigrants," presents a helpful overview of early-twentieth-century immigration to Utah.

45 Cleverley, "The Development of an Urban Pattern," 551.

Incursions, 1: Leon Goulet Saloon, Salt Lake City, Utah.

"quasi-legalized prostitution." In fact Salt Lake City had long had a prostitution problem, and gentile mayor John Bransford was simply trying to limit the trade's presence by establishing a designated district. Rather than allowing prostitutes to walk the entire downtown, as they were, he ordered a city block walled. This zone, popularly called the "Stockade," held prostitutes' living quarters, a dance hall, a saloon, stores, and other amenities. Prostitutes who relocated there were guaranteed freedom from city interference, though they were expected to undergo regular health examinations and abide by specific rules that limited their mobility and accept the direction of a long-time Salt Lake City madam (invited to this office by the mayor). Outrage soon led to the Stockade's closure in 1911, but the project had by then received such lurid press that nothing would have set the Mormons' minds at ease.[46]

Though the temptations of Salt Lake City were real, it's important to realize that in these fifteen rural communities the threat of youthful corruption

46 Ibid. and MacKell, *Red Light Women*, 301–13.

Incursions, 2: Building the Stockade, Salt Lake City, Utah.

was largely in residents' heads. Scattered evidence of gentile invasion did exist in a few of these hamlets—a pool hall in Preston, a saloon in Murray City, and both in Tooele thanks to gentile miners—but their children, on the whole, continued to lead extremely sheltered lives by Intermountain West standards. Not only did the region's largest cities (Spokane, Reno) tempt young men with red-light districts, saloons, gambling, and gangs, but most medium-sized communities struggled also with vice, including Boise, which had a thriving prostitution culture.[47] The newspapers of numerous small towns, including Baker City and Rock Springs, periodically reported criminal mischief, violence, property crime, and youthful vagrancy.[48] These

47 Prostitution has been estimated to have been the largest occupational group for women in the Mountain West, behind paid domestic service (MacKell, *Red Light Women*, 4). Land and Land note that Reno's downtown was so dangerous that college students were forbidden to go there (*Reno*, 36). For details about Spokane's vice and crime, see chapter 7.

48 Baker City even possessed a consolidated zone of vice, where "young people and ladies were warned against straying onto that side of the street," Baker County Historical Society, *The History of Baker City*.

fifteen Utah towns, in contrast, saw few reports of any actual juvenile misbehavior outside of minor mischief, as when some boys got drunk in Cedar City in 1913.[49]

Still, rural Mormons *feared* that their children were in danger. Though they bravely proclaimed their moral superiority to Utah's largest, now-corrupted cities (Tooele's newspaper chided Salt Lake for calling itself "great" when it had six saloons in one block[50]), they also expressed substantial anxiety about what might happen in their own communities. "Matters [must] be regulated and the pernicious evil purged from our midst," wrote the editor of Preston's *Franklin County Citizen* on January 31, 1913, speaking of the pool hall. The editor of the *Panguitch Progress* went so far as to claim in 1915 that a crisis point had arrived. Citizens had to decide whether boys' "strength" was to be "wasted in mischief-making, deviltry, dissipation, and destructive works, or shall be diverted to good ends."[51]

As Driggs, Jacobsen, and Downey promoted Carnegie libraries in rural Mormon villages, they spoke directly to such fears of outside corruption. Establishing a Carnegie library, Driggs assured his listeners, would mean taking control of what their children read, and thus assuring that their character would be appropriately shaped. He even issued a thinly veiled suggestion that Carnegie libraries would function as necessary correctives to secular public education, whose administrators were "spending vast sums of money in teaching the children to read and very little teaching them what to read."[52]

---

49 *Iron County (Cedar City, UT) Record*, Dec. 19, 1913. Tooele had the greatest cause to fear change among this group of towns, for a smelter constructed in 1910 did draw an influx of rowdy gentile labor. Newspaper reports indicate that ladies were occasionally "insulted" downtown, though the miscreants were promptly arrested – see *Tooele (UT) Transcript*, Apr. 22, 1910. Some miners drank heavily, but their number was slightly reduced after several died in a drunken accident as they walked to town to buy more liquor. See, *Tooele (UT) Transcript*, Apr. 1, 1909. Still, Tooele remained governed by Mormon city officials, and Mormon Church news dominated the local newspaper. See, for example, the *Tooele (UT) Transcript*, Feb. 5, 1909.

50 "Great," the editor argued, should equate with "clean" in *Tooele (UT) Transcript*, Feb. 12, 1909.

51 *Panguitch (UT) Progress*, Apr. 5, 1915.

52 Though Mormon tradition celebrates the culture's reverence for reading, the actual texts read were always supposed to be selected to agree with church values. "Unclean" reading was explicitly discouraged. One early church leader remarked that if he had to choose whether Mormon children would be proficient in traditional school subjects or in church teaching, he would always choose the latter (Author, *Journal of Discourses*, 286–90). Children weren't the only ones considered at risk of being seduced by unsuitable books. Around the time of Cedar City's Carnegie application, the local newspaper

So compelling was this argument that it supplanted economic pro-Carnegie library rhetoric even in several pairs of rural Utah towns that were competing for intra-regional supremacy with a vigor reminiscent of the communities described in the previous chapter. As the largest towns in southern Utah, St. George and Cedar City had long been contesting their claims as market center for the "Dixie" region when they applied in the same year for Carnegie libraries. Rather than emphasizing their communities' bright economic futures, however, Carnegie library applicants from both bragged about their status as centers of wholesome learning. Cedar City's initial inquiry letter to Carnegie described the town's normal school and St. George's detailed its Mormon Stake Academy and high school. Both claimed to need a Carnegie library because they served "a considerable number of students from other places." Local rhetoric followed this theme. "The artistic new building will of itself be an inspiration and an elevating influence for hundreds of young people," Cedar City's citizens were told.[53]

Competition proved even more bitter between the other pair of towns south of Salt Lake, Manti and Ephraim, communities contesting not only a theoretical supremacy but the tangible advantage of designation as the county seat of central Utah's Sanpete County and home to the county high school.[54] Like the communities described in chapter three, Manti and Ephraim regularly maligned each other in their respective presses. "Ephraim has eight telephones, against forty for Manti. Ephraim has no waterworks system, insufficient hotel accommodations, no electric lights, no bank, and not even a first-class public school building," sniped the *Manti Messenger* in 1904. When it came time to promote Carnegie libraries, however, youth-centered rhetoric trumped economic competition. A Carnegie library, the *Messenger* told readers, would provide an "attractive and elevating" influence providing "added mental strength . . . and a protection against the allurements of vice" to boys. Conceding that taxes were already high, the editor reminded readers that "Our children are everything to us." Though

editor cautioned women against privileging reading of any kind over other duties. "If there is anything that seems out of place and disorderly," he wrote, "it is a mother or grown daughter leisurely reading while the children are unkempt in appearance," *Iron County (Cedar City, UT) Record*, Mar. 1, 1912.

53 Letter from Kate P. Macfarlane to Andrew Carnegie, Mar. 16, 1912; letter from Thomas Judd to Andrew Carnegie, 14 May 1912; *Iron County (Cedar City, UT) Record*, Dec. 19, 1913.

54 Antrei, *The Other Forty-Niners*, 400–2. Boorstin discusses the frequence and intensity of "County-Seat Wars" in newly settled districts in *The Americans*, 161–68.

Ephraim's editor remained a bit more competitively oriented, he still emphasized the child theme. "Ephraim's reputation as an educational center is at stake!" he challenged readers of the *Ephraim Enterprise*.[55]

The Local Logistics of Rural Utah Carnegie Applications

Invested with such symbolism, Carnegie libraries found ready support in rural Utah. When Howard Driggs visited Brigham City, citizens immediately and "unanimously" decided to pursue a grant. Richmond and St. George applied on the heels of Karen Jacobsen's visits. The latter town even established its own library-gymnasium board in imitation of the state model to ensure that its application progressed efficiently.[56]

While some who took charge of rural Utah communities' Carnegie library applications were prosperous business or professional men like the leaders of economically motivated applications, others were not. Instead, the constant variables in rural Utah were maleness and prominence in the local Mormon Church. Though women had occasionally been involved in founding church-related pre-Carnegie libraries and often served as community librarians, adult male church leaders or the adolescent boys in Mutual Improvement Associations were more typically associated with library establishment in their capacity as community moral guardians.

When Carnegie library campaigns began, this patriarchal tendency prevailed. In Ephraim, Tooele, Richmond, Lehi, Murray City, American Fork, and Brigham City, library boards were all-male.[57] Now and then a female librarian served on a board as secretary and shared correspondence duties, as did St. George's Ida Miles. The primary direction of applications, though, was inevitably assumed by men who already held Church-related offices, men whom others had become accustomed to following. D. H. Morris of St. George was a member of the church's High Council and principal of

55 *Manti (UT) Messenger*, Oct. 20, 1904, Nov. 3, 1911 and *Ephraim (UT) Enterprise*, May 8, 1913.

56 Letter from Ida Miles to James Bertram, May 14, 1912, CCA and letter from Kate P. Macfarlane to the Carnegie Corporation of New York, Mar. 16, 1912, CCA.

57 Hepworth, "Carnegie Libraries," 58; Lidell, "Libraries,"104; letter from Samuel L. Goodwin to Andrew Carnegie, Aug. 4, 1917, CCA. Lists of library board members appear in Centennial Book Committee, *Ephraim's First 100 Years*, 108 and in Peters, "History of the Brigham City (Utah) Library," 21.

the Mormon St. George Stake Academy, while Joseph S. Geddes of Preston served as president of the Oneida Stake. Such men sometimes also held positions related to secular education. Tooele's correspondence was conducted by the school principal and Lehi's library committee chair was president of the town Board of Education. Some Carnegie library leaders commanded particular prestige as descendents of the men initially "called" to settle their towns, including Thomas Sevy of Panguitch and George Hendricks of Richmond.[58]

These library application leaders echoed the pro-library rhetoric which Driggs and his associates had used to sell the projects. Brigham City's Carnegie library was promoted as "a splendid institution where . . . children could go and read the best books." Tooele's application was said to be the centerpiece of a concerted campaign "now going on for the intellectual and moral improvement of the young people of this city."[59] An applicant from Parowan noted that a Carnegie library would "diffus[e] the influence of good books," and members of St. George's Carnegie Library Committee emphasized that while the town's current library was "doing much good," it was inadequate to the needs of local youth.[60]

Thanks to leaders' connections, communities in this cluster rarely had difficulty obtaining suitable building sites. Indeed, sites were regularly donated outright by institutions or people who endorsed the agenda they symbolized. Mormon stake presidencies in Parowan, Ephraim, Mt. Pleasant, Smithfield, Murray City, Cedar City, and Preston donated lots, as did the widow of Richmond's founder (and mother of its library board present), and the school board in St. George. In keeping with the libraries' perceived significance, these sites were invariably near Mormon church property. Parowan's Carnegie library arose in the same block as a ward

58 These men are identified in various sources, including Judy, "A History of Preston," 77; Tooele County Chapter, Daughter of Utah Pioneers, *History of Tooele* County, 17; Bair, *History of Richmond*, 39.

59 *Box Elder News (Brigham City, UT)*, May 30, 1912 and *Tooele (UT) Transcript*, Feb. 18, 1910.

60 Letter from Kate Taylor to Andrew Carnegie Oct. 27, 1914 and letter from Ida Mills to Andrew Carnegie, Oct. 27, 1912. The connection between Carnegie libraries and children was embodied in the later stages of Ephraim's Carnegie library construction when schoolchildren went door-to-door collecting money for books, and eighth-graders physically transferred the old church library books to the new facility, see, *Ephraim (UT) Enterprise*, March 20, 1915.

Panguitch, Utah, Carnegie library, a corrective to "mischief-making, deviltry, dissipation, and destructive works."

chapel, a ward tabernacle, and a Mormon recreation hall, while Murray's was adjacent to a chapel. Smithfield's, St. George's, Manti's, and Panguitch's abutted tabernacles.[61]

Contention over library levies was as rare as dissention over site selection. Brigham City's citizens supported their levy by a margin of three to one, Richmond's proposition passed ninety-five to twelve, and Lehi's triumphed by "a large majority."[62] In a few places where additional levies were simultaneously proposed (as in Parowan, where the vote on municipal waterworks came up simultaneously with the vote on the library levy), or where citizens felt overburdened already with debt (as in Murray City), projects were delayed, but not for long.[63]

Citizens even came forth in a spirit of tithing reminiscent of their church obligation where the costs rose beyond available resources. When bids for

61 Hepworth, *Carnegie Libraries*, 42–43.

62 *Box Elder News (Brigham City, UT)*, July 11, 1912; Bair, *History of Richmond*, 39; letter from William Gurney to Andrew Carnegie, Aug. 21, 1917, CCA.

63 Hepworth, *Carnegie Libraries*, 30 and Winterowd, "Murray City Library History," 39.

Cedar City's building exceeded the amount that Carnegie had promised, a mass meeting of citizens unanimously authorized the city council to "raise any sum needed" through an additional tax levy.[64] When Carnegie would only give $6,000 for Panguitch's library, Mayor Thomas Sevy told Bertram that "the individual members of the Council and Library Board have guaranteed to raise the difference in cost of the building."[65] St. George's citizens rallied to make up a shortfall after their library cost more than Carnegie was willing to give.[66]

With such enthusiastic local support and with help from the Utah Library-Gymnasium Commission, Carnegie public library applications from these fifteen towns stand as models of efficiency. Some Utah communities even completed the preliminary steps toward a promise before they wrote the Carnegie, thanks to the guidance of Driggs, Jacobsen, and Downey.[67] Applicants appear to have been told approximately how large a promise offer to expect from Carnegie, given their valuation and population, and to have framed their support resolutions accordingly.[68] The initial letters from Panguitch (April 5, 1915), Smithfield (Sept. 10, 1917), and Richmond (Aug. 14, 1912) emphasized that these cities had already passed tax levies equivalent to 10 percent of the gifts they sought. Richmond's board even enclosed a completed "Schedule of Questions" with its initial inquiry, triggering a question from Bertram about how the community had procured the blank.[69]

---

64 *Iron County (Cedar City, UT) Record*, Apr. 25, 1913.

65 Letter from Thomas Sevy to James Bertram, Apr. 29, 1916, CCA.

66 Miller, *The Immortal Pioneers*, 117.

67 Staff members, particularly Downey, stepped in to help Utah applicants where they encountered opposition from Bertram. She advised St. George's library board on appropriate building materials, for example, when Bertram objected to expenses, see, letter from John T. Woodbury to James Bertram, Nov. 5, 1914, CCA. Clearly loyal to the Utah towns under her direction, she expressed a pragmatic, unsentimental attitude toward the program's grand benefactor and his apparatus. "Something [must] be done very soon," she advised Mt. Pleasant residents when they considered applying for a grant in 1916, "as Mr. Carnegie is an aged man and not likely to hold out much longer," quoted in the *Mt. Pleasant (Utah) Pyramid*, Jan. 28, 1916.

68 In a very few cases, Library-Gymnasium staff members seem to have encouraged applicants to ask for inappropriately large amounts, as when Brigham City first requested $20,000 at Driggs's suggestion but settled for $12,000, see, *Box Elder News (Brigham City, UT)*, May 30, 1912.

69 Letter from James Bertram to George Hendricks, July 31, 1912, CCA.

Initial inquiry letters from these towns sound a distinctively confident, professional note, even when they came from the tiniest places, like the letter written by Parowan's mayor Joseph McGregor:

> We have been informed that the terms of the Carnegie grants are that the city council agree to appropriate by taxation, annually, ten percent of the amount asked for the building, as a maintenance fund. We have recently voted a tax here that will bring us something over $600, annually, and possibly, this may be increased, so we should like to make application for a $6,000 building. Will you kindly send us blanks?[70]

Here and there library design did temporarily retard progress. A few of these communities, like their counterparts elsewhere, dreamed of grander libraries than Carnegie would allow for their populations (Smithfield) or requested money for climate-specific enhancements about which Bertram was skeptical (St. George). The most distinctive and significant disagreements in the group, however, resulted when local preoccupation with serving children conflicted with Bertram's notions of proper library architecture. Murray City's application stalled when Bertram complained that the children's reading room had taken the place usually assigned to adult facilities. American Fork's slowed when he noted that the building had been designed to give children a full 25 percent of main floor space, supplanting an adult lecture room.[71] Both communities eventually compromised on design.

The dedication ceremonies that celebrated completion of these fifteen libraries took on a quasi-religious character. Citizens were directed from the pulpit to attend, while officials who had supervised the grants offered prayers and quoted Howard Driggs. Driggs himself sometimes attended and other guests included prominent out-of-town church officials and educational administrators.[72] As might be expected, children were featured at

---

70 Letter from Joseph McGregor to Andrew Carnegie, July 7, 1912, CCA.

71 Letter from James Bertram to P. M. Kelly, May 23, 1921 and letter from James Bertram to A. Bird, Feb. 17, 1915, CCA.

72 See, for example, the descriptions of ceremonies in Lehi in, Lehi Centennial Commission, *Lehi's Centennial History*, 347 and in Manti in, *Manti([UT) Messenger*, Jan. 5, 1912. Ephraim sent Bertram a personal invitation to its ceremony (letter from P. C. Anderson to James Bertram, Mar. 22, 1915, CCA), an offer that might have been motivated by an attempt to surpass neighboring Manti, which had hosted Driggs and Utah's governor at its Carnegie library dedication.

these ceremonies. Arriving in organized processions from their school or the church, they sat together on stage or at the front of the crowd. They sang and offered recitations. They trooped across the stage to sign up for the library cards as their doting parents watched.[73]

Thus these fifteen morally motivated applications reflected communities' specific contemporary preoccupations no less than the cluster of applications discussed in chapter 3. Rather than marking these Mormons as people destined for earthly prosperity, however, they reassured them that they had remained faithful to the "Zionic character" and "communitarian single-mindedness" Leonard Arrington and Melvin Larkin have noted as hallmarks of Latter-day Saint self-definition.[74] While the rest of Utah might be changing, as these rural Mormons gazed at their new Carnegie library buildings (especially when the same gaze took in a Mormon church), they could take comfort and pride in believing that they were still united in a vital and living culture, a culture whose priorities were in the right place.

Such sentiments were voiced directly in an article published in a special Christmas edition of the *Iron County Record* which appeared as Cedar City's Carnegie library was nearing completion. Contributed by the town's librarian, Jean Brown, the article complemented citizens warmly for their support of the project.[75] For many years, she acknowledged, Cedar City's residents had made "a library of good books" available to young people. But the new Carnegie library demonstrated that they were enduring considerable sacrifices to take such stewardship to a new level, so proving themselves "far ahead" of most other communities "in social and moral conditions." The library, she concluded with pride, would stand as a visible expression of the "cohesive force of love."

---

73 High school students were especially evident in Manti, where they presented their school "yells" in celebration of the new building, *Manti([Utah) Messenger*, Jan. 5, 1912.

74 Arrington and Larkin, "The Logan Tabernacle," 301–2.

75 Significantly for this chapter's argument about the locally assigned signification of Carnegie libraries, this article does not appear in the section devoted to business expansion or population growth, but in the section titled "The Moral and Social Conditions of Cedar City, Utah," see, *Iron County (Cedar City, UT) Record*, Dec. 19, 1913.

5

Carnegie Libraries in Religiously Diverse Utah Communities

"An enlightened people"

THOUGH AROUND THE TURN OF THE TWENTIETH CENTURY, rural Latter-day Saints perceived that their culturally hegemonic way of life was being challenged by a gentile invasion, outsiders had in fact lived in Utah for many years. Among the earliest gentiles to arrive were the military occupation forces of Johnston's Army, soldiers assigned to surveillance in 1857–58 because the federal government feared Mormon sedition. During the Civil War, a military division under Colonel Patrick Connor camped above Salt Lake City, gaining notoriety for its harassment of residents. Utah's territorial officials were not Mormon and their relationship with the people whom they were superintending was often contentious. After the Civil War gentiles came to Utah in increasing numbers. Missionaries settled in the territory to attempt to convert Mormons. Miners, freighters, and railroaders emigrated to take advantage of new economic opportunities. Utah's largest cities—Salt Lake City, Ogden, and Provo—held substantial non-Mormon populations by the turn of the twentieth century; so did some smaller places like Eureka, Price, and Springville.

Utah's non-Mormon minority found itself uneasily integrated into the state's predominant culture. Gentiles protested discrimination in hiring and blue laws and they complained that Mormon religion was being taught in community schools. They found themselves excluded from the social life of their towns and they protested that their children were shunned by Mormon children. They claimed that community officials were more interested in collecting church tithing and building church structures than initiating civic improvements. They argued that the cooperative stores Brigham Young promoted were designed to discourage gentile entrepreneurship. Mormons, in their turn, accused these outsiders of challenging their freedom of religion, inciting violence, and corrupting their young people.[1]

Given this history of suspicion and discontent, it is absurd to imagine that identifying Carnegie public libraries with the LDS church would have fostered universal support for grant applications in Utah's mixed-religion communities. No gentile uneasy about the separation of church and state would ever have pledged tax support to an institution promoted, as Howard Driggs once suggested in a Latter-day Saint periodical, as "a help to . . . the Church."[2] No non-Mormon would have stood by gratefully while a stake president decided which were the "best books" and prohibited literature he considered inappropriate. No non-Mormon would have imagined a Mormon Sunday school committee as the appropriate governing body for a free public library.

When citizens of Utah's religiously diverse communities sought to interest others in Carnegie libraries, they were thus obligated to devise other arguments in favor of the institutions and to constitute their governing boards in different ways. This chapter explores the various shapes Carnegie library applications assumed in several clusters of such Utah communities, arguing that, once again, reading the local mindset was crucial to pitching a library successfully. No matter how religiously and ethnically varied a town's population was, if library proponents could find a way to symbolically connect their Carnegie library with some common community agreement about "who we are" or "who we want to be" that resonated with a significant proportion of the population, their applications stood a good chance of succeeding.

Small Mixed-Religion Towns

Local history would have made citizens of one cluster of four small Utah towns especially sensitive to the dangers of sectarian divisiveness. As geographically isolated towns, Springville, Mt. Pleasant, Price, and Eureka City

---

1 For the history of early Mormon-gentile relations in Utah see Dwyer, *The Gentile Comes to Utah* and Alexander and Allen, *Mormons and Gentiles.*

2 This quotation comes from Driggs, "The Utah Library-Gymnasium Movement," 514.

understood the necessity of community self-reliance, yet obvious fault lines in all four offered the threat of paralyzing civic disagreement and stalemate.

Like the communities described in the previous chapter, Springville and Mt. Pleasant had been established as Mormon agricultural settlements and still made their livings primarily from agriculture at the turn of the twentieth century. Their insular culture changed, however, when they were selected as mission sites by protestant denominations engaged in a coordinated effort to proselytize in Mormon Utah.[3] Presbyterians established a church and academy in Springville, both of which quickly gained a foothold. Baptist and Episcopal churches joined them. Mt. Pleasant proved an even richer ground for missionaries, for there Swedish Mormon immigrants had already apostatized, disaffected because LDS services were not held in their language. Once a minister arrived, it was a short step from the "Liberal Hall" they had built (named for Utah's anti-Mormon political party) to Presbyterian services. A Presbyterian secondary school, the Wasatch Academy, was established in Mt. Pleasant and soon became the second-largest non-Mormon school in Utah. Methodists followed, building a church in Mt. Pleasant in 1886.[4]

As mining centers, Eureka City and Price were also much more diverse than the communities described in chapter 4, and they faced particularly volatile situations. Utah's mining communities had always been associated in the public mind with anti-Mormonism, thanks to the fact that the state's earliest miners were members of Connor's occupation force and to their raunchy lifestyle featuring saloons, gambling, and prostitution. Robert Dwyer describes an occupational segregation in which agricultural work in Utah was conducted "almost entirely by Mormons" and mining "almost entirely . . . by anti-Mormons."[5] Yet both Eureka City and Price included Mormons along with gentiles, setting the stage for potentially contentious civic life.

While Price had been settled in 1879 as a Mormon agricultural colony, its economic life transformed radically in 1893 when the Denver and Rio

3 Lyon and Leonard, 317–55 and Dwyer, 30–41, 161–89. A history of the Methodist Church in Utah describes how Presbyterians, Methodists, Congregationalists, and Baptists formally coordinated their efforts (United Methodist Centennial Committee, *The United Methodist Church*, 91).

4 For the history of Mt. Pleasant, see Longsdorf, *Mt. Pleasant*, and Antrei, *The Other 49'ers*.

5 Dwyer, *The Gentile Comes to Utah*, 62.

Grande Western Railroad laid track through the region and coal mining became profitable in Carbon County. As the new hub of a lively mining district, Price drew numerous non-Mormon immigrants, including Finns, Italians, "Austrians" (Serbians, Croatians, and Slovenians), and Greeks. Working in dangerous conditions for low wages in company towns to the north and east of Price, these miners voiced discontent, welcomed union organizers, and went on strike several times. Violence and threats of violence drew the National Guard to Carbon County. Already-festering antagonisms between new and old residents were exacerbated when some LDS leaders, according to one historian, "assisted in recruiting strikebreakers among the farmers and residents of surrounding communities."[6]

Eureka City also included an uncommonly large number of Mormons for a Utah mining town, thanks to the fact that its dominant operation, the Bullion Beck Company, was run by Jessie Knight, one of the rare Mormon mining magnates. Knight employed Mormon miners, and the community held enough Mormon wards for a stake.[7] The enormous output of the mines around Eureka, however (an early smelter was said to have produced 172 tons of silver bullion in sixty days), demanded a large workforce. Irish settled in the area after the transcontinental railroad was completed, along with Cornish, Welsh, Germans, and Finns. By the turn of the twentieth century the community held Protestant churches (including Methodist, Episcopal, Baptist, and Lutheran), a Catholic church, and parochial schools staffed by Sisters of the Holy Cross, leftists groups, and more than a dozen fraternal orders.[8]

As had happened in Price, labor unrest opened divisions in this mixture, in particular the Mormon-gentile dichotomy. The strike of 1893 brought tensions to a head. After Bullion Beck stood firm against collective bargaining, union men and townswomen brought pressure to bear on strikebreakers. Federal marshals were imported to keep order. Accusations began to circulate that Bullion Beck was not only hiring Mormon farmers

6 Powell, "Coal Industry," 130–35. Papanikolas discusses statewide labor conflict in "The New Immigrants," 447–62, and describes conflict in the Price area in particular in "Women in the Mining Communities of Carbon County," 80–102. See also Notarianni's "Utah's Ellis Island." Price's history is recounted also in Watt, *A History of Carbon County*, in Madsen, *Carbon County, A History*, and in the Carbon County Chapter, Daughters of Utah Pioneers, *Ecclesiastical History of Carbon County*.

7 McCune, *History of Juab County*, 17.

8 Notarianni, "Tintic Mining District," 344–49.

as scabs but using Mormon bishops as employment agents. The Secretary of the Eureka Miners Union, John Duggan, demanded that the Mormon Church President "use his influence to stop church 'meddling' in the labor problem."[9]

Apparently realizing that their actual or incipient tensions could not be allowed to continue—that their very municipal survival depended on détente—residents of all four communities attempted to bury their differences in the years immediately prior to their Carnegie library applications. Notarianni suggests that a conscious attempt at reconciliation took place in Eureka City. After a citizens' committee survey found overwhelming sympathy for unionized miners, "the Beck Mine management and business approach changed, becoming more compatible with community interests."[10] Fostering cooperation, voters took pains to return a balanced "triumvirate" of city officials term after term, with Catholics, Protestants, and Mormons sharing governance. The community's Mormon choir sang at midnight mass at Catholic St. Patrick's, and Catholics, Mormons, and Methodists jointly prepared food for public celebrations. When various churches cooperated to plan a common trip to the Lagoon amusement park, so many people joined the intramural fun that the town was effectively deserted.[11]

Price's various denominations also extended public hands of friendship to each other. The city's Methodist Episcopal minister attended the local Mormon tabernacle's dedication and registered in the press high praise for the sacrifices his LDS neighbors had made to build it. A few years later that tabernacle was chosen as the site for joint Methodist Episcopal Academy and public high school graduation exercises.[12] Although Price's municipal government declined to donate land for a Greek Orthodox church, a coalition of businessmen from a variety of religious groups soon raised enough money to purchase a lot. Price consequently became, in the judgment of one commentator, a place where no single religion "was really dominant, an unusual situation in Southern Utah."[13]

9 Ibid., 349–51 and Notarianni, "Tale," 155–58.

10 Notarianni, Tintic, 352.

11 Notariani, "Tale," 121, 166–69.

12 Watt, 232, 262.

13 Ibid., 7. Discussion of the Greek community's efforts to build a church in Price appears in the pamphlet "Hellenic Orthodox Church of the Assumption, Price, Utah."

Prosperous Eureka, Utah, around the turn of the twentieth century.

Springville and Mt. Pleasant's newspapers also suggest comfortable inter-religious mingling. Springville's gentile club women socialized with their Mormon counterparts in joint meetings featured in the newspaper; Mt. Pleasant's Mormon women's organization went so far as to give a banquet for its gentile Twentieth Century Club, involving a Presbyterian minister in the occasion.[14] Mt. Pleasant gained such a reputation for tolerance that the newspaper editor in Manti suggested the former town offered a corrupting influence on young people.[15]

In the minds of citizens of these four communities, however, open-mindedness was a positive thing, a feature of town culture so positive that it was used as promotion. "The utmost tolerance in spiritual matters prevails," the Springville *Independent*'s editor declared proudly in a special issue lauding the town's advantages. Speaking of the benefits of living in Carbon County, a civic leader in Price noted that "most people are tolerant of each other's religious views and appreciate their differences."[16] The local politics of Carnegie public library building grant applications in all four of these communities were shaped by this atmosphere. As supporters urged their

14 *Springville (UT) Independent*, Jan. 4, 1924 and *Mt Pleasant (UT) Pyramid*, Feb. 25, 1916.

15 *Manti (UT) Messenger*, Aug. 19, 1910.

16 *Springville (UT) Independent*, Mar. 27, 1906 and Watt, *A History of Carbon County*, 247, 255. For an example of balanced new coverage in Price, see the *Carbon County (Price, UT) News*, Oct. 3, 1912, which includes extensive detail about an LDS Conference along with a first-page account of a Methodist-Episcopal wedding.

Diversity in Price, Utah, Greek Orthodox Church congregation.

fellow citizens to pursue applications, they avoided rhetoric that might have been identified with specifically Mormon concerns, and they chose committee members who represented a broad cross-section of the population. Library support in these communities had never been the exclusive work of the Mormon Church. Labor unions had established Eureka's sizeable pre-Carnegie public library. Presbyterians had founded a reading room as soon as they arrived in Mt. Pleasant. Springville's mixed-denomination women's clubs worked with city council to establish the reading room that grew into that town's Carnegie library, and they had been aided by donations "from various religious, civic, and social organizations, and . . . individuals," as a correspondent to Carnegie emphasized.[17] Price had a substantial library in a non-Mormon secondary school, as did the other three.[18]

The library boards which handled these four towns' Carnegie public building grant applications were diverse in their affiliations. Eureka's

17 Letter from Claude K. Davis to James Bertram, Dec. 7, 1915, CCA.

18 Notarianni, "Tale," 166; Longsdorf, *Mt. Pleasant*, 176; Finley, *A History of Springville*, 94.

board included Catholics, Mormons, Protestants, and men not obviously affiliated with any particular religious group, including the town's mayor, J. D. Stack.[19] This effective, proactive board obtained a promise from Carnegie in 1908—two months before Howard Driggs came to town with his message about the need for public libraries. Rather than proselytizing, Driggs found himself congratulating. Though he chose a Mormon church for his address, Eureka's gentiles seem to have ignored this potential sign of special interest, for a variety of churches helped with fundraising.[20]

Similarly balanced leadership directed the other three applications in this cluster. Price's initial inquiry letter was written by the local Methodist Episcopal school principal, but once negotiations began the project leaders were chosen from several interest groups. The city council appointed Mormon Church official Carlos Gunderson as head of the library committee and Mormon bishop A. W. Horsley to the building committee, along with a prominent Methodist Episcopal schoolteacher and members with other affiliations.[21] Mt. Pleasant's Carnegie library committee was constituted as a group of "representative . . . citizens;" it included Mormons and non-Mormons, religious and secular teachers, and members of the town's gentile women's clubs. When both Presbyterian and Mormon churches offered land for Mt. Pleasant's library, board members made a public show of their open-minded impartiality, with one admitting that a public hearing had changed his opinion. "Whatever the people want," he declared, would guide his decision.[22]

Springville's Carnegie public library building grant application was not only distinguished by its democracy, but also by the nature of its prime mover, Sebrina Lund Cropper (Mrs. Mark) Reynolds, a Mormon woman. Though Springfield's Presbyterian minister wrote the community's initial inquiry letter, Mrs. Reynolds assumed charge of conducting the application.

---

19 The list of committee members appointed by J.D. Stark in 1908 is cited in McCune, *History of Juab County*, 199. Religious affiliations of board members throughout this study have been determined by scanning contemporary newspapers and by consulting biographies in Warrum, *Utah Since Statehood*, along with local newspapers.

20 *Eureka (Utah) Reporter*, Oct. 15, 1909.

21 Letter from W. H. Frye to the Carnegie Corporation of New York, Dec. 11, 1911, CCA. In the very beginning, the application does seem to have been conceived as a sectarian project. Frye's initial letter appears on the stationery of the Methodist-Episcopal Academy and suggests that the library be constructed on his school's grounds. As the text notes, however, Mormons were soon given a full share in the project.

22 *Mt. Pleasant (UT) Pyramid*, Jan. 28 and Apr. 26, 1916.

Sebrina Reynolds was a remarkable woman, one who managed at once to be thoroughly Mormon and thoroughly independent. No rebel, she served on the Relief Society Board, taught theology classes, and apparently delighted in the role of wife and mother. She also, though, had studied at Brigham Young University, and she continued to teach high school after her marriage and after the birth of her four children in an era when few Mormon mothers worked outside their homes except from necessity. Sebrina Reynolds's occupation seems to have been voluntary, for her husband ran a successful business and held the office of Springfield fire chief. She also sought wider service than that provided by the local Relief Society, maintaining a high intellectual profile in the community's women's clubs and its cultural life. A biography describes her as "very prominent in literary work" and reports that she gave "many public readings."[23]

When Springville's Carnegie application nearly foundered on the rocks of unsuitable plans and too-high bids, it was Sebrina Reynolds whom the educational leaders, businessmen, and city officials on the board trusted to negotiate with Bertram. So skillful and composed was she that she seems to have single-handedly preserved Springville's opportunity to build a Carnegie library. Like Twin Falls, Springville was still negotiating its grant amount when World War I foreshadowed the end of the library building grant program. In contrast to the Idaho city officials who simply spoke more loudly about their coming greatness, however, Reynolds assembled statistics and anecdotes to demonstrate that building costs were atypically high in south-central Utah. Though Bertram did not raise Carnegie's offer, he was apparently inspired enough by Reynolds's polite, businesslike manner to offer her a solution he did not suggest to many other applicants, the same solution that had made him so angry when adopted independently by Umatilla County, Oregon's Judge Charles Marsh. "I sympathize with you," he wrote with uncharacteristic gentleness, "but in similar cases the difficulty has been solved by the community raising the additional money required itself."[24] Reynolds took his advice and became the major spokesperson in the bond referendum that followed. The vote was unanimously in favor of community buy-in, even though at $13,000 the bond issue entailed a greater

23 Information about Reynolds's life is taken from obituaries in the *Deseret News (Salt Lake City, UT)* and the *Salt Lake (UT) Tribune*, both Jan. 20, 1948.

24 Letter from Bertram to Mrs. Mark Reynolds, Oct. 1, 1917. Bertram's anger at Marsh is noted in chapter 2.

The Springville, Utah, Carnegie library, whose application was directed by Sebrina Reynolds.

obligation than Carnegie himself was incurring.[25] Springville's Carnegie library, which opened for business in 1922, was one of the very last in the nation constructed under the terms of the then-defunct grant program.

These four communities constructed pro-Carnegie-library rhetoric as diplomatically as they framed their building committees. Though Howard Driggs "plead[ed] the cause of the young people" in Eureka and the newspaper editor in Mt. Pleasant inserted the typically Mormon argument that the library would provide "a better place for boys or girls than the streets or worse" in the midst of his list of twenty-one reasons to support a Carnegie library, public arguments from this cluster otherwise avoided any hint of sectarianism, instead evoking locally relevant concerns.[26] The dominant strain in Eureka emphasized the institution's potential effect on miners' and immigrant's lives, with the town's Catholic priest praising libraries' ability to build industrious habits and self-education among workingmen. Another Eureka library proponent suggested that a Carnegie library would function

25 Finley, *A History of Springville*, 94.

26 Driggs's remarks are quoted in the *Eureka (UT) Reporter*, Oct. 15, 1909 and the *Mt. Pleasant (UT) Pyramid*, Apr. 26, 1916.

as an agent of Americanization for miners recently arrived in the country, fostering love of "country and home." Pride in transcending raw mining camp stereotypes was also exploited. Eureka was said to deserve its Carnegie library as a community soon to take its place among the large and prominent cities in Utah. A similar note was sounded during Price's Carnegie campaign, where the institution was proclaimed appropriate to "the greatest little city on earth."[27] Mt. Pleasant's editor democratically emphasized that a Carnegie library would serve all of the town's people (listing debate clubs, literary societies, and businessmen among its beneficiaries, rather than dwelling on Mormon church organizations), adding "a new tone" of polish and dignity to the community.[28] Using language so carefully generic that its signification almost disappears, Sebrina Reynolds proclaimed, "The building will stand as a monument of high ideals and worthy aims and aspirations."[29]

Such tact paid off, for despite the potential for partisan antagonism in these religiously diverse towns, Carnegie library building grant applications enjoyed the same high level of support as they did in Mormon agricultural villages. Miners in Eureka and Price put aside any labor-based resentment they might have harbored toward Carnegie in the name of municipal common good; Mt. Pleasant's citizens approved their library tax levy by a two to one proportion. Dedication ceremonies continued the cooperative theme. A Wasatch Academy professor and a non-Mormon clergyman joined a Mormon bishop on the podium at Mt. Pleasant's. In Eureka City an Episcopal bishop gave the opening prayer while a Catholic priest and Mormon bishop both presented major remarks. In that community Howard Driggs sat onstage alongside the state's gentile governor, and the latter made a point of congratulating the town on the "amenity" of the application process.[30]

---

27 *Eureka (UT) Reporter*, Oct. 15, 1909 and Feb. 21, 1908; *Carbon County (Price, UT) News*, Jan. 23, 1912; letter from W. H. Frye to the Carnegie Corporation of New York, Dec. 11, 1911, CCA.

28 *Mt. Pleasant (UT) Pyramid*, Apr. 26, 1916.

29 Letter from Mrs. Mark Reynolds to Bertram, Sept. 22, 1917, CCA. Sadly, all issues of the local newspaper contemporary with Springville's application disappeared in a newspaper office fire, and without them only scattered evidence exists to suggest how this competent woman rallied local support.

30 *Mt. Pleasant (UT) Pyramid*, Mar. 17, 1916 and Feb. 16, 1917 and *Eureka (UT) Reporter*, Oct. 15, 1909.

Large Cities with Significant Gentile Populations

"Amenity," however, is not a term which could be applied to the Carnegie library applications from Utah's two largest cities. The Mormon bishops who championed Carnegie libraries in Utah's agricultural settlements would have been flabbergasted—and appalled—had they imagined the symbolism being assigned to Carnegie libraries in Salt Lake City and Ogden. Not only were those two applications not projects designed to extend LDS values, they were conceived as aggressively *anti*-Mormon projects.

Salt Lake City's Application for a Main Library

Salt Lake City made two applications to Andrew Carnegie, one for a main library in 1899, the other for the Chapman Branch Library constructed in 1918. While suspicion and antagonism informed both, it is the first that was driven primarily by religious tension. Salt Lake City had long constituted an epicenter of sectarian mistrust in Utah. It was home to the state's anti-Mormon territorial government and held a significant non-Mormon population. The city also functioned as a control center for Protestant denominations that came to Utah to proselytize after the Civil War. Following Presbyterian minister Norman McLeod's advice that the best way to "Christianize" Mormons would be to educate their young people, missionaries channeled their energies into founding schools, like the one in Mt. Pleasant noted in the previous section. Many of these schools attempted to make themselves more attractive to thrifty Saints by eliminating tuition, where many Mormon-dominated "public" schools charged tuition. By 1885 nearly two thousand students, about two-thirds of them from Mormon homes, attended twenty-eight Congregationalist schools in Utah; nine hundred children were enrolled in thirty-one Presbyterian schools, and about three thousand more attended Methodist, Episcopal, Catholic, and Baptist schools across Utah. Salt Lake City was home to several non-Mormon high schools and a gentile teacher-training institute.[31]

While gentiles welcomed Mormon children to their schools, they were usually not so hospitable to adults in their clubs and benevolent organizations. The Young Men's Literary Institute, founded in early territorial days, became famous for its derogation of Latter-day Saints and the city's Masons banned Mormons from membership. Salt Lake City's most elite women's

---

31 Clark and Scott, "From Schoolmarm to State Superintendent," 233–48.

club, the Ladies Literary Association, did not allow Mormons to attend even as visitors until the 1890s.

Whether Mormon women would have wanted to attend, actually, is doubtful, for Salt Lake's Latter-day Saint and gentile women soon clashed over polygamy. Believing the practice of plural marriage to constitute immoral exploitation of women, the city's gentile women formed the Anti-Polygamy Society in 1878, designed to combat "the nefarious influence of the Mormon priesthood." Members sent a statement to the wife of the President of the United States, Mrs. Rutherford B. Hayes, affirming, "With the cordial co-operation and concentration action of the Christian women of the land, we may confidently hope that the great sin of polygamy will be abolished." Mormon women immediately responded, petitioning Congress to uphold polygamy and arguing that "We, the women of the Church of Jesus Christ of Latter-day Saints have been misjudged and misrepresented to the nation by those in our midst of our own sex."[32] Not until the formation of the Utah Federation of Women's Clubs issued in a "decade of détente" later in the century did the general tension begin to relax.[33]

Salt Lake City's earliest pre-Carnegie library was a thoroughly gentile project, established in 1870 as a study club library by women vocal in the anti-polygamy movement.[34] After a few years, the city's anti-Mormon Masons assumed its management. This "Pioneer Library" included not only a selection of reference works, classical and modern literature, and specialized magazines (including *California Architect* and *Book Buyer*), but a collection of "popular books on Mormonism"—scurrilous rants and sensationalized exposes like *Wife Number 19*, a memoir written by an apostate wife of Brigham Young.[35]

32 Dwyer, *The Gentile Comes to Utah*, 191–92, 195–96.

33 For a discussion of the city's women's clubs and cross-religion politics, see Madsen, "Decade of Détente," 298–319. Derr also touches on this subject in "Scholarship, Service, and Sisterhood," 249–94.

34 Parsons traces this history of the Ladies Literary Club in *History of Fifty Years*.

35 Dwyer discusses the Masons in Utah and notes the presence of "popular works" on Mormonism in *The Gentile Comes to Utah*, 155–56. Evans traces the history of the book collection as it passed to the Masons and then to city hands in "A History of the Public Library Movement," 35–45. A partial list of library resources as of June 1, 1898, appears in a report to the "Honorable Board of Directors of the Public Library of Salt Lake City," included as a supporting document submitted to Andrew Carnegie at the time of initial application for a library building grant, CCA.

Such books were guaranteed to offend Salt Lake City's Latter-day Saints. So it is predictable that when municipal support was requested for the institution, Salt Lake City's officials (Mormons, in contrast to the gentiles who staffed territorial government) declined. The collection faced a "hard struggle" to survive for decades. Only in 1897, after a mixed-religion coalition of women associated with the Utah Federation of Women's Clubs gathered 1,000 signatures on a petition, did the Salt Lake City public library first receive tax support.[36]

The institution continued to struggle, however. Part of the problem, given how conservative Salt Lake City's Mormon government was at that point, may have been the institution's apparent refusal to compromise. The anti-Mormon books stayed on the shelves, and a female Protestant minister, the Rev. Mrs. Maynard, was enlisted to give the keynote address at the dedication, where an invitation to a Mormon Church leader might have inspired LDS confidence in the institution as friendly to their interests.[37] Whatever the reason, tax support was minimal, and the city council ignored effective governance to squabble over the proportion of Mormons and non-Mormons on the library board.[38]

Just a year after Salt Lake City's public library received municipal support, a member of the library board decided to take matters into his own hands. This man was presumably a Mormon, given his position as manager of the LDS-oriented *Salt Lake City Herald* (a newspaper derided as "The Mormon Herald"), but he was clearly a liberal Mormon, given his support of the public library. This man (whose signature is illegible on the *Salt Lake Herald* stationery he used but who is later referred to as "Mr. Ingelhart") wrote to William McKay, a gentile federal judge and former Salt Lake City attorney who was an acquaintance of Carnegie, complaining that the city council was sabotaging the Salt Lake City's municipal library and requesting that McKay begin a Carnegie library building grant application. The rooms assigned to the collection in city hall were inadequate, he contended, plus there was no money for acquisitions, and books were being allowed to deteriorate because of city officials' misguided parsimony. Most of the city

36 The library's struggle for survival is discussed in Oyler, "Events in the History of the Salt Lake City Free Public Library." Alexander and Allen also mention this subject (*Mormons and Gentiles*, 118). The women's cooperative efforts are discussed in Parsons, *History of Fifty Years*, 84, and in Madsen, "Decade of Détente."

37 Oyler, "Events in the History of the Salt Lake Free Public Library," 5.

38 Evans, "A History of the Public Library Movement," 43.

councilmen, he told McKay, "Could not understand the value of money applied to this use because they belong to the older, pioneer class—the non-progressive element which has been a drag on the educational institutions of the city and state for years . . .The antagonism which one class of our people has toward the spread of liberal culture . . . has blocked the more progressive element . . . completely."[39] No one even vaguely familiar with Utah could have failed to miss the implication: conservative Mormon opposition was killing the library.

While the editor's words presented nuanced argument for cultural divisions within "our people," when McKay wrote to Carnegie he chose more unilateral and alarmist rhetoric that certainly would have offended the editor had he been aware of it, no matter how liberal he was. Attempting to persuade Carnegie of the urgent need for a Salt Lake City grant (and perhaps voicing his own prejudice), McKay drew on classic anti-Mormon arguments that generalized the culture into a unilateral menace. Of course the city's Mormon leaders were hostile to a public library, he suggested. Mormonism was known for desiring ignorant, tractable followers, so it was in the church's interest to keep Utah "sadly deficient in all that aids or makes for intelligent public opinion." The judge also raised the specter of polygamy. "I believe if properly administered, [a library] will . . . go a long way toward solving that unmentionable problem which legislation had thus far failed to accomplish," he wrote.[40] For the sake of citizens' morals as well as their right to be free of "priestcraft," he pleaded with Carnegie in companionable faux-Scots dialect, the philanthropist should "cast [his] bread upon the drumly waters of benighted Utah."[41]

By coincidence, another Salt Lake City gentile also enlisted an influential man to approach Carnegie at the very end of the nineteenth century. Dr. Thomas Gordon, President of the city's Presbyterian Sheldon Jackson College, urged his friend John Eastman, former US commissioner of education, to lobby for a Carnegie grant to Salt Lake City. A public library would

39 Letter from the [ill.] [Iglehart] to Judge William McKay, Dec. 4, 1899, CCA.

40 For a discussion of polygamy's continuation after the Woodruff Manifesto, which nominally ended the practice, see Van Wagoner, *Mormon Polygamy*, 153–76.

41 Letter from William McKay to Andrew Carnegie, Dec. 11, 1899, CCA. McKay's contention that Mormons were anti-education contrasts with Mormons' own self-perceived emphasis on education, discussed in chapter three. Evans acknowledges this disconnection, calling it "ironic that Utah's first permanent public library would be established by Salt Lake City's non-Mormons" given "the Mormon tradition of education and enlightenment," Evans, "A History of the Public Library Movement," 32.

never have proper support under Mormon leadership, Gordon suggested, because that culture was unsympathetic to liberal education. Jackson's letter picks up that theme with a vengeance, suggesting that any city agency in Salt Lake was "in danger of being perverted to the purpose of this modern Mohammedanism." Jackson reminded Carnegie that Salt Lake City was "the seat of Mormon headquarters" from which the church extended its influence "to every part of the civilized world and thence gathers its obedient followers." It would constitute a tremendous, far-reaching public service, he suggested, to contribute libraries that would serve as "centers of light against the darkness of Mormonism."[42]

It is hard to imagine, given such vitriolic private rhetoric, how such men might have spun a public library's symbolism so that Salt Lake City's Mormon majority would have been convinced to support a Carnegie grant. Fortunately they were never required to sell the project to the public. Within a year, before either correspondent had obtained a promise or raised the issue of a tax levy with local government, city council members received a sudden, unforeseen offer that "nearly carried them off their feet," according to the *Salt Lake Tribune*. John Q. Packard, a Salt Lake City philanthropist and mining magnate about to retire to California, announced that he was giving the city an extraordinary parting gift—a prime city lot worth $20,000 and $75,000 cash—on the condition that the city use these resources to construct a public library. "It took the Council only a few minutes to accept the grant" reported the *Tribune*.[43] The city's magnificent new library opened on Oct. 27, 1905—without Carnegie's assistance and without public exposure of the rancorous sentiment that lay behind at least some citizens' support for books and reading.

Ogden's Application

Ogden's Carnegie library building grant application was also proposed by gentiles and conceived as a corrective to Mormon influence. Since no fairy godfather stepped forth in this case, however, Ogden's pro-library forces struggled with the very problem Salt Lake City's gentiles avoided: how to convince the Mormons in their community to support an institution sought for the very purpose of undermining their cherished culture.

---

42 Letter from John Eastman to Andrew Carnegie, Nov. 28, 1899, CCA.

43 Evans, "A History of the Public Library Movement," 58 and *Salt Lake (UT) Tribune*, Oct. 10, 1900.

Gentiles had a particularly strong presence in Ogden. Originally founded by Mormons, Ogden became contested space in the 1860s after the community of Corinne, a freighting point for the Idaho and Montana mines and a self-proclaimed "Gentile City," lost its economic importance. In its heyday Corinne was a defiant, aggressively "open" town, headquarters of Utah's Liberal Party, an organization dedicated to overthrowing Mormon political domination in Utah (and the source of the name of the social hall constructed by Mt. Pleasant's disaffected Swedes). Once the rail connection at Ogden and branch lines made freight traffic obsolete, most of the population of Corrine moved *en masse* to Ogden, now on the main coast-to-coast route and booming with industry.[44]

Railroad-inspired prosperity drew migrants from other regions to this famous "golden spike" town. Soon Ogden hosted Methodist, Episcopal, Presbyterian, Catholic, and other non-Mormon churches. Liberal Party members preached anti-Mormonism while newcomers frequented saloons and insisted on Sunday recreation. Ogden's original Mormon settlers fought back, attempting to maintain a viable presence but generating hard feelings. When Mormon leaders instructed the rank-and-file to do business only at Latter-day Saint establishments, gentile merchants complained of a boycott.[45]

In 1889, about a decade before Ogden's Carnegie library application, the city elected a member of the Liberal Party as mayor. He appointed men known to be hostile to Mormons as city officials, then (in a gesture of symbolic insult) attempted to rename all of Ogden's streets, substituting word-names for the customary Mormon village north-south-east-west grid. He ruled that no schoolhouse could be used as a place of religious worship, complicating the lives of those who sent their children to the same ward-house room for Mormon public school and Sunday school. He approved funding for badly needed city services, including waterworks, a sewer system, and a city hall, leading gentiles to sneer that the community's Mormons at last would have to place civic quality of life above their tithing obligation. Furious Latter-day Saints mobilized to elect their own ticket at the next election, but that government was overturned at the following election. For

44 For a history of Corinne, see Madsen, *Corinne: The Gentile Capital.*

45 Ogden City Commission, *A History of Ogden*, 49–51. Brigham Young's choice of Ogden in 1869 for the first branch of the Mormon-Church-affiliated store, the Zions Cooperative Mercantile Institute (ZCMI), may have been an attempt to strengthen LDS unity in the city.

several decades, control of city government swung between Mormon and gentile, with policies made and canceled with dizzying rapidity.[46]

Ogden's Carnegie library application began in the midst of this turmoil. Like Salt Lake City, Ogden contained a pre-Carnegie library, a modest collection established by a gentile women's club and supported by a gentile board. This library had with great effort achieved some municipal support, but board members, as in Salt Lake City, were convinced that Mormon city administrations neglected the institution. In 1901 the library board organized a committee to approach Carnegie. The rhetoric these correspondents chose, like the arguments used from Salt Lake City, was frankly anti-Mormon. "Unhealthy religious practices," Carnegie was told, had limited "intellectual advancement" in the city; "sectarian" thinking had thwarted "public and united effort[s] for . . . social and united opportunities." It was crucial to "forever prevent any sectarian control" of a library, for such control currently resulted in a "limited supply of books" and "limited room." These writers assured Carnegie that they were *delighted* that the pledge mandated a constant, ongoing level of support, for this would insure that the institution could not be sabotaged by temporary shifts in the religious composition of city government. "It is doubtful whether there is any place in the United States where so much good could be done or where such a gift would be more appreciated," they concluded.[47]

Ogden received a $25,000 promise within a few weeks.[48] In these pre-1907state-library-reform days, few Utah municipalities could have levied a support tax of $2,500, but the amount was well within the power of booming first-class-city Ogden, and gentile newspapers triumphantly announced the award. The problem was that the city council at the time happened to be Mormon, and it at first resisted imposing a new tax for library purposes. "Keep up the agitation!" urged the editor of the Ogden *Standard*, warning of "a great deal of apathy" on the part of local government towards the library. Officials did finally pass a support resolution, but only after weeks of pressure, several postponements, and many meetings.[49]

46 Ibid., 50–61.

47 Letter from Thomas Goshen and Judge W. L. Maginnis to Andrew Carnegie, Feb. 22, 1901, CCA.

48 Attorney J. A. Howell writes to Carnegie thanking him on behalf of the board for this offer on Mar. 20, 1901, CCA.

49 In this period before Utah's library law was emended, a general vote was not required in a first-class city in order to levy a library tax.

With Ogden's council less than enthusiastic, the project took a long time to complete. Decisions were postponed, site selection caused "turmoil" in extended meetings, every expenditure was debated, and unspecified "unpleasant features" in application logistics delayed progress. When ground was finally broken, contractors discovered that the site contained quicksand and construction costs rose exponentially. Bertram refused to appropriate additional monies and so did Ogden's city council. In order to complete any structure at all, the building committee was forced to compromise on interior features.[50] The budget for books, in particular, was so limited that one speaker at the library's dedication ceremony likened the new structure to "a beautiful cage" with no bird. The *Standard*'s editor attempted to shame residents into filling the embarrassingly empty shelves. Few, he admitted, had even attended the dedication ceremonies. "Now stop this knocking," he urged, asking for donations. "The library board has had trouble enough in completing the building." But Ogden citizens did not open their pockets as had the residents of St. George and Springville, and the library opened with woefully short resources.[51]

"The equipment," librarian Zoe Faddis wrote in an appeal to Carnegie for additional funds, "is most inadequate to the demands made upon it . . . There seems to be no possibility of help from local sources."[52] Municipal economic woes certainly played a role in the library's troubles, for Ogden's city council was at the time involved in a lawsuit against its own waterworks company, and residents were routinely protesting new taxes. But Ogden's Carnegie library proponents also had not used the most diplomatic public rhetoric in promoting the project. Rather than crafting some appeal to the common interests of Ogden's Mormon and gentile residents, they had touted the library as an instrument of educational reform—not the wisest tactic to enlist support from a population still angry about the changes that came with statehood. Supporters had even edged toward McKay's and Jackson's rhetoric by suggesting in not-very-veiled terms that the library

50 A history of the project published at the time of the building's dedication traces this history of difficulties, see, *Standard (Ogden, UT)*, Apr. 22, 1903. The contentious city council meeting where the site was debated is described in the *Standard*, Apr. 17, 1901.

51 *Standard (Ogden, UT)*, Apr. 22, 1903.

52 Letter from Zoe Faddis to Andrew Carnegie, CCA. Though this letter bears no date, it was presumptively written in April/May 1904, since Faddis notes that she has served as Ogden's librarian for one year.

would help citizens escape thought control, enabling "an enlightened people [to] live more rationally." A newspaper editorial had suggested that the project would promote "liberty of thought and freedom of speech" and "individual responsibility." In America, the editor declared, "no class has the right to control others."[53]

Administration of the project had also remained under gentile direction, with the building committee and the first library board after construction comprised thoroughly of gentiles. Not one person identifiable in retrospect as a Mormon leader had spoken at the dedication ceremony, though several Protestant clergymen, a Catholic priest, women's club officers, past board members, and Zoe Faddis did. Mormon officials had been relegated to a role that might have seemed demeaning: the stake presidency, the highest-ranking Mormon body in the city, had been asked to arrange the reception following the presentations, a task customarily assigned to women.[54] Ogden's Mormons would have certainly noticed.

Perhaps worst of all, the new librarian the library board had hired from Chicago was rabidly anti-Mormon. "The great mass of converts to the Mormon faith," Zoe Faddis asserted to Carnegie during one of her perennial but unsuccessful campaigns to secure supplements to the initial gift, "are from the most ignorant classes of Europe." Such people, she suggested to Carnegie, were naturally reluctant to support a public library, having "never seen [one] before." She then played the polygamy card, putting a very interesting spin on the then-future Utah Library-Gymnasium Commission argument about young people and public libraries:

> The old system of polygamy, indulged in by the generation that is passing away, and the evil effects of which constitute a blighting heritage upon the younger generation, can only be eradicated by education—by reading. Every book a Utah boy or girl may read, whether history, biography or a novel breathes unconsciously the spirit of monogamy which is contrary to the faith of his fathers. In behalf of these boys and girls, whom this nation expects to lead monogamous lives, I ask your further aid. The magnificent gifts you have made in all parts of the world will do untold good, but none will have greater

53 It should be remembered that at the time of Ogden's application, the Utah Library-Gymnasium Association—with its solidly Mormon pro-library arguments—was still six years in the future. The arguments quoted appear in the *Standard (Ogden, UT)*, Mar. 19, 1901 and Apr. 22, 1903.

54 Ibid., Apr. 17 and 22, 1903.

> results than this of yours to Ogden if it does, as I believe it will, tend to blot out polygamy and mold the future citizens of this part of Utah to live the lives of the other citizens of this country, and not as in the past of some European country.[55]

It is hard to imagine that such missionary zeal would not have influenced Faddis's daily dealings with the Mormon children who entered her library—and equally difficult to imagine that Mormon patrons would have felt comfortable with a woman who held these opinions, or her institution.

Ogden's Carnegie library proponents thus failed to symbolically identify their project with some common vision of their community, some common value that seemed immediately relevant to everyone. This mistake hurt their library long beyond Faddis's tenure. Despite attempting to cater to schoolchildren, businessmen, and tradesmen through evening and Sunday openings and relevant book and journal selections, Ogden's Carnegie library remained chronically short of funds for decades. At one point the building held only 3,500 volumes for 3,108 readers.[56] Backers continued to plead with the populace in fundraising efforts, using rhetoric which alternately cajoled and attempted to shame. Why pay taxes and have on the shelves "only a few books that would be a discredit even to Salt Lake City?" asked a Catholic priest. Such appeals, however, failed to instill a broad sense of ownership, and it was only many years later, after the sectarian tinge of its genesis was forgotten, that the library gained its feet.

Salt Lake City's Chapman Branch Library Application

Salt Lake City's second Carnegie library application was also motivated by a spirit of reform, but it met considerably less opposition because its agenda was one on which gentiles and Mormons could agree: unassimilated working class "foreigners" posed a significant danger to their community's health and safety.

Salt Lake City's "Terminal District," a poor neighborhood west of downtown, cut off by railroad lines and viaducts, was the benefactor of the city's second Carnegie library application. In this district rail shops, heavy manufacturing, and substandard housing intermingled, giving the

55 Letter from Zoe Faddis to Andrew Carnegie, n.d. [Summer 1906?], CCA. As a trained librarian who came West full of energy and ideals, Faddis represents the type described in Passett, *Cultural Crusaders*. Her aggressive prejudice, however, seems not to have been typical.

56 Hepworth, *Carnegie Libraries*, 69.

neighborhood a thrown-together look compared to Salt Lake City's characteristically neat grid. While people of northern European descent dominated the city's population at large, the Terminal District held large concentrations of Italians, Greeks, Syrians, and other distinctive ethnic minorities—groups whom contemporary anti-immigration literature labeled as a backward and potentially violent leftist presence in the city.[57] So lightly were the district's residents regarded that the city's mayor located the Stockade (the walled red-light compound noted in chapter four) there in 1908, declaring that "most of the better class of residents were leaving the area anyway." Terminal District residents were blamed for epidemics of disease and accused of organized crime.[58] An early twentieth century University of Utah master's thesis even declared them unilaterally the cause of "the Housing Problem in Salt Lake City." Open violence against district residents occurred, both spontaneously and at the direction of the Ku Klux Klan.[59]

In 1912, however, city officials were surprised by a request from this supposedly disreputable neighborhood. The residents respectfully submitted a petition asking for a branch public library. During the two decades since Salt Lake City's main library had been constructed with Packard's funds, earlier branch libraries had been established in solidly middle-class neighborhoods and genteel suburbs. But no one had imagined that the Terminal District's residents might want one. Cautious funding was approved to rent two rooms in a department store, with the provisional institution named for Annie Chapman, Salt Lake's first salaried librarian, whose good works had included teaching English to Chinese immigrants.[60]

By 1915 the tiny branch had become one of the most enthusiastically patronized in the city. City officials balked, however, at Salt Lake City librarian Joanna Sprague's request that they allocate funds for a purpose-built library in this suspect neighborhood, when other branch libraries patronized by solid citizens were still operating in rented buildings. With the blessing

57 Discussions of ethnic minorities in Salt Lake City appear in Zeidner, "From Babylon to Babylon," Papanikolas, "The Exiled Greeks," and "The New Immigrants," and in Notarianni, "Italianite in Utah."

58 McCormick, *Salt Lake City: The Gathering Place*, 61 and Harris, *Salt Lake City: A Regional Capital*, 152.

59 Groebli, "The Housing Problem." Papanikolas discusses Klan activity in "The New Immigrants," 458.

60 Oyler, "Events in the History of the Salt Lake City Public Library," 11-12 and *Salt Lake (UT) Tribune*, Oct. 10, 1900.

of the city's forward-looking library board, Sprague approached Andrew Carnegie directly. Presenting convincing arguments about these deserving immigrants (a cause dear to Carnegie's heart) and mustering strong statistics about Chapman Branch patronage, the altruistic Sprague soon received good news: Carnegie would promise $15,000 for a new public library building, an amount quickly raised on her request to $25,000.[61]

Delighted with the offer, Terminal District residents once again gave the lie to those who characterized them as lazy and debauched. When municipal officials delayed allocating funds to procure a building site, the neighborhood Parent-Teacher Association began independent fundraising. Within nine months these citizens had gathered enough money to buy a site outright—a site they proudly donated to the city for library purposes. After some debate about the building's design with Bertram (its corner location dictated an eccentric entryway), work progressed quickly. Thanks to Joanna Sprague and Terminal District residents themselves, the neighborhood possessed a completed Carnegie library building by 1918, just three years after the application process began.[62]

Until this point Chapman Branch Library application had been conducted with dignity and respect relative to neighborhood residents. Sprague and the other board members had welcomed Terminal District citizens as partners in the project, and letters to Carnegie and news releases had emphasized their genuine hunger for books. At the building's dedication ceremony, however, city officials changed the tone. Apparently afraid that middle-class citizens might wonder why tax dollars were being spent literally across the tracks rather than in their own neighborhoods, they framed the ceremony's action and rhetoric to suggest that the project was really about Americanizing the neighborhood's suspiciously foreign children, a cause whose worthiness no one could debate.[63] Early on opening day, the District's multi-ethnic children were marched from their schools to the new

61 Letter from Johanna Sprague to James Bertram, Nov. 6, 1915, CCA; letter from James Bertram to Johanna Sprague, Mar. 21, 1916, CCA; letter from James Bertram to Johanna Sprague, Feb. 3, 1917, CCA.

62 Oyler notes the PTA's contribution in, "Events in the History of the Salt Lake City Public Library," 68. J. D. Spencer also mentions it in his letter to James Bertram, Dec. 1, 1916, CCA. A series of letters between Spencer and Bertram discussing library design continued through 1916–17, CCA.

63 Van Slyck suggests that Americanizing immigrants was a perceived benefit of big-city Carnegie libraries in other communities also, including Pittsburg, Pennsyvania (*Free to All*, 106).

The Chapman Branch Library, Salt Lake City, Utah, accomplishes its mission: serving Terminal District children.

library building. There they enacted a choreographed display, solemnly raising and saluting the flag and singing "America." Speakers addressed them and their parents in a tone more admonitory than celebratory. "The library stands for bigger and better citizenship," lectured Salt Lake's mayor Mont Ferry. "The degree to which the people use it will show the measure of their appreciation of good government and of liberty."[64] The irony, of course, is that the dedication ceremony would not have been taking place at all had not those being admonished already possessed a pro-active sense of civic responsibility.

Bearing symbolic associations that ranged from tolerance to intolerance, from affirmation of the status quo to agency for change, Carnegie libraries in Utah's religiously diverse communities stood for a dazzling, self-contradictory variety of agendas and were supported by wide range of

64 *Deseret News (Salt Lake City, UT)*, May 28, 1918.

people. The turn-of-the-twentieth-century Intermountain West, they collectively suggest, was not the unilateral frontier of legend, but a multi-cultural place even among Anglo-American residents, a place where values and priorities were determined by distinctly local circumstances. In this culturally complicated region, the "outlaws" believed to threaten civic harmony were most often the people next door.

6

Women's Role in Bringing Carnegie Libraries to Settled Communities

"A monument to the women"

> The Entre Nous Club of Mountain Home, a women's organization, are trying hard to build a public library for the town. An excellent site has been donated and the Club has accumulated a small fund, to which they are constantly adding, for the purchase of books and furniture, but if we have to rely upon our own limited resources of money to build the building it will necessarily be years before we can get it.[1]

When Bertha Stull Green wrote these words to Andrew Carnegie from a high-desert hamlet in southwestern Idaho in 1906, she might have been voicing the hopes and frustrations of hundreds of her Intermountain West peers. Like women across the region—indeed, women across the United States—Green and her friends were so dedicated to bringing library service to their town that they had practically made a profession of the effort. As Green explained to Carnegie, they had opened a subscription library on their own initiative in a "well-lighted" sixteen foot by twenty foot second-story room above a store, staffing it themselves though they were also responsible for domestic duties, other volunteer work, and even paid occupations. Through dedicated canvassing for donations and frequent fundraisers—talent shows, dances, food sales—they had managed to amass seven hundred books. They had even convinced the man who owned the store to donate two empty lots for a purpose-built library and the city council to institute a modest appropriation. Now it was time to seek the

1 Letter from Bertha Stull Green to Andrew Carnegie, Feb. 7, 1905, CCA.

outside patronage that might miraculously crown their efforts with a modern library building.

Outside of rural Mormon Utah, where most pre-Carnegie libraries were established as local Mormon Church projects, women's clubs like Green's established nearly all of the initial public libraries in the region's future Carnegie library communities. Convinced—as Sandra Haarsager, a historian of Pacific Northwest women's clubs puts the case—of "the importance of reading to [their] vision of culture and community . . . women turned to libraries as both a resource and a gift of permanent opportunity and enrichment to their communities."[2] Though these initial libraries were typically modest, Carnegie library statistics from the region suggest a direct correlation between the women's efforts and Carnegie library application success, for the pre-existence of an ongoing, women-supported library was one of the strongest predictors of success in regional Carnegie building grant applications. Only *one* Intermountain West community whose initial library had been started by women failed to bring its Carnegie application to fruition and more than half of the region's nine unsuccessful applications came from communities with no extant libraries. As Haarsager has argued, such women "built the bridges" that made Carnegie libraries possible[3] by establishing institutions that demonstrated to their fellow citizens the value of books and reading.

And yet, as previous chapters have suggested, the public face of Carnegie applications *per se* was male in a majority of Intermountain West applicant communities. Though it was often women who informed themselves about the opportunity and pitched their case to city officials—sometimes after writing initial inquiry letters to Carnegie themselves—men typically took over the application business and shaped the public rhetoric that assigned local symbolism to the institutions. In only sixteen of the region's seventy-eight applicant communities did women (including Green and her compatriots) retain control of the process: Boise, Caldwell, Idaho Falls, Lewiston, Moscow, Mountain Home, Nampa, and Pocatello, Idaho; Delta, Durango, and Grand Junction, Colorado; Hood River and Ontario, Oregon; Ellensburg and Goldendale, Washington; and Prescott, Arizona. In other communities women either voluntarily ceded leadership to men or were shouldered aside. Sometimes they were welcomed onto library

2 Haarsager, *Organized Womanhood*, 154.

3 Ibid., 163.

boards, but the task of negotiating matters of grant size, library site, and library architecture largely fell to their male counterparts. Only such duties as choosing library furniture and arranging refreshments for the dedication remained reliably theirs.

Scholars have offered convincing arguments about why this transfer of power occurred. "Carnegie was careful to formalize every step of the negotiations with the elected officials of the local government," Abigail A. Van Slyck notes, arguing that since women could not hold public office they were necessarily excluded from playing public roles in the applications, though their status and relationship to leaders insured that "their disenfranchisement was never automatic and seldom absolute." She points out also that the turn-of-the-twentieth-century's growing emphasis on professionalism devalued volunteerism of the sort the women practiced[4]—and negotiations with an Eastern capitalist would certainly have been perceived as not a matter for amateurs. So long as library development remained modest and local in scale, women were assumed to be appropriate leaders. When a community was called to negotiate with powerful male outsiders, however, and to manage statistics and significant amounts of money, only about a fifth of communities in this sample trusted women to do that work. Male dominance of Intermountain West Carnegie library grants reveals a fundamental skepticism about women's business sense, a basic assumption that the proper sphere for women's work was among people whom she knew.

How, then, did sixteen groups of women manage to retain public control of their libraries? What gave them the confidence to negotiate both Carnegie's procedures and prevailing cultural norms?

The History, Economic and Social life of Communities Where Women Led

Carnegie Library Efforts

A fundamental answer to these questions lies in the distinctive history and contemporary status of these sixteen communities—circumstances that allowed a particular kind of woman to flourish there. All of these communities were characterized by relative longevity at the time of their Carnegie applications. In contrast to the boom towns described in chapter 3 (eight of which had existed for fewer than ten years when they approached

4 Van Slyck, *Free to All*, 134.

Carnegie), the median span between town foundation and Carnegie library application in these sixteen communities was 27.5 years, and only one had as history of less than twenty years. Economic stability also distinguished them. Hood River, Idaho Falls, Delta, and Grand Junction sat confidently in the centers of long-established and well-developed irrigated districts and on main shipping lines. Lewiston was the market and supply center for a substantial mining district. Prescott served as a hub for lumbering as well as mining operations. Pocatello contained crucial railroad shops. All were county seats, and Boise was the state capital. Several featured colleges, normal schools, or academies, and all boasted at least high schools.[5]

If these communities had experienced booms, that phase of their development was safely in the past. The railroad had reached Goldendale nine years before its Carnegie application and the opening of an Indian reservation that triggered Grand Junction's land rush was more than twenty years in the past. Many towns in this group could congratulate themselves on a history of economic resilience. Lewiston and Prescott had survived the loss of the state or territorial capital designation, while Durango had rebounded from the collapse of silver prices, and both Delta and Grand Junction had survived severe agricultural depressions.[6]

Such places self-consciously defined themselves as mature at the time of their Carnegie library applications. While their residents, like all who lived in the Intermountain West at the turn of the twentieth century, were experiencing rapid change, they corporately defined this transformation as mellowing. Grand Junction's newspaper announced a self-proclaimed "golden era" at the time of the town's Carnegie application.[7] Lewiston's mayor declared, "The conditions under which we are now living are so different from the

5 For a history of Hood River, see Hood River County Historical Society, *History of Hood River*. Several writers discuss early Idaho Falls, including Horton, *Beautiful Bonneville*, Marker, *Eagle•Rock U.S.A.*, and Fritzen, *Idaho Falls, City of Destiny*. Doherty's *Delta, Colorado* tells the story of that community; Mueller's "Natives, Migrants, and Immigrants" traces the history of early Lewiston; Toney, *The Prescott, Arizona Story* and Weiner, *Prescott Yesterdays* discuss that town. Pocatello's history is documented in Kissane, *Pocatello Memories* and in Gittins, *Pocatello Portrait*. For a history of Boise, see Wells, *Boise*, and Hart, *Life in Old Boise*.

6 Ballou, *Early Klickitat Valley Days* and May, *100 Golden Years* trace Goldendale's history; Underwood recounts Grand Junction's in *Town Building*, and Smith, *Rocky Mountain Boom Town* tells Durango's.

7 *Grand Junction (CO) Daily Sentinel*, Jan. 7, 1899. As chapter 1 documented, however, a correspondent from that community was not above exploiting the "new country" argument in her letter to Carnegie.

Courtesy of History Colorado, Orig. Photos collection, scan #20004355.

A settled, stable place: Delta, Colorado, at the time of its Carnegie application.

conditions that confronted us [in the earliest days of settlement] that it is almost like a story of another age or another land." An Ellensburg application supporter said, "In past years, it seems to me that the people have given over a great deal of their time to procuring bread. But now the indications are that we may turn our attention a little more toward mental conditions."[8] Such communities obviously had a great deal more to offer educated, financially secure settlers than did raw boom towns or rural hamlets. By the time of their Carnegie applications, these sixteen places held significant concentrations of lawyers, doctors, engineers, college professors, educated public school teachers, administrators, prosperous businessmen, and clergymen. They had developed a comparative wealth of cultural resources. Their educational institutions offered debates, concerts, and plays. Their theaters staged performances beyond music-hall entertainment; their opera houses occasionally even presented actual operas. They hosted Chautauquas in the summer and sponsored music societies, literary clubs, and fraternal

8 Underwood, *Town Building*, 51–63; *Lewiston (ID) Tribune*, Apr. 15, 1905; *Ellensburg (WA) Evening Record*, Jan. 21, 1910.

organizations.[9] Religious life was also diversified in these places. Moscow, representative among them, contained Baptist, Methodist, Presbyterian, Catholic, Christian, Lutheran, and Episcopal churches by 1890.[10]

The Women Who "Led Out" in Carnegie Library Applications

The men who relocated to these diverse, secure communities to work in established industry, state and county government, education, law, or medicine brought their wives and daughters, typically educated and cultured women whose expectations about community lifestyle and tastes had been formed in longer-established parts of the country. These were the women who "led out," as one of them put it, during Carnegie public library grant building applications. Determined to shape their new hometowns into places that supported not only basic safety, civility, and hygiene but also self-improvement for children and adults, they embraced a Progressive spirit of civic activism.

Some of these women stood at the highest social and economic levels of the region, like Julia Goldwater of Prescott, daughter-in-law of the already wealthy and influential Arizona Goldwaters. Others were wives of locally prominent men. The two leaders in Nampa's Carnegie application were Mrs. E. H. Dewey, wife of an irrigation developer who organized the Idaho Northern Railroad and built a $70,000 hotel in Nampa, and Belle Kurtz, whose capitalist husband Mark Anthony made important Paleolithic discoveries in the course of excavating for the city's water supply. Catherine Murray, who helped direct Ellensburg's application, was married to a rancher/capitalist who served as county commissioner and city councilman.

9 The cultural resources in these towns could be quite extensive. Tiny Delta, for instance, located on the Rockies's western slope, was home to a Chataugua Literary and Scientific Circle that presented an ongoing Lyceum Lecture Course series (Doherty, *Delta, Colorado*, 34). Lewiston, with the resource of a small college, had not only a Chautauqua Club but also a Handel and Haydn Club that specialized in presenting oratorios, a Tennyson Club, and a study club dedicated to Greek and Roman culture (Idaho Writers League, "Tsceminicum," 7). Prescott's cultural resources were among the best in the region, for settlers from "the Yankee, eastern faction" brought with them enough books to stock the territorial library, literally "carry[ing] a good deal of their culture west" (Toney, *The Prescott, Arizona Story*, 11–12).

10 Moscow's religious diversity is described by David in *Moscow at the Turn of the Century*, 20 and Prescott's in Weiner, *Prescott: A Pictorial History*, 50.

Murray reportedly lived in "one of the prettiest residences in [Ellensburg], replete with evidence of luxury and wealth."[11]

Rosters of groups of women who cooperated in Carnegie library efforts read like town social registers. In Durango the work was shared among the wives of high-ranking officers of two different banks—one of whom was also the city's mayor—and a judge's wife.[12] In Moscow a coalition of state university professors' and business men's wives successfully negotiated the town-and-gown division. Correspondence with Bertram was jointly conducted by Kate Henderson, wife of a botany professor, and Mrs. M. J. Shields, whose merchant husband was prominent in the Business Men's Association.[13] The cadre of women behind Boise's Carnegie application, all members of the city's Columbian Club, were particularly well-connected, including Mary Beatty, a federal judge's wife, Gertrude Hays, wife of a man who became Boise's mayor and Idaho attorney general, and society leader Mary Ridenbaugh, married to one of the city's wealthiest businessmen. The club's first president and long-time leader, Victoria Louise Eoff, was a banker's wife and famous Boise hostess.[14]

Beyond the status they acquired from their husbands, the women active in Carnegie library applications often boasted impressive educational and occupational resumes in an era when professional training and higher education were relatively rare for women. Louise Dorman of Goldendale had earned a doctorate, Ethel Bear of Delta held an MA, Pocatello's Eva Standrod attended Cornell University, and the same city's Minnie Howard had earned an MD *after* her marriage.[15]

Many pursued professional careers. Bear had served as principal of Pasadena High School, Julia Goldwater had taught, and Howard had

11 Smith details the lives of Julia Goldwater and her husband in *The Goldwaters of Arizona*, 116–20; details about the Dewey family appear in "The Dewey Dynasty"; information about the Dewey and the Kurtz families appears in "History of Nampa and Vicinity"; Murray's status is discussed in "History of Washington, 804."

12 Ayres, "History of the Durango Public Library," 4. Throughout this chapter, the women's husbands' occupations have been identified by consulting news stories, business cards, and advertisements in contemporary local newspapers.

13 David, *Moscow*, 68–71. He explicitly terms this class of women "aristocrats" (p. 46).

14 Haarsager, 198–200.

15 Dorman is identified as "Doctor" in the *Klickitat County (Goldendale, WA) Agriculturalist*, June 15, 1912; details on Bear's life are taken from "Miss Ethel Bear, 16 August 1972"; details about Standrod's life come from Hodsett's *The Golden Years*, 21–22. Haarsager profiles Howard in *Organized Womanhood*, 168–70.

Idaho State Historical Society, photo #75.2.44.

Women of wealth and influence: Mary Ridenbaugh's home, Boise, Idaho.

practiced medicine until the pressure of raising four sons became too great. Green herself was a lawyer and member of the Idaho bar. Some held influential positions in the media, including newspaper editor Estelle R. Dodge of Ontario and reporter Eva Dockery of Boise.[16] In several of these communities nearly all of the women involved in Carnegie library efforts worked outside their homes. Delta's female-dominated library committee was compelled to schedule its meetings in the evenings to accommodate the professional obligations of the teachers, businesswomen, and town postmistress who were members.[17]

Women like these knew how to organize time and resources. They were accustomed to speaking in public and had experience managing people and influencing others' opinions. Anecdotal commentary suggests that they could have strong public personas. Mary Forney of Moscow was said to

16 Haarsager presents a biography of Green in *Organized Womanhood*, 306–8, see also Hodsett, *The Golden Years*, 86–91. For information on Dodge, see Gregg, *Pioneer Days in Malheur County*, 372–24. Dockery's connections with the *Idaho Statesman* are noted in an article that appeared in that newspaper on Dec. 15, 1937.

17 Henshaw, "General Federation of Women's Clubs," 1.

Idaho State Historical Society, photo #69.153.2

Victoria Louise Eoff of Boise.

be "a natural leader in the community," to whom "men and women alike turned . . . for guidance." Ethel Bear was termed "a go-getter, one to whom you didn't say no."[18]

They also possessed a strong sense of civic responsibility. Many came from families with traditions of service, including Forney, a preacher's daughter, and Green, a judge's. Many had seen their mothers involved in the burgeoning women's club movement, which encouraged women to think of themselves as appropriate agents for particular kinds of progressive change. Many had themselves been members of such clubs in the East, Midwest, and Far West before they moved to the Intermountain West. As a history of a Nampa women's club remarks, "Such women could not be contented to spend their leisure in idleness."[19] Some held public office, including Adelia Scott of Idaho Falls, "A woman of determination and strong character," who served as justice of the peace, police judge, county treasurer, and school board member. Lillie Wertz of Mountain Home served

18 Hodsett, *The Golden Years*, 37 and "A Historical Narrative of the Delta Public Library," 3.

19 Kenneke, "History of the Nampa Women's Club," 2.

as county superintendent of schools, and Ella New of Delta ran for state superintendent.[20] Katherine Truitt of Moscow served as the first forewoman of a jury in Idaho and Mary Ridenbaugh of Boise was appointed as a regent of the University of Idaho. Belle Kurtz of Nampa acted as Idaho's hostess at the Portland Exposition in 1905, the Yukon Pacific Exposition in 1909, and the Panama Pacific Exposition in 1915. Victoria Louise Eoff founded the Idaho Children's Home and St. Luke's Hospital in Boise.[21]

Local Women's Clubs

Women's clubs proliferated turn-of-the-twentieth-century America (membership in the national General Federation of Women's Clubs grew from one hundred thousand in 1896 to eight hundred thousand in 1910),[22] and most Intermountain West Carnegie library applicant communities held at least one women's organization between 1898–1920. These clubs were particularly important for idealistic middle class and upper-middle-class women in a region comparatively poor in cultural and educational resources. They provided a community of like-minded spirits to newcomers who missed the comradeship of club members in their former home towns by allowing women who longed to learn but lacked access to higher education an opportunity to expand their knowledge and broaden their worlds. They fed educated women's intellectual hunger and gave idealistic, determined women the power to influence the shape of their developing communities. Under the cover of "municipal housekeeping"—in which civic activism was defined non-threateningly as a legitimate extension of women's concern for others and high moral character—these clubs afforded women significant power to forever alter the social, political, and cultural shape of their communities.[23]

20 Scott's accomplishments are recounted in Cox and French, *Second Stories*, 14–17. Wertz's office is mentioned in the *Mountain Home (ID) Republican*, Dec. 26, 1905 and New's in Hodgin, "A Historical Narrative of the Delta Public Library."

21 Truitt's accomplishments are described in the *Idaho Digest and Blue Book*, 901–2; Ridenbaugh's in the *Boise (ID) Statesman*, Feb. 19, 1978; Kurtz's in Crain, "Nampa Nears 40th Birthday Celebration," 3; Eoff's in Haarsager, *Organized Womanhood*, 196.

22 Altbach, *Women in America*, 115–17.

23 Among those who have made this argument are Blair, *The Clubwoman as Feminist*, Haarsager, *Organized Womanhood*, and Scott, *Natural Allies*. See Ring, "Outpost of New England Culture," for a case study suggesting how feminism and the ideology of "True Womanhood" combined to inspire Michigan club women to establish a public library and lecture series. At least some clubwomen in the Intermountain West

Women's clubs supported both civic improvement and study.[24] In the first category, they undertook projects (often with their own hands) designed to make their communities more attractive, safe, and convenient places to live. As noted earlier in this book, the Idaho Falls Village Improvement Society planted trees and flowers, grubbed sagebrush and weeds from the cemetery, cleaned canal banks, and numbered houses.[25] Other clubs lobbied for public drinking fountains, established city parks, organized downtown clean-up campaigns, worked to enforce ordinances against public spitting, and complained about suspect drinking water until something was done. The motto of Lewiston's Tsceminicum Club, "Seize the opportunity,"[26] might have been the motto of them all. Nampa's club was so influential that a local historian judged that it had "accomplished more than any other organization Nampa has ever had; the municipality included." Boise's Columbian Club went beyond local activism (establishing a city park, a curfew, and child study meetings for mothers) to influence state legislation, including a bill that enabled the state's first traveling library.[27]

Study clubs promoted intellectual ambition, assigning members to research and present reports on particular topics. The Round Table Club of Idaho Falls chose art as its subject in 1911–12 and heard presentations including "Paintings in the Catacombs of Rome," "Rembrandt," and "Watteau."[28] Some broke into special interest groups, each meeting on a different schedule so that members could attend more than one if they chose. In 1915–16 members of Delta's Women's Club might have attended the Literature Department twice a month to hear papers on American authors, or the Art Department, which discussed such topics as the architecture of Canterbury Cathedral, or the Home Economics Department (which heard

---

appear to have been consciously aware that they were involved in a balancing act: when the women of Prescott, Arizona organized their club, they chose as its name "Monday Club" instead of "The Women's Club of Prescott," which they judged to be "too aggressive." "Might someone, from the name, infer its object to be, not culture, but the ballot?" one woman asked, in Sewell, "An Historical Gem," 5.

24 In some communities one club engaged in both kinds of activities and in others multiple clubs focused on one or the other.

25 Crowder, *Tales of Eastern Idaho*, 126.

26 Mueller, "Natives, Migrants, and Immigrants," 3.

27 Cottingham, 31 and Haarsager, 195–206.

28 "Secretary's Record of the Round Table Club, Idaho Falls, Idaho, 1909–[15]."

Idaho State Historical Society, photo #66.36.49.

Book Cases for the Idaho Free Traveling Library established by Boise's Columbian Club.

papers on matters including "Understanding Rugs and Period Furniture" rather than discussing cleaning tips or recipes).[29]

It might be tempting to think of such study as dabbling, and one woman's club organizer seeking to propel the movement forward did warn against a year's agenda involving "a grotesque range from Life in Early Egypt to the Waverley novels, and from the Panama Canal to Spring Flowers."[30] Yet these Intermountain West clubwomen took their study very seriously. "This group is not a social club that sits around and gossips," the policy statement for the Idaho Falls's Round Table Club warned prospective members. The Monday Club of Prescott actually forbade a member to resign "without first completing the work assigned to her or providing a satisfactory substitute." Each Monday Club meeting included "a critical review of the previous program, in which words mispronounced, errors in grammar,

29 "Program of General Meetings, The Woman's Club of Delta, Colorado, 1915–16."

30 Benton, *The Complete Club Book for Women*, 1–2.

Idaho State Historical Society, photo # 79-129.2

The Pleiades Club, Moscow, Idaho.

or any misinformation was corrected."[31] Meetings of Mountain Home's Sub Rosa Club "frequently took the better part of a day," for they involved answering roll call with quotes from an author being studied, discussing a magazine article, hearing papers presented, listening to classical music, and studying parliamentary procedure.[32] Some promoted general cultural literacy beyond the club rooms, including a Pocatello club that cooperated with the Idaho Federation of Women's Clubs to bring traveling art exhibits from the Chicago Water Color Society and the New York Society to thirty Idaho towns.[33]

Membership in a women's club offered training in skills that prepared women to promote and manage Carnegie public library applications. Even if a woman did not hold college degrees or professional positions, the study clubs accustomed her to framing presentations carefully, speaking in public, and dealing with criticism. The civic improvement clubs taught members managerial and fiscal-management skills, along with lessons in the logistics and politics of municipal decision-making. Whatever their mission, as

31 Author, "Table of Knowledge" and Hall, "The First Woman's Club in Arizona."

32 Haarsager, *Organized Womanhood*, 170–71.

33 Ibid., 168.

clubwomen set agendas they experienced debate and consensus building. They learned to work together and to trust each other's capacities.

While all women's clubs taught such lessons, in these sixteen communities the organizations maintained a particularly high profile. Not content with social-column coverage of their activities, their secretaries submitted lengthy reports to local newspapers detailing matters discussed and actions taken. Club members themselves, as in Ontario, were themselves newspaper editors, and in such cases publicity appeared on front pages. Consequently, in these communities residents had become accustomed to accepting clubwomen as active, competent people—as natural leaders—long before Carnegie applications began.[34]

Networking Through State Federations of Women's Clubs

The women who assumed and maintained control of Carnegie applications also shared the sort of broader connections that would today be called "networks." In contrast to clubwomen elsewhere who were obliged to puzzle out the process's daunting technicalities on their own, women in these sixteen communities were blessed with access to direct coaching. As members of state federations of women's clubs, they could have their questions about application logistics answered by women experienced in process. Thus, with the help of insider tips, these women were able to present themselves as confident experts from their very first inquiry letters.

Most Intermountain West states held state federations of women's clubs by the early twentieth century , but those umbrella organizations were especially active in Idaho and Colorado, the states which contained the majority of the applicant towns in this group (eleven of sixteen). In contrast to some other western state federations, Idaho's and Colorado's organized regular district and state conventions where women mingled, devised coordinated statewide initiatives, and gained a clear sense of unified mission. These two federations also published substantive state magazines containing practical suggestions for accomplishing goals, inspirational messages by state presidents, and columns in which local clubs shared their triumphs with their sisters.

From their inception, these two federations encouraged women to exercise power beyond the local level. The Idaho Federation evolved from the

34 For a sample of a well-reported account of club business, see the *Nampa (ID) Leader-Herald*, Apr. 17, 1906. Both the *Hood River (OR) Glacier* and the *Pocatello (ID) Tribune* frequently made women's club business front-page news.

Idaho Equal Suffrage Association, an assembly of local clubs which had achieved the vote for women within a decade of statehood.[35] At the very first Idaho Federation convention, these women—so confident in their power that they had announced to a national suffrage meeting "We stand as a great bulwark of strength to the states around us, higher in altitude and higher in attitude!"—were framing bills relevant to women's concerns and placing them on legislators' desks. The state's enabling legislation for public libraries resulted from their efforts, as did reforms relating to married women's property, child labor, juvenile courts, teacher education, and divorce law.[36]

Even these women, however, were jealous of the power the Colorado Federation wielded. When an outgoing president of the Idaho Federation sought a way to challenge her sisters to more enthusiastic action, it was the former group's record she posed as an example:

> The Colorado State Federation convention endorsed eleven measures [in 1912] The Legislative committee later endorsed ten more. Eleven of these were passed. Among those endorsed were child labor law, eight-hour law for women, library amendment, school election, more effective law for support of traveling library, providing for teaching of adult blind, anti-polygamy resolution, anti-cigarette law . . . Their legislation committee has 57 members with 15 associate members. They meet every week in the morning during the legislative session with an average attendance of 55.[37]

It is significant that the women who led applications in these sixteen communities were also leaders in their state federations. While they were clearly already natural leaders, playing on this larger stage would have enhanced their assertiveness, business sense, and confidence. Delta's New served as District President in Colorado, Green wrote a regular column on legislation for the *Idaho Clubwoman*, Pocatello's Minnie Howard, Idaho Falls' Adelia Scott, Moscow's Mary Forney, and Boise's Mary Beatty and Mary Ridenbaugh all served as presidents of the Idaho Federation.

Carnegie's public library building grant program was selected by both of these strong federations as a special priority. Women who had participated in successful Carnegie applications before coming to their current

35 Larson discusses the women's suffrage movement in Idaho in "The Woman's Rights Movement" and "Idaho's Role in America's Woman Suffrage Crusade."

36 Hodsett, *The Golden Years*, 15–6.

37 Author, "Mrs. Bowerman's Address," 6–9.

homes led the effort, inviting others to dream of a community library constructed with outside funds and convincing them that they could negotiate the process. The queen of these women in the Intermountain West was Mary Beatty, who as president of the Salt Lake City Women's Literary Club had helped her former place of residence make unprecedented "advance(s) in systematic and improved methods of literary work." Beatty (a "woman of great executive ability" who could "speak or write six languages") was already familiar with Carnegie application procedures when she came to Idaho, and she traveled the state as a consultant to women's clubs interested in Carnegie applications.[38]

Friendly competition between federation member clubs helped spark applications. Delta's initial inquiry letter was written after women attended a Colorado Federation meeting in Salida held in a newly completed Carnegie library. The very sight, a Delta woman later recalled, "fired our ambition to prove that we could do the same."[39] The Delta club also consulted during the application process with Durango's, which had recently completed its own Carnegie library. Idaho clubs proudly announced their application milestones to each other in the *Idaho Clubwoman*'s "What the Clubs are Doing" column.

Clubwomen Leading Carnegie Grant Applications

Bolstered by social cache, education, life experience, confidence, and coaching, the women in these sixteen communities proved effective leaders in Carnegie public library building grant applications. They established forthright public personae, straightforwardly requesting—or demanding—what they wanted from both their fellow citizens and Carnegie. In Delta, members of the Woman's Club "marched into a meeting of the County Commissioners and asked for a gift of land"—a prime parcel on the courthouse square—for a library site. They got it. "Using similar tactics," they convinced the city to pass a support levy.[40] After Ellensburg's city officials cited an already high tax

38 Beatty's work in Salt Lake City is mentioned in Parsons, *History of Fifty Years*, 13, 37 and her accomplishments are noted in Turner, *The Golden Dream*, 16. Letters from applicants in both Mountain Home and Nampa credit her as a consultant in Carnegie library applications, see, letter from Lillie B. Wertz to Carnegie, July 25, 1907, CCA and letter from Belle Kurtz to James Bertram, June 28, 1906, CCA.

39 Mrs. John E. Hillman, quoted in the retrospective "Federated Women's Clubs."

40 "A Historical Narrative of the Delta Public Library," 7.

burden as an obstacle, the town's Mutual Improvement Association secured title to a site and donated it to the city. Club members also raised more than a thousand dollars to cover architect's fees and purchase books and furniture.[41]

These clubwomen also exploited their connections to powerful men beyond their communities. Some enlisted US senators and representatives, state governors, and federal officials to plead their towns' causes to Carnegie.[42] Others were able to supplement community funds with generous donations from outsiders. Prescott's Julia Goldwater, for example, procured monies essential to that library's completion from the editor of the well-known national magazine *The Youth's Companion*, who published her sister-in-law Sarah Winter Kellogg's children's stories.[43]

These women's political acumen is evident in their internal cooperation. Where communities held more than one club, the groups joined forces, insuring that all possible energy and expertise would be used and that everyone felt valued. As Grand Junction's Carnegie application began, the town's two clubs merged into the Woman's Library Association of Grand Junction, allowing fifty "energetic ladies" to work on the project without jealousy.[44] In all of these communities except Idaho Falls (where contention over rival sites led to temporary hard feelings between women belonging to various factions), they presented a united public front, whatever their disagreements may have been in private. Nor were they shy about soliciting the aid of men who possessed competencies necessary to supplement their own, as in Delta, where "one man was appointed [to the library board] because of his business and building experience."[45]

---

41 Ryder, "Ellensburg Public Library," 15–6.

42 Carnegie correspondence reveals that Delta's energetic women called on all of the above.

43 Prescott's application began in 1899, very early in Carnegie's grant program, and seems to have operated on different principles than became standardized later: in this case Carnegie accepted a cash match as earnest money for the project, see, Weiner, *Prescott, A Pictorial History*, 93.

44 While Grand Junction's women's clubs buried their sense of rivalry during the application process, their underlying sense of competition did not disappear. In 1987, a historian noted that "the controversy over which women's club set up the Grand Junction public library is still being argued" in, Underwood, *Town Building*, 155.

45 The club was careful to ensure that this man would not represent an opening for male take-over. The club's president retained the right to appoint the site selection committee, and the library board's charter stipulated that at least one representative of the woman's club would always sit on the board, see, Author, "A Historical Narrative," 8.

As had happened in the rural Utah communities coached by the Utah Library-Gymnasium Commission, these women anticipated Carnegie's questions before they were asked. The initial inquiry letters they wrote assured Carnegie that tax support already existed or was certain, that a site had already been obtained with a clear title, and that money had already been collected for books and furniture. When the women themselves filled out the "Schedule of Questions," they avoided the sort of inflated claims that delayed applications elsewhere. When Mrs. C. W. Shaff calculated Lewiston's population, for example, she estimated the population conservatively at the five thousand documentable people living permanently within the city limits. Though a boomtown booster might have inflated his estimate to include the "many hundreds" of miners who wintered in Lewiston, the students at the state Normal School, and the citizens of Clarkston-Vineland, a community of four thousand people who might also use the library, Mrs. Shaff wisely only mentioned them in passing.[46]

To explain to their fellow citizens why a Carnegie library was desirable, these women emphasized the personal enrichment that a public library would provide to adults and children. A public library, one of them wrote, would promote "the development of the highest culture" and ensure an informed citizenry.[47] "We need a working library where . . . young people can go for reference study as well as a quiet, refined place for seekers after knowledge at such times as they may select," a letter from Delta told Carnegie.[48] Such arguments had the political advantage of aligning neatly with the concept of "municipal housekeeping," the idea that mothering one's community and fellow citizens was a natural extension of women's domestic role, thus heading off others' potential concerns about uppity presumption.[49]

So focused and obviously competent were these clubwomen that only in two of these sixteen communities, Caldwell and Nampa, Idaho, did they

46 Letter from Mrs. C. A. Shaff to Andrew Carnegie, Mar. 4, 1913, CCA.

47 Mansfield et al., "Our Library—The Object," 1.

48 These words appear in a support letter to Carnegie requested by the club, letter from Philip M. [Condal?] to Andrew Carnegie, Feb. 23, 1910, CCA.

49 The clubwomen who worked for Carnegie library building grants in the Intermountain West seem to have been very concerned with maintaining their own and their friends' personas as "womanly women." A tribute to Mary Forney notes that "with all her public interests and duties, she was always a gentle and beloved homemaker, a devoted wife and mother" in, Hodsett, *The Golden Years*, 38. A friend of Green described her as "tall and slender and very feminine, a woman who could wear flowers in her hair with great charm," in, Haarsager, *Organized Womanhood*, 308.

encounter the sort of attempted application take-over that regularly relegated women to supporting roles in other communities' Carnegie applications. Caldwell's women began by writing to Carnegie themselves after city officials brushed aside the suggestion of a Carnegie application. The women received a "Schedule of Questions," consulted with sympathetic men, and completed and returned the form themselves. After they received a promise, community pressure became so great that officials had little choice but to theoretically pass a support levy, that is. Assuring the women that they were now the proper ones to conduct Carnegie applicant business, the city council proceeded to ignore Bertram's letters, then conveniently to "lose" all of the correspondence. Only when the women and their supporters managed to muster enough public sentiment to oust these foot-draggers did a new city administration more sympathetic to the library cause follow through on the offer the women had obtained.[50]

Like Caldwell's women, Nampa's obtained a promise and formed their own library committee to oversee the project. Facing a more reasonable city council, they also obtained a sincere municipal levy commitment. But then the library application was nearly wrenched from their hands, as city officials summarily appointed a male board "to conduct all the business and oversee the expenditure of money" for the remainder of the application process. "The appointment of this second committee aroused the ire of the functioning committee," a local historian writes. After unsuccessful local protest, the women consulted the state attorney general and on his advice they hired a lawyer to contest their right to retain control. They won their case when the lawyers declared the second committee void and stipulated that a joint committee be appointed since "the Century Club secured this fund."[51]

Case Study: Mountain Home, Idaho

The extensive records that exist regarding Mountain Home, Idaho's, 1906–8 application provide a useful illustration of how all these distinctive factors came together in a women-directed Carnegie library campaign.

---

50 Gipson presents the history of the Caldwell Forward Club's struggle to establish a municipally supported library is presented in "A History of the Library and Reading Room."

51 This story is told in "Early Objective of Woman's Century Club in 1900 Was Establishing of Nampa's Public Library."

Like other towns in this group, Mountain Home was economically secure.[52] It had won county seat designation in 1881, more than two decades before its application. Government-funded irrigation works had been completed and were functioning effectively, ensuring the town's status as the center of a prospering agricultural district with a comfortable, stable economy. Mountain Home also boasted an active cultural life, including a small city-supported circulating library established by one of the town's three women's literary societies.[53]

The women who led Mountain Home's application were members of the town's privileged class and active in women's club affairs beyond the local level. Lawyer Bertha Stull Green, said to have been the first woman to practice law in Idaho, was a member of the local school board, belonged to all three local clubs, headed the legislative committee of the Idaho Federation of Women's Clubs, and compiled a booklet in 1909 containing all Idaho laws relating to women and children. Working alongside Green was Emily Pence, the wife of a prominent banker/sheep rancher. Pence had served as toastmistress and gave the welcoming address when a district meeting of the Idaho Federation was held at Mountain Home. The clubwoman who conducted the bulk of the correspondence, Lillie Wertz, was a teacher who became Elmore County Superintendent of Schools and faithfully attended state federation meetings.[54]

Coaching contributed directly to these women's facility in managing their Carnegie library application. Mary Beatty encouraged Green and the others to apply, then traveled to Mountain Home for an in-depth consultation about procedures. Friendly competition with member clubs (as in Delta's application) seems to have played a role in motivating the application. "I can't see why we could not have a Carnegie Library if Nampa and Boise can have one," Pence remarked at a library board meeting. "Why don't we ask for one?"[55]

Despite the reservations of one male library board member (reported to have said "it never hurt anyone to try for the moon, but it doesn't do

52 Groefsema recounts the history of Mountain Home in *Elmore County*.

53 The *Mountain Home (ID) Republican*, July 18, 1907, notes that the clubs have joined forces in the library effort.

54 Details about Pence's husband appear in French, *History of Idaho*, 3:964 and her activities at the district meeting are noted in the *Mountain Home (ID) Republican*, Oct. 10, 1905. Wertz's activities are also described in the *Republican*, Dec. 26, 1905.

55 Groefsema, *Elmore County*, 203.

much good"), the clubwomen who formed the group's majority voted to pursue a grant. Green's initial inquiry letter reveals her familiarity with the process. She requested a specific amount appropriate to the town's population and Carnegie's formula and informed Carnegie that a site had been donated. Further, she implied that Mountain Home knew enough not to expect Carnegie to buy books and furniture; the town's Entre Nous Club had such things under control already, she assured him. Mountain Home simply needed construction funds in the amount, exactly, that Carnegie was prepared to offer.[56] Another club member, Mrs. E. C. Helfrich, enlisted "a very dear friend" who also happened to be a US Senator to write a support letter for Mountain Home. Before filling out the "Schedule of Questions," club members canvassed for books from house to house "in order to make a creditable report to Mr. Carnegie as to the number of volumes on hand."[57]

When a promise arrived, it was the clubwomen themselves who phrased the support resolution for the city council, noting a levy amount equal to exactly 10 percent of Carnegie's gift. City officials obediently signed. The women also insured that Mountain Home's grant would not be delayed by quibbles about library architecture. Knowing that "the donor . . . is very exacting as to the character of the plans," Wertz went to Boise to consult with the firm that had designed that city's Carnegie library. When plans were completed, the ladies presented them to the village board at a face-to-face meeting, insuring that the men's questions were promptly answered.[58] This care paid off, for Bertram approved Mountain Home's plans the first time around. As construction moved briskly along that summer and fall of 1908, the clubs held entertainments to furnish the library.[59] When the library opened on November 28, 1908, it was stocked and functional. "In this day of achievement," the editor of the *Mountain Home Republican* wrote, "[the city's women] may well feel proud of their success." Fittingly, the library's cornerstone held the histories of the Entre Nous, Sub Rosa, and Artemesia Clubs which had worked so effectively for its construction.[60]

---

56 Letter from Bertha Stull Green to Andrew Carnegie, Feb. 7, 1906, CCA.

57 Groefsema, *Elmore County*, 202–3 and letter from Senator Fred T. Dubois to Andrew Carnegie, Apr. 3, 1906, CCA.

58 Letter from James Bertram to Lillie Wertz, Dec. 13, 1907, CCA; letter from Lillie Wertz to Andrew Carnegie, Jan. 15, 1908, CCA; *Mountain Home (ID) Republican*, Feb. 6 and 15, 1908.

59 Groefsema, *Elmore County*, 203.

60 *Mountain Home (ID) Republican*, Nov. 28, 1908.

Idaho State Historical Society, photo #62.50.86.

The Mountain Home, Idaho, Progressive Club and its library.

Clubwomen as Negotiators: Hood River, Pocatello, Boise

A few applications in this group did not progress quite as smoothly as Mountain Home's. Still, the women who directed them did manage to see their projects through to completion, relying on tactics tailored to local circumstances, tactics that reveal these women's political deftness and suggest just how boldly they could assume power in the service of a worthy cause.

Hood River's story has been sketched in chapters 1 and 2—a tale of well-connected clubwomen who easily convinced their male relatives and friends on the city council to pass a library levy, then, when a working-class taxpayers' revolt precluded spending municipal funds for a site, raised the funds themselves from their local elite.[61] Secure in their powerbase, these women did not waste time attempting to convince detractors—they simply ignored these less-powerful citizens and worked over their heads.

61 The Hood River Historical Society's *History of Hood River* gives the basic outline of the women's campaign for a Carnegie library (120–21) but does not discuss the local difficulties the process faced. I have reconstructed that narrative from news stories in the *Hood River (OR) Glacier* of Apr. 10, 17, and 24, 1913 and in the *Hood River (OR) News*, Apr. 16, 1913.

Pocatello's women faced a more daunting challenge, for they initially lacked the sort of insider connections to local government that Hood River's women possessed. Their community's municipal officials belonged to a lower class than they did. The men were long-time residents, less cosmopolitan than the more recently arrived doctors, school principals, and well-educated wives of affluent professional men who made up the city's women's clubs. The town's mayor, a storekeeper on record as saying that life experience was vastly "more necessary than college educations," was so notoriously cheap that one of the women who led the library effort called him "Hetty Green" to Carnegie, referencing a miser famous in current popular culture. He presided over a council of like-minded small-town businessmen, uniformly resentful that these privileged women were attempting to impose their expensive tastes on hardworking residents.[62] One councilman remarked in a meeting that he thought "not 5% of the citizens" really wanted a Carnegie library or would use it. Another called the project "all a humbug."[63]

These women were formidable and persistent, however, and the councilmen eventually understood that just saying no would not make them go away. Instead, they attempted to impose impossible conditions. They would sign application forms, they said—but only if the women could obtain signatures of a majority of voters and the approval of the city's trade unions. One can almost imagine them rubbing their hands in glee at their craftiness, for Pocatello was a center for railroad shops where sympathy to organized labor ran high, and antagonism for the Carnegie name could be expected to be general and vehement.[64]

The Women's Civic Club was not intimidated. Led by Dr. Minnie Howard and Eva Standrod, members undertook a carefully crafted publicity campaign and petition drive. Howard had for several years been writing a weekly column, and she used that forum to firmly associate public libraries with issues sacred to labor. Libraries were not for the few, she proclaimed; indeed, they exemplified egalitarian democracy, and anyone who would block them was no friend of the workingman. "A life-long education," she

62 Kissane quotes Cleare's no-nonsense philosophy of life, expressed in an advertisement entitled "A Message to the People of Southern Idaho," in *Pocatello Memories*, 90–92. Other city councilmen's profiles have been determined from advertisements and business cards in the *Pocatello (ID) Tribune*.

63 *Pocatello (ID) Tribune*, Aug. 22 and 21, 1906.

64 Uhland, "Progress," 2.

wrote, was the people's right, and a public library was "an essential part of a broad system of education."[65]

The women took that message to the streets, personally approaching union leaders. To ease fears that Pocatello might seem to be honoring the man behind Homestead, they pledged that the inscription over the library door would read "Public Library," not "Carnegie Library."[66] So persuasive were they that the leaders signed. With such endorsements prominently displayed on their petitions, they made short work of collecting a critical mass of additional signatures. They also collected $2,500 in pledges to purchase a library site, including several sizeable pledges from unions. Howard, of course, thanked these organizations publicly in her newspaper column.[67]

With no choice, the city council grudgingly approved the petition, and Pocatello's Carnegie application moved forward. But instead of trusting previously reluctant men to take over the application in good faith as the women of Caldwell had done, Pocatello's women kept control of the process. Howard conducted all of the correspondence, preventing "mistakes" or delays which might sabotage the application, and she moved briskly and competently through various negotiations to fruition in a mere two years.

The wisdom of declining to delegate was demonstrated in the very week the library was dedicated in 1908, when city officials made one last try to undercut the project. This one was financial. In 1906, when Pocatello officials had signed the contract under duress, Carnegie's support levy language had been less precise than it later became, so they'd been allowed to pledge a mill amount rather than a dollar amount. One mill in 1906 had amounted to $1,200, 10 percent of Carnegie's gift. In the intervening two years, however, property values in Pocatello had risen so much that "one mill" now netted a much greater amount. Surely, officials said, they didn't have to spend the whole current "one mill" on library services. Informed of this ploy, Howard and her friends hired lawyers, and the men were warned that their proposed action would be illegal and they would be prosecuted if they proceeded. With much grumbling, they backed down.[68]

---

65 *Pocatello (ID) Tribune*, Nov. 21, 1905.

66 Uhland, "Progress," 2 and *Pocatello (ID) Tribune*, Nov. 18, 1906.

67 Uhland, "Progress," 2 and *Pocatello (ID) Tribune*, Nov. 21, 1906.

68 *Pocatello (ID) Tribune*, Aug. 21, 22, and 28, 1908. Another place where women contended with cheap city officials over a Carnegie library was Pendleton, Oregon. In this case, however, they deferred to men in the actual pursuit of a building grant. While a laudatory article in a woman's magazine (Monroe, "When Women Will")

Idaho State Historical Society, photo #SG-202/23.

Dr. Minnie Howard, Pocatello, Idaho's Library Leader.

Boise's women were not troubled by local attempts at sabotage but by the sort of opposition from Bertram that quelled many an over-ambitious Intermountain West library hopeful. These women, however, persisted where some men backed down. Along the way, they demonstrated themselves to be remarkably skillful spin-doctors.

Several accounts of Boise's Carnegie library campaign exist, all presenting the project as a triumphant effort by idealistic women. And so it was. But when one begins comparing library board minutes and newspapers with Carnegie correspondence, another layer of narrative appears, for

gives complete credit to the town's Civic Club for procuring a Carnegie library, Carnegie Corporation records and a fact reported in the article itself qualify that claim. The city's negotiations with Carnegie were handled by Umatilla County Judge Charles Marsh, who worked not simply as the Club's champion but as a man with his own ideas about how the project should evolve (see the mention of his negotiations for increased funds in chapter 2). The decisive blow that overcame city officials' objections was struck not by the women, but by members of the city's commercial club, who sued councilmen when the latter attempted to divert endowment funds that should have gone to the Carnegie library to a separate city library. These women's energetic devotion to the library cause cannot be disputed. But Pendleton's application functioned differently than the applications described in this chapter, and thus this book does not categorize it with them.

these women seem to have been feeding different people different stories at the same time. Boise's application began in 1901, when Mary Beatty was deputized to lead the Columbian Club's effort to win a Carnegie building. Beatty wrote an initial inquiry letter to Carnegie in March 1902, enlisting an enthusiastic support letter from a judge known to Carnegie.[69] Bertram replied positively and sent a "Schedule of Questions."

The women returned the form and began promoting a bond issue to raise money for a library site. Nothing, certainly, prohibited them from doing so. But one might question the propriety of the public announcements they made in conjunction with this campaign. A perusal of Carnegie Corporation files makes it clear Carnegie had not replied to their communication at all at this point, much less made a promise. Yet on May 8, 1902, the day before the vote was to be taken, the *Idaho Statesman* trumpeted, "On this site the $25,000 promised from Mr. Carnegie will be used in erecting a library building. It will be one of the most useful improvements of the city."[70]

This statement—with its future tense—could have come from nowhere but the women, since they were the only ones who had been in communication with Carnegie and only their long-standing publicity committee (including reporter Eva Dockery and Fanny Cobb, wife of the *Statesman*'s publisher) could have disseminated these "facts." And the implication that the application had been successful was not the only misleading element of this communication. The figure "$25,000" existed only in the women's minds, for Bertram had never suggested this number in any of his letters. Yet a $25,000 grant was also suggested as a *fait accompli* when the Columbian Club-dominated library board convinced Boise's city council to approve a maintenance pledge for $2,500 in October, 1902, still in the absence of any definite promise from New York.[71]

One can only imagine the women's chagrin when Bertram's offer finally arrived, in February, 1903, and the amount offered was $15,000,[72]

69 Letter from William M. Morrow to Andrew Carnegie, Aug. 25, 1903, CCA. Morrow's friendship with Carnegie and his part in Boise's library building grant application are noted in Turner, *The Golden Dream*, 10–11.

70 *Boise (ID) Statesman*, May 8, 1902.

71 This action is recorded in the "Boise Public Library Minutes 1902–55," Dec. 27, 1902 as Ordinance #425, approved Oct. 9, 1902.

72 "Boise Public Library Minutes," Feb. 16, 1903. Also alluded to in a letter from James Beatty to James Bertram, March 1903, CCA.

well below both the Columbian Club's grand hopes and the figure they'd assured the public was Boise's share of Carnegie's bounty. They did thank the philanthropist, but they also began immediately to lobby Bertram for a larger grant, arguing in a circular fashion that since a site had been set aside worthy of a $25,000 building, $25,000 was their due. Mary Beatty's husband was enlisted to compile numbers of potential patrons in unincorporated suburbs and to testify to the inevitability of Boise's growth as Idaho's state capital. Even from a federal judge, however, such arguments had little effect on Bertram's jaundiced ears. Carnegie could consider only current census-documented population in the city proper, he wrote, and the census said that number was 5,957 people, so Boise could receive only $15,000.[73]

Rather than continuing to stubbornly argue with this subordinate, Boise's women determined to go straight to the top. Mary Beatty traveled to Sacramento, California to consult a mutual friend of her husband's and Carnegie's, Justice William M. Morrow of the US Circuit Court of Appeals. Morrow wrote directly to Carnegie at his private home in Scotland. As a personal favor, Carnegie agreed to increase Boise's offer to $20,000 total.[74]

This was unusual largesse, but it was not enough to satisfy Beatty and her friends. They had assured the public of a $25,000 library, and they were determined that Boise would have one. Fortunately for them, this all took place in 1903–04, before Carnegie required a pledge to stay within the promise amount—a pledge their actions certainly helped inspire. Blithely ignoring the $20,000 ceiling, they chose an architect's plan bid at $24,000 and commenced construction.[75]

This discrepancy accounts for the fact that when all Carnegie's money had been spent, in June, 1905, Boise's library still lacked some little things, including wiring and covering for the exposed pipes of the heating system.[76] It also had no furniture, but Beatty and her compatriots had collected funds for this purpose—a fact that she employed when she wrote to Carnegie

73 Letter from James Beatty to James Bertram, Feb. 28, 1903. Bertram became angry enough during the ongoing negotiations that he scrawled "5957"—the census-verified population of Boise—over Mary Beatty's appeal (letter from Mary Beatty to James Bertram, Aug. 11, 1905, CCA).

74 Letter from James Bertram to W. M. Morrow, Nov. 18, 1903, CCA.

75 "Boise Public Library Minutes," Feb. 9, 1904.

76 Letter from Mary Beatty to James Bertram, Aug. 11, 1905, CCA and "Boise Public Library Minutes, Sept. 26, 1905. Boise's mayor commented on the building's unfinished condition, calling the heating system "the homeliest and most unsightly arrangement" he had ever seen, see, Turner, *The Golden Dream*, 14.

admitting "unanticipated" overruns during construction. The good news, she told him, was that the city had managed to pay off contractors with the $5,000 the women had with great effort raised for furniture. Sadly, though, now those funds were unavailable to buy the tables and chairs they needed. Couldn't Carnegie help them out?[77]

Bertram raged. Nothing more would be forthcoming, he said—indeed, Boise was lucky it wasn't getting sued for not disclosing that it already had a fund for library construction available.

Once again, however, it wasn't Bertram who made the final decision. Justice Morrow again entered the lists and pleaded Boise's case directly to Carnegie. On September 15, 1905, Carnegie granted Boise an additional $5,000, bringing the total donation to $25,000 – exactly the grant that the women had wanted all along.[78]

Whether they achieved success by stratagem, as in Boise, by deft public relations, as in Pocatello, by fortunate connections, as in Hood River, or simply by dogged hard work, as in Mountain Home and Delta, the women who directed successful Carnegie library campaigns had a great deal to be proud of. Their new Carnegie libraries provided spacious, comfortable, and fiscally secure quarters for books and expanded collections for women's own reading. Best of all, perhaps, somebody else would be responsible for running them.

Beyond those practical considerations, Carnegie libraries also offered lasting testimony to women's effective cooperative work. Contemporary sources make this symbolism explicit: a Prescott newspaper noted that "the . . . library will stand for many years as a monument to [the women's] generosity and labors."[79] Carnegie libraries could also serve as poignant reminders of sisters departed in one way or another. Some who had joined in the efforts moved away as their husbands' work called them elsewhere, including Mary Beatty, while others died young, including a Prescott woman who moved away in mid-application and expired before its completion. That community's library was dedicated to her.[80]

---

77 Letter from Mary Beatty to James Bertram, Aug. 11, 1905, CCA.

78 Letter from James Bertram to William M. Morrow, Sept. 15, 1905, CCA.

79 *(Prescott) Arizona Daily Journal-Miner*, Nov. 3, 1903.

80 Ibid., Jan. 7, 1902 and "Minutes of the Board of Directors, Public Library, Prescott, Arizona," Mar. 4, 1902.

Had these women known how atypical they were in leading their communities' Intermountain West Carnegie library applications, they would have been even prouder, if that were possible. For in addition to securing the structures, they'd made points of principle central to the ethos that drove the entire women's club movement. They'd succeeded in convincing others that women's concerns deserved concrete municipal support. They'd established a bulkhead of "higher ideals" in their communities. They'd proved themselves worthy of the trust extended to them as managers and negotiators in a high-stakes project with outsiders, viable leaders in a culture where most men assumed women's incompetence.

They had also, we might say today, validated their communities as "progressive"—a term that would have pleased them very much.

7

Oligarchies and Carnegie Libraries in Transitional Towns

"A healthy and elevating influence on the community"

Most Carnegie public library building grant applications in the turn-of-the-twentieth-century interior American West might be called status quo projects in terms of their locally assigned significance. Proponents spoke of potential libraries as institutions which accorded seamlessly with extant values, institutions that would move the community into more perfect alignment with the essential nature it already possessed.

In a small subset of Intermountain West communities, however, Carnegie applications functioned as components of deliberate campaigns to reinvent local identity. Opinion leaders in these communities played not to residents' pride in perceived strengths, but to their embarrassments or awareness of current limitations, seeking to convince them that their homes could become radically different and better sorts of places. Rather than reinforcing extant assumptions about civic identity, Carnegie libraries in these five towns became symbols of transformations-in-progress, simultaneously agents and evidence of positive change.

These reinventions were related to the Intermountain West's evolution at the turn of the twentieth century from an American outback to a more settled, civilized region. All five were seeking to become less distinctively "Western" by fitting themselves into a more mainstream, self-consciously modern American community model. Two of these communities, Spokane and The Dalles, were attempting to put their frontier reputations as "wide-open towns" behind them. Two others, Tucson and Yuma, were engaged in spurning their Hispanic roots. Phoenix was seeking to claim new status as a place of national importance, courtesy of the US Department of Reclamation.

What distinguishes these applications besides their ideological trajectory is the breadth of the coalitions that worked on their behalf. In Spokane, The Dalles, Tucson, Yuma, and Phoenix, the work of applying for a Carnegie library grant was cooperatively conducted by men and women, business and professional people, leaders of various faiths, and representatives of multiple interest groups.[1] What these people shared was a deep conviction that their communities needed to reshape their images in order to thrive.

Respectability and Moral Reform: Spokane and The Dalles

Daniel F. Ring has written that the public library in the rowdy mining town of Butte, Montana was championed as "an instrument to convince the East that Butte was a civilized place to live," an institution citizens hoped would radically improve the city's disreputable image.[2] Such was also true in two Intermountain West communities that sought Carnegie libraries, Spokane, Washington, and The Dalles, Oregon. Spokane's image problem was particularly desperate, for the city held a reputation for vice so notorious that even San Franciscans spoke with awe of its "wide open," lawless character.[3] A substantial district containing brothels, saloons, and gambling halls flourished along Front, Bernard, Main, and Howard Streets. Daily reports of burglaries, drunkenness, armed robbery, and battery crowded the communities' newspapers. Juvenile gangs terrorized the citizenry, including one headed by a vicious young thug nicknamed with Dickensian relish "Lidgerwood Red."[4]

In Spokane's early years, the lawlessness had seemed inevitable, a product of the community's proximity to mining districts. But as the city

1 Only in the small religiously diverse Utah towns discussed in chapter 5 were the groups of citizens who united to pursue Carnegie libraries equally diverse. Ring's discussion of Montana Carnegie library applications suggests a correlation between social control motives and diverse leadership there also in, "Carnegie Libraries as Symbols for an Age," 8–9.

2 Ring, *The Origins of the Butte Public Library.*

3 Youngs, *The Fair and the Falls*, 76.

4 Stimson, *A View from the Falls*, 41 and *Spokane (WA) Spokesman-Review*, Jan. 10, 1901.

University of Washington Libraries, Special Collections, WAS0107.

"Wide-Open Spokane" just before its Carnegie library application.

grew, doubling in population between 1890 and 1900, so did its aspirations. Wealthy residents constructed elaborate mansions and cultural amenities increased.[5] Frontier rowdiness began to seem like an embarrassing anachronism in a city that aspired to be the most important community in its region. Spokane's newspapers began lobbying for reform using shaming tactics as well as direct argument. When a headline announced on February 6, 1910 that Seattle—a city considered one of Spokane's chief rivals—had banned open gambling, the editor suggested that Spokane should follow that commendable lead. But, he taunted, those who profited from vice in Spokane would never let that happen. If such a thing were even proposed the "saloon men" would "unite and throw their influence in favor of men who will manage the city as they desire."[6]

This sneer would have touched a particularly raw nerve in those who patronized the city's public library. Though the institution received city support and operated on a secure footing, it was housed downtown in the tenderloin district, in a room in city hall. Those who wanted to take advantage of its services were "compelled to run the gauntlet of two blocks of saloons, variety theaters, gambling halls, and houses of ill fame," "where vice in its most flagrant form [was] presented on every side"—including

5 Stimson, *A View From the Falls*, 35–39 and Meinig, "Spokane and the Inland Empire," 17–23.

6 *Spokane (WA) Chronicle*, Feb. 7, 1901.

prostitutes, who solicited by calling from windows as well as by openly walking the streets clad in showy garb. Unconcerned about the desperate lives of these women—who often died young from violence, suicide, disease, or the drug and alcohol abuse coincident to depression—Spokane's citizens focused on their own outrage and their children's innocence.[7]

In early 1901, the city's librarian, Mrs. Emma Wheatley, issued an "urgent request" that the institution be relocated. The *Spokane Chronicle* evoked this plea, arguing that "the present location of the city library cripples, if it does not destroy, half of the usefulness of that institution."[8]

A group of well-off citizens agreed, including members of the city's women's and men's clubs and city officials, and they united to seek Carnegie funds for a new library building. Their effort initially got off to a bad start, however, after someone enlisted an old acquaintance of Carnegie to write a support letter. This correspondent did not know the city and apparently misunderstood what he was told, for he implied that Spokane already had an adequate library building. It was simply, he suggested, in the wrong location.[9] Carnegie replied that he could not consider a request to replace a perfectly good building, however thoughtlessly sited it was.

The advocate apparently did not communicate this rationale to Spokane's library proponents, nor did Bertram. They were simply told that their request was denied. For almost two years they sought an explanation, but none was forthcoming, not even to a senator who went to New York on their behalf only to be "discourteously rebuffed."[10]

In the meantime, Wheatley was succeeded by Estelle Deffenbaugh, a librarian determined to declare war on the institution's disreputable neighbors. In October 1902 she announced that business owners in the tenderloin must either donate funds to relocate the library or move themselves. "We are going to have a library in this city which will be accessible to all people, and there are just two ways to do this," she wrote in an article contributed to the *Spokesman-Review*. "Someone must move out of that part of

7 Ibid.; letter from Mary Munson Shaw to James Bertram, Dec. 16, 1901, CCA and letter from George R. Wallace to Andrew Carnegie, Jan. 28, 1903, CCA. MacKell discusses the difficult lives of Mountain West prostitutes in *Red Light Women of the Rocky Mountains*.

8 *Spokane (WA) Chronicle*, Feb. 7, 1901.

9 Letter to Andrew Carnegie from W. D. Wrighten, Feb. 8, 1901.

10 Gengler, "Spokane's Public Libraries," 45.

town. We will go if we can. If the people on whose account we are obliged to go will not make this possible, they will be forced to leave."[11]

Before that showdown could take place, Rev. George Wallace, a member of the city's library board and Congregational minister, finally received an explanation from Bertram. Wallace immediately corrected the misunderstanding, describing the small rooms that housed Spokane's current library and emphasizing city support for a purpose-built library. On April 3, 1903, Spokane received a long-awaited promise of $75,000.[12]

The board which worked to complete this initial main library project and the three branch Spokane Carnegie libraries that followed in 1913–15 was composed of a variety of influential citizens. Clergymen of many denominations contributed their efforts, including Wallace, Catholic priest Father Verhagen, Rev. J. W. Allen of the Johnson Avenue Christian Church, and Mayor W. J. Hindly, pastor of the Pilgrim Congregational Church. Professional men and women also worked on the project, including M. M. Higley, President of the Northwest Business College, and Kate B. Reed, Preceptress of the high school. Women's club representatives served on the committees that helped decide the library's location and design.[13]

The choices made about the latter two factors underline the library's symbolic connection with a civic new beginning. Rather than struggling to clean up the dirty, crime-ridden neighborhood that previously served as the center of municipal operations, Spokane had already corporately turned its back on the past. Instead, a new core district was rising west of the old downtown, a neighborhood of ornamented stone public buildings, landscaped green spaces, and lavish houses constructed according to the "City Beautiful" model. Anyone visiting this district would have been unlikely to imagine that he or she was in a lawless western town. A building lot in this neighborhood, near the new cathedral, was set aside for Spokane's Carnegie library. The library was designed in Classical style complete with a two-story portico, an antithesis of frontier architecture, and an emblem of the civilized new Spokane.[14]

11 *Spokane (WA) Spokesman-Review*, Oct. 24, 1902.

12 Letter from James Bertram to George R. Wallace, Feb. 13, 1903, CCA and Gengler, *Spokane's Public Lbraries*, 46–48.

13 Participation is described in Gengler, *Spokane's Public Libraries*, 55 and in the *Spokane (WA) Spokesman-Review*, Sept. 16, 1909.

14 Details about Spokane's City Beautiful district come from an application for National Register of Historic Places status for the Riverside Avenue Historic District, in which

The speeches given when the library's cornerstone was laid in 1904 make explicit connections between the institution and the city's rebirth. "May its dedication or consecration today mark a new era of educational, social, and moral advancement in the environment of our beautiful city," offered one speaker. J. M. Comstock, a former mayor, assured his listeners that "the perfection of character which flows from the study of the selected volumes contained therein so far transcend[s] its outward ornamentation . . . that the masses throughout the coming ages will ever bless the donors and the people who today lay this cornerstone."[15] Similar themes marked the building's dedication a year later. A triumphant Estella Deffenbaugh reviewed the library's history and proclaimed that a new day had arrived in the lives of all Spokane's readers. Seattle's head librarian, Charles Wesley Smith, offered remarks that must have been highly satisfying to those who had feared Spokane would never outgrow its unsavory reputation. The library's construction, Smith confirmed, had changed the way that outsiders perceived the community. When Spokane had modernized its public school system a few years before, the world had sensed that the city was moving toward maturity; this new Carnegie library confirmed that Spokane had arrived.[16]

While Spokane was attempting to overcome long-standing infamy, The Dalles was mobilizing to regain lost respectability at the time of its Carnegie library application. Established as a Methodist mission in 1838, The Dalles had long considered itself more virtuous and civilized than the average western town. As a supply point at an important location on the Oregon Trail, the community had prospered in the mid-nineteenth century, attracting a stable population, many churches, and a lively network of social and benevolent organizations.[17] By the turn of the twentieth century, residents were congratulating themselves on having long ago "passed through the trials of pioneer life," and they bragged that the community resembled an Eastern town in its high proportion of well-educated and cultured citizens.[18]

---

the city's main Carnegie library was constructed. The form (#7 in a series of similar forms) is held in the Northwest Room of the Spokane Public Library.

15 *Spokane (WA) Chronicle*, Dec. 12, 1904.

16 Ibid., Dec. 19, 1905.

17 For a history of The Dalles, see McNeal, *History of Wasco County*. Haarsager notes that over twenty women's organizations existed in The Dalles, including those associated with Congregationalist, Methodist, Catholic, Christian, Baptist, and Lutheran churches in *Organized Womanhood*, 104–5.

18 Letter from Mrs. Roxie S. Shakelford to Andrew Carnegie, Dec. 8, 1904, CCA.

Oregon Historical Society Research Library, image #62757.

Citizens of The Dalles, Oregon, gather socially in 1893, about a decade before the temporary invasion that brought rowdiness and crime to their community.

This satisfaction, however, vanished around 1906 as railroad construction brought rowdiness and crime to town. Construction on a Northern Pacific Railroad track down the Columbia River to Portland and an Oregon Trunk Line extension to Bend simultaneously neared The Dalles that year, and the community became a base of operations. Railroad workers and speculators jammed the town, and new saloons, gambling dens, and prostitutes quickly followed. Cheap lodging houses, thrown up overnight, allowed disorderly conduct. "The night life in The Dalles," writes a local historian, "reverted back to that similar to the gold rush days of the 1860s" with drinking, crime, and vice flourishing. The "free love" newly available in the city particularly shocked long-time residents.[19] Worst of all for the town's readers, this burgeoning downtown vice district grew up downtown near the city's extant public library, and those who sought to patronize the institution repeatedly encountered rowdy behavior that reminded them of how their once-quiet community had changed.

19 McNeal, *History of Wasco County*, 22.

The citizens of The Dalles fought back. Troops were called in to keep order, and a curfew was established. The city passed laws outlawing gambling and prostitution and severely regulating saloons.[20] At the same time, citizens decided to relocate their library. For years the institution had functioned in a "delapidated," "cramped," "old frame" building with almost nobody complaining.[21] But now that eyesore in the midst of eyesores apparently seemed a particular embarrassment, yet one more sign of entropy. As in Spokane, a coalition of middle and upper-middle class citizens dedicated to civic reform—including educators, professionals and businessmen, city officials, and women's club members—worked together to secure The Dalles's Carnegie library building grant.[22] In a rare show of shared governance, the president of the local women's club, Mrs. R. S. Shakelford, and the town's mayor, J. L. Kelly, took turns corresponding with Carnegie. Commercial Club members contributed their public-relations skills by circulating a petition in favor of a support levy. Within a year, cooperative effort had secured The Dalles a $10,000 promise, and men with particular talents in negotiation were deputized to deal with Bertram's questions.[23] All possible local human resources, in other words, were mobilized to ensure that this application—and the crucial larger cause it symbolized—succeeded. The project's perceived importance is suggested by the fact that four hundred citizens of The Dalles, a crowd that would have been large even in a much larger community, attended the dedication ceremony in 1910. News reports of the festivities themselves emphasized their high tone. "The intelligent and representative audience appreciated the scholarly and intellectual lecture delivered by a man of magnificent brain power," *The Dalles Semi-Weekly Chronicle* wrote of talk presented by a former president of the University of Oregon. The building's "orderly arrangement" and "well-grown lawns" were described, making the building into an emblem of civilization.[24]

Within five years railroad construction moved elsewhere, and with it the railroaders, the prostitutes and the gamblers, and, after The Dalles

20 Ibid.

21 The structure is described in a letter from J. L. Kelly to James Bertram, Apr. 3, 1907, CCA.

22 Lists of board members appear in Ibid., 26, and in *The Dalles (OR) Semi-Weekly Chronicle*, Feb. 8, 1905.

23 Letter from John Gavin to James Bertram, Apr. 3, 1907, CCA and *The Dalles (OR) Semi-Weekly Chronicle*, Sept. 23, 1910.

24 *The Dalles (OR) Semi-Weekly Chronicle*, Sept. 23, 1910.

attempted to ensure future peace by outlawing saloons, the drunkards. As the city became again quiet,[25] citizens undoubtedly breathed a sigh of relief for what they had lost. But they could also take pride in what they had gained: a sturdy little library standing as a permanent reminder of the years they'd fought successfully for their community.

Carnegie Libraries as Agents of Americanization: Tucson and Yuma

Tucson and Yuma possessed their share of frontier rowdiness at the time of their Carnegie applications—both had been military towns, compounding the draw for prostitutes in particular—but the people behind their Carnegie library applications were more concerned with race than with morality. Nearly every western town contained vice, after all, but only in Arizona could communities be tarred with the brush of their Hispanic history. Eager to attract the population and capital that would help their communities move into the American mainstream, these civic promoters were working to spread the news that their communities were not lazy, backwards "Mexican" towns but "wide-awake" modern places.

A venerable town by Intermountain West standards, Tucson came by its Hispanic reputation honestly: it had been established as a walled presidio by the Spanish in 1775 and became a US possession only after the Gadsden Purchase of 1853. Even after this transfer, however, a constant threat of Apache attack limited the community's appeal to Anglo settlers. A US military post, Camp Lowell, mitigated that problem between 1867 and 1891, the year the Apaches were finally defeated, but not until the Southern Pacific Railroad reached Tucson in 1880 and made the city its southwest center of operations did substantial development begin. Finally, thirty years after Arizona had become a US territory, new settlers flocked to the area, drawn by copper mining, milling, commerce, and the community's self-constructed reputation as a healthseeker's mecca.[26]

In 1900, however, Tucson still looked very different than most American cities. European American citizens constituted less than 40 percent of the population, Mexican Americans 55 percent. Tucson's architecture was

25 McNeal, *History of Wasco County*, 22.

26 Mabry et al. discuss Tucson's history at the time of its Carnegie library application in *Tucson at the Turn of the Century*, as does Magie in "Carnegie Free Library."

Arizona Historical Society, Tucson, photo #BN205430.

Old Tucson: Adobe construction.

dominated by modest adobe dwellings and many residents exclusively spoke Spanish. The old Military Plaza, site of the former Camp Lowell, functioned as a casual south-of-the-border-style shantytown.[27]

Anglo residents eager to achieve statehood feared that such "foreignness" in the territorial capital would work against them. And so they embarked around the turn of the twentieth century on an initiative to transform their community from "a Mexican village to a modern city."[28] Shunning adobe construction (or "mud," as they called it), they built their own two-and-three-story houses from brick in the new and wealthy "Snob Hollow" neighborhood. These houses flaunted Tucson's first front lawns, in contrast to the characteristic Hispanic-style interior courtyards. Anglo residents also instituted civic improvements befitting a modern American city. They upgraded the city's water system, laid the first sewer lines, hired a professional fire department, and attempted to impose white middle class moral standards

27 Mabry et al, *Tucson at the Turn of the Century*, 21.

28 The phrase comes from the *(Tucson) Arizona Daily Star*, Nov. 17, 1900.

New Tucson: Snob Hollow.

on the city's population, closing down Tucson's red light district and instituting a law that prohibited women from singing in saloons.[29]

Tucson's Carnegie application occurred in the midst of this transformation. An early correspondent sent Carnegie "maps showing our city as it formerly was and as it is now" and bragged about the modern architecture that demonstrated how forward-looking the population had become.[30] The same sort of people who were working to modernize Tucson directed the library project, an Anglo coalition that shut out even the community's most influential and respected Hispanics. Those who participated in the Carnegie application included members of the male cultural elite (newspaper editor G. W. Pittock, state legislator E. J. Trippel, medical doctor and University of Arizona regent Hiram W. Fenner, and Professor S. M. Woodward), prominent members of the city's women's clubs, city officials, and businessmen. In a gesture at once convenient (the land was available) and symbolic, this coalition selected the old Military Plaza as the ideal library site, and slum clearance began. Soon the shantytown squatters were gone with their

29 *(Tucson) Arizona Daily Star*, June 18, 1899 and Mabry et al., *Tucson at the Turn of the Century*, 4–21.

30 Letter from Rochester C. Ford to Andrew Carnegie, Dec. 5, 1899, CCA.

haphazard hovels replaced by a plot neatly landscaped in what was locally termed the "American" style.[31]

Tucson obtained a $25,000 promise from Carnegie on June 28, 1899. "It is as liberal an offer as that extended to San Diego," wrote the *Arizona Daily Star* proudly, suggesting that Tucson's Anglo citizens were already thinking of themselves as competing on a broadly American stage. Chicago's cutting-edge Henry C. Trost, one of the most revered modern architects of the day (a man guaranteed not to use "mud" in his design) was chosen as architect.[32] At the completed library's dedication a few years later, the library's physical shape was heralded as certain to "exercise a healthy and elevating influence on the community, especially the young and rising generation." The community's new Carnegie library, one celebrant proclaimed, was certain to inspire further "progress."[33]

So powerful was this symbolism twinning library and modernization that it persisted for many decades. As late as 1981, a history of Tucson's evolution entitled "From Mud Village to Modern Metropolis" features the library prominently as milestone in the city's transformation."[34]

Yuma's 1917 Carnegie library application was also the work of an Anglo oligarchy consciously working to Americanize the town's image. Like Tucson, Yuma had been first established in 1779 at the confluence of the Gila and Colorado Rivers as a Spanish mission to the Quechan Indians. Permanent Anglo settlement began in 1849 when a United States military post was constructed to protect travelers enroute to the California goldfields. A formal survey of the townsite was conducted in 1854, and by 1859 the community (then called Colorado City) had a post office and was the hub of river steamboat traffic.[35]

To many Anglo immigrants Yuma seemed a foreign town culturally dominated by Hispanic residents. Mary Elizabeth Post, a schoolteacher who came to Yuma from New England in the 1870s, remembered that during her first decades in town the little girls wore "long, peculiar," Indian-style dresses because "the Spanish mothers of this isolated country did not know

31 Magie, "Carnegie Free Library 1900–1990."

32 *(Tucson) Arizona Daily Star*, Nov. 15, 1899 and Magie, "Carnegie Free Library."

33 *(Tucson) Arizona Daily Star*, June 9, 1901.

34 Bufkin, "From Mud Village to Modern Metropolis."

35 Trafzer, *Yuma: Frontier Crossing*, and Crowe and Brinckerhoft, *Early Years* trace Yuma's history.

Arizona Historical Society, Yuma, photo #65.937.3.

Mary Elizabeth Post, Yuma's "High Priestess of Americanization."

what little girls in other places were wearing." Post remembered just how difficult it had been to bring the rudiments of what she considered civilization to Yuma. She was forced to teach the Spanish wives of "American" men how to bake cakes and to teach the children how to sing "American" Christmas and patriotic songs.[36]

By the second decade of the twentieth century Yuma was prospering, Hispanic culture or not. Reclamation Act projects (including the Laguna Dam [1909] and a large network of canals [1912]) had expanded agricultural land in the area by 80 percent. Large-scale farming became possible for the first time. "The promise of the twentieth century seemed bright," writes historian Jay Dexter Pierson, describing a building boom inspired by "great confidence in the future of [the] town."[37] Yuma's initial inquiry to Carnegie came in the midst of this period of prosperity, when the Yuma City Women's Club deputized city attorney H. Wupperman (the husband of a member) to inquire about Carnegie's requirements.[38]

36 These reminiscences are reported in Boehriger, "Mary Elizabeth Post," 96.

37 Pierson, "The Growth of a Western Town," 4–6.

38 Westover, *Yuma's Parade*, 96–97.

Arizona Historical Society, Yuma, photo #80.6.14.

Inadvertent demolition: the flood that aided Yuma's transformation.

City officials' inertia and debate over a library tax temporarily stalled the application, however, until a catalyst literally swept Yuma off its feet. That event was the winter flood of 1916–17, "the greatest catastrophe in the history of Yuma," when the Colorado River rose thirty-five feet, inundating the community. A third of the city's citizens were left homeless, 150 buildings were destroyed, the city's mayor was flattened by a heart attack, and the newspaper office was ruined. No trains were able to reach Yuma for four days.[39]

This devastation inspired transformation. The Yuma *Sun* roared back from a twenty-one-day hiatus urging residents to respond with "a new life, a new energy and determination, a progress unprecedented." And they did, seizing the occasion as an opportunity to modernize their community. After the rubble was cleared, the reconstructed streets were paved and sewers were constructed. The red light district was forced to relocate outside the city limits. Ordinances restricted adobe construction and "frame houses began lining city streets." Yuma was being transformed from a former military outpost and Indian village "to resemble small town America."[40] In the midst of this literal and figurative rebuilding, Yuma's city council proved

39 Pierson discusses the flood and its aftermath in "The Growth of a Western Town," 10.

40 Ibid.

more receptive to a Carnegie library application than it had previously, and Carnegie was petitioned. Like the other applications described in this chapter, Yuma's building grant application was a coalition effort. Participants including prominent men (Wupperman and mayor Frank Stanley, who negotiated with Bertram) and women's club members, including the wife of the *Sun*'s publisher, who served on the board that supervised construction and landscaping. The head of the building committee was none other than Mary Elizabeth Post, the "High Priestess of Americanization" in Yuma.[41]

In early 1921—with Yuma sparkling in its reconstructed glory—the city's commercial club hosted a junket for to show capitalists from San Diego that the city was, as a correspondent had put the matter to Carnegie, "assured of one of the greatest futures that will not be found in any other part of the country."[42] During the businessmen's visits, they were treated to the sort of festivities one might expect: balls, fancy dinners, speeches. One celebration, though, was a bit more unusual. They were also invited to tour Yuma's new Carnegie library, and to participate in its dedication ceremonies, which had been delayed for six months after the building's completion so that this symbol of their hosts' forward-looking spirit could be highlighted as evidence that a thoroughly modern Yuma was fit to be San Diego's "right hand of power."[43]

From "Hamlet" to "Great Regional Capital": Phoenix's Carnegie Library

Phoenix's Carnegie library application was associated with one of the most rapid and radical civic transformations which occurred in any Intermountain West city in the early twentieth century. In 1885, Phoenix was a village with no rail link to the outside world, its 1,300 citizens living in fear of Apache raids. By 1920 it had acquired a population of nearly 30,000 people. As historian G. Wesley Johnson, Jr. puts it, the city bourgeoned from an "obscure . . . desert hamlet" into a "great regional capital" in less than forty years.[44]

41 Westover, *Yuma's Parade*, 98.

42 Letter from [illegible signature, Town of Yuma stationery] to Andrew Carnegie, June 13, 1913, CCA and letter from Rev. Lawrence Kelly to James Bertram, July 23, 1917, CCA.

43 *Yuma (AZ) Daily Sun*, Feb. 20, 1921.

44 Johnson, "Directing Elites," 14 and Luckingham, "The Promotion of Phoenix," 84.

In contrast to Yuma and Tucson, Phoenix lacked a Hispanic heritage since it had been established from the ground up by civil war veterans in the early 1870s. Boosters were proud of this difference, fond of contrasting their "wide-awake American city" with "the sleepy Mexican town" of Tucson. Phoenix achieved a Southern Pacific connection in 1887 and it won the state capital designation from Prescott in 1889.[45] Surrounded by vast tracts of undeveloped land and boasting a warm climate, it seemed destined for a great influx of immigrants and money.

Agriculture proved difficult in the area because of water problems, however. In the spring Phoenix's irrigators had access to an abundance of water—indeed, too much water, for the Salt River's flood-level flows regularly washed out irrigation ditches and drowned new crops. For the rest of the growing season there was very little water, especially during the droughts of the 1890s that parched thousands of acres of cultivable land. Without water for farming and ranching—or enough water to reliably serve the needs of an urban population—the city's growth potential appeared limited.[46]

During the very end of the nineteenth and beginning of the twentieth centuries, however, a handful of wealthy speculators from the East and Midwest began to acquire large tracts surrounding Phoenix, gambling that they could somehow make this difficult (and thus extremely cheap) land pay. Among them were two men who moved their families to Phoenix and played leading roles in Phoenix's Carnegie library campaign as well as in its economic development. These were Benjamin A. Fowler, a Yale-educated book publisher who had lived in New York and Chicago before he came to Phoenix in 1899, and Dwight B. Heard, the heir to America's largest hardware company, who immigrated to Phoenix from Chicago for his health.

Fowler, Heard, and other aggressive developers—including bankers, entrepreneurs, and wealthy civil war veterans—began a concerted campaign to develop Phoenix.[47] Heard assembled a promotional booklet published by the Board of Supervisors of Maricopa County, including an article somewhat prematurely titled "Phoenix: Center of Farming

45 Mawn, "Phoenix, Central City of the Southewest," 171.

46 Luckingham discusses the early history of water problems in Phoenix in "The Promotion of Phoenix," 85, as does Zarbin, *Salt River Project*.

47 Johnson identifies these men and notes their coordinated efforts in "Directing Elites," 17–19.

Arizona Historical Society, Tucson, photo #8099.

B. A. Fowler of Phoenix, Arizona.

Paradise-1901." As a very different kind of "developer" than the provincial boosters described in chapter 3, these men did not simply bluster, they exploited wider networks to secure the improvements that would allow their community to grow.

Heard spoke with his personal friends Theodore Roosevelt and Gifford Pinchot, noting that the territory held almost limitless economic potential for America if a strong American presence could be established to discourage Mexican incursion. In Heard's argument, federal assistance in developing the desert became almost equated with patriotic duty.

While Heard laid the ideological groundwork, Fowler worked with the technicalities of federal support for irrigation. Something creative had to be done, for as a territory Arizona was not eligible for Carey Act funds—those were available only to states. Recognizing Fowler's political savvy, the six hundred members of the new Salt River Valley Water Storage Association elected him permanent chair in August 1900, and sent him to the nineteenth National Irrigation Congress in Chicago. There Fowler joined other westerners in promoting a National Reclamation Act tailored to the region's particular needs. He also engaged in more narrowly partisan lobbying, discussing Phoenix's problems with Charles Walcott of the US Geological Survey and George Maxwell, Executive Director of the National Irrigation Association.[48]

Fowler, Heard, and the other members of the city's "directing elite" (as G. Wesley Johnson terms them) worked to improve the city's cultural resources as well as its economy around the turn of the twentieth century. At their insistence and with their patronage, better schools and Phoenix's first hospital were built, theaters and churches were constructed, and luxury hotels lured wealthy convalescents. A neighborhood of expensive homes and parks was developed to the north of downtown. Literary and fraternal societies flourished. The city's first public library also appeared in 1897, established by the exclusive women's Friday Club, which counted Fowler's wife Etta Frances ("a woman of marked attainments, great executive ability, and an exceptionally good speaker") among its members.[49]

In 1901, the Phoenix Library Association was formed for the express purpose of soliciting a library building grant from Andrew Carnegie. B. A. Fowler headed the group and served as the main correspondent. Etta Fowler and her friend Dorothy McClintock, wife of a judge (who herself had earned an MA in Botany), also wrote letters as the application progressed.[50] Committee members included lawyers, clergymen of several denominations, and businessmen. The group initially received a promise of $15,000 in 1902. As in so many other communities, Phoenix's library board thought it deserved a higher amount, but as members considered how they might obtain $25,000 they discovered that extant state library legislation would not allow a $2,500 yearly support tax. That problem was easily solved, for Fowler had been elected to the state legislature. Two library board members drafted a new bill, Fowler presented it, and it became law. The city of Phoenix imposed a $2,500 library tax on itself.[51]

48 Smith discusses the politicking that led to federal aid for Phoenix's irrigation needs in *The Magnificent Experiment* and Zarbin describes Fowler's lobbying in "In Pursuit," 148.

49 Mawn, "Phoenix, Central City of the Southwest," 170–82. Details about the life of Etta Frances Fowler appear in her obituary, *Phoenix (AZ) Sun*, Aug. 26, 1943 and in Gertz, "Biography of Mrs. B. A. Fowler." The quote comes from an article on B. A. Fowler in *Who's Who in Arizona 1913*, 796–97.

50 Dorothy O. McClintock's life is sketched in her obituary (*Phoenix) Arizona Republican*, May 26, 1941.

51 Downing, "History of the Carnegie Public Library in Phoenix," 12–13.

Now the only obstacle to a $25,000 library was convincing Bertram that Phoenix would inevitably grow. Once again, Phoenix found this less an obstacle than most other Intermountain West communities, thanks to an incredible windfall. In the same year as the initial Carnegie promise, the National Reclamation (Newlands) Act passed Congress, incorporating revisionist language suggested by Fowler and Heard that allowed the government to fund not only projects promising to deliver irrigation to previously unbroken lands (the original drafters' intent) but also to deliver water to land already in private hands. Thus land in the Salt River Valley was eligible to benefit, including Fowler's and Heard's holdings.[52]

As Secretary of the Interior Ethan A. Hitchcock began weighing proposals from Montana, Colorado, Wyoming, Nevada, and Arizona vying for initial Newlands funds, Fowler traveled to Washington DC, and, sharing surveys completed under Walcott's direction, he succeeded in getting the Salt River Project selected as the first to be undertaken.[53] Planning for the Roosevelt Dam and Tonto Reservoir high on the Salt River began. Land speculation accelerated, with so many city subdivisions platted between 1905 and 1910 that the city engineer had to redraw his map five times.[54]

The Salt River Project proved exactly the ammunition that Phoenix's Carnegie library supporters needed to convince Carnegie to raise his library building grant offer. Phoenix's friend Charles Walcott happened to be a member of the Carnegie Institute as well as head of the US Geological Survey, and he assured Carnegie that construction of the Tonto Reservoir on the Salt River would certainly "more than double" Phoenix's population virtually overnight and insure continued growth.[55] Fowler visited Franks in New York several times to make sure Carnegie staff understood the effect that the Salt River Project would have on Phoenix's growth. Bertram issued a revised promise for a $25,000 library in 1904.

Heard, now head of Phoenix's real estate board, insured that the city council phrased an appropriate resolution of support—not much of a problem, for the city was already taxing at the required rate. Plans and bids were handled with great efficiency. Site selection did slightly delay the project, as developers on the library board with competing interests contested with

52 Zarbin, "In Pursuit," 148–53.

53 Smith, *The Magnificent Experiment*, 23.

54 Mawn,"Phoenix, Central City of the Southwest," 348.

55 Zarbin,"In Pursuit," 148–53.

each other for this prize. In the end, the city council chose Neahr's Park, a prosperous new addition planned in Beaux Arts style with plenty of green space and wide boulevards.[56]

At this, Phoenix's rank-and-file citizens attempted to have a say in their new library, though the project had to this point progressed without their input. The Neahr's Park site, protesters claimed to city council, was unsuitable, for the very people who needed the library the most would be the farthest from it. Traveling out to the western suburbs would prove so time-consuming for Phoenix's working class and those with homes in the old central core that patronage would inevitably suffer. "Not less than a dozen taxpayers made stirring speeches before the council," the *Arizona Gazette* reported. One man complained that the site "would be well for the 500 [Phoenix's wealthy citizens] and for the real estate developers nearby, but what about the 14,500? Have they no rights?" Phoenix was hardly a democratically constituted community in 1904, however, and the library was constructed where the board had recommended.[57]

By the time that the Carnegie library was dedicated, in February, 1908, the city's elite citizens were in the mood to celebrate a transformation-in-progress. Construction had begun on the Newlands Act-funded Tonto Reservoir and Roosevelt Dam, though the latter would not be completed until 1911. Land values inside and outside the city had soared as homeseekers and investors were arriving daily.[58] Phoenix was no longer "the land of tradition, the Aztec, the Apache, the veritable Wild West with all its weird romance and story," B. A. Fowler assured the crowd at the dedication ceremony. "What a difference" was apparent "in the people, in the domestic and public life, in the educational advancement, in the degree of civilization, in the Christian development."

The new Carnegie library, Fowler pronounced, stood as a physical representation of the "permanent and enduring" character Phoenix had now achieved. It would "open a new vista" in citizens' personal lives as well, bringing the potential for Horatio Alger-style transformation. He advised his listeners that;

> The library unfolds the lives of great men who, by their own exertions and will power, have conquered obstacles, infinite almost, and whose

56 Historical information on Neahr's Addition is available at http://www.historicphoenix.com.historic-district/woodland-historic-district/history-woodland-historic-district.

57 *(Phoenix) Arizona Gazette*, Dec. 8, 1904 and Downing, "Directing Elites," 15–17.

58 Mawn, "Phoenix, Central City of the Southwest," 348.

> victories have become an inspiration to hundreds and thousands. Through its windows the yearning boy or young man can see visions, and dream dreams, as he looks out on the uncounted fields of art, science, literature and commerce, in all their branches, in which his fertile brain and highest ambitions can find room for activity with as good a chance for success as any ever had. To such, there may come new hopes, new aspirations, new determination to win, coupled with a solemn vow to toil, if need be; to suffer pain and deprivation, if called upon; to bear scoffs and criticism patiently, and, keeping his eye on the goal, to "learn to labor and to wait," and then "to hustle while he waits."[59]

In voicing this spirit of "hustle," Fowler was sounding a theme that the other coalitions described in this chapter would have approved. Social progress, Mary Elizabeth Post, Estella Deffenbach, et al. would have agreed, did not happen accidentally—it came at the cost of focused and deliberate work.

And, as the Carnegie library proponents of The Dalles knew all too well, it required constant vigilance. Fowler himself emphasized this latter point to his listeners, suggesting that even Phoenix could not afford to rest on its laurels. "While today is better than yesterday," he said, borrowing words that Carnegie himself had once spoken, "tomorrow should be better still."

59 Fowler's speech is transcribed in Downing, "History of the Carnegie Public Library in Phoenix," 7–9, 19.

8

Carnegie Libraries in the Service of Personal Power

"The most cordial congratulations on all sides"

AMONG THE MOST DISTINCTIVE INTERMOUNTAIN WEST CARNEGIE APPLICATIONS are those that were undertaken as personal projects by individual powerful men, or by individual men who dreamed that procuring a library for their communities would make them powerful. Conceived as solitary initiatives, managed as conclusively by one person as Carnegie's procedures allowed, these library building grant projects contrast sharply with the community-driven applications that formed the region's norm.

In a sense, though, the five applications that took this shape *are* similar to the others, for they too mirror a particular local spirit. All were conducted in communities where grassroots (or even oligarchical) action was not the customary way things got done, communities where corporations controlled not only the economy, but the day-to-day decision making that shaped municipal circumstances. Citizens of these communities had become accustomed to waiting for the powers-that-were to decide when crucial civic improvements would take place and they'd become convinced that those who held life-and-death power over their communities didn't always have their best interests at heart. Thus the initiative of independent minded men—often outsiders newly come to town—was required to break the inertia and begin Carnegie applications.

Three Carnegie Library Leaders Who Won Local Respect

Robert Morris, Green River, Wyoming

Robert C. Morris of Green River, Wyoming, seems to have been the most altruistic in this group of local Carnegie library patrons, and the most genuinely interested in a library for its own sake. A bachelor, Morris had led a distinguished but solitary and peripatetic life before he settled in Green River in 1902. His relocations began in childhood, when his family brought him to South Pass City, Wyoming, in 1869.[1] His family quickly became active in serving the state, especially his mother Esther Hobart Morris, who became "the mother of woman's suffrage" in Wyoming and the model for the statue representing Wyoming in the nation's capital. She also served briefly as the first female justice of the peace in the United States, with the eighteen-year-old Robert working as her clerk.[2] Robert was sent back to his mother's native New York for his higher education. Trained as a lawyer, he served as a court reporter, then as private secretary to Albert Bigalow, New York's Secretary of State, a position which required him to "investigat[e] the financial management of the state charitable institutions," including Carnegie's. After two years with Bigalow, Morris returned to Wyoming to work as a stenographer for the Wyoming district courts and as private secretary to three Wyoming governors. He then migrated east again to work in Washington, DC as clerk of the United States Senate Committee on Education and Labor from 1891–94. Then he came west once again to become clerk of the Supreme Court of Wyoming in Cheyenne.

This wandering ended temporarily in 1902, after his twin brother Edward's death. Edward had been overseeing several businesses the brothers held in common in Green River, including a bank and a store, and Robert Morris returned to his home to take them in charge. The community he found had not evolved much beyond the town of his boyhood. Established as a Union Pacific station point in 1872, Green River remained at the turn of the twentieth century still economically dependent on the railroad and mining operations associated with it. Coal produced in the surrounding area was shipped out through the city, and local fortunes rose and fell with

---

1 A brief account of Robert Morris's life appears in the Green River Historic Preservation Commission's "Self Guided Tour of Historic Green River" and in the *Green River (WY) Star*, Feb. 22, 1907.

2 Denice Wheeler, *The Feminine Frontier*, xvii, 162 and Larson, *History of Wyoming*, 89–94, profile Esther Morris.

Robert Morris of Green River, Wyoming.

Wyoming State Archives, Department of State Parks and Cultural Resources.

its supply and demand. Civic development had lagged. The city had only recently established a fire department and it still lacked many amenities common in newer Intermountain West communities, including an organized program of town beautification, a commercial club, and a public library.[3]

Raised in a family with an ethos of confident activism, armed with decades of organizational skills and knowledge of business practices—and, perhaps, inspired by a wanderer's desire to be accepted and loved by citizens of the place where he had spent his formative years—Morris began taking steps to move his home town into the new century. He initiated a tree-planting campaign and encouraged his fellow businessmen to form a club.[4]

He also began working for a public library, an effort for which he was particularly well prepared. While a resident of Cheyenne, Morris had helped to write the legislation that enabled Wyoming counties to impose taxes for public library purposes, then had participated in Cheyenne's successful Carnegie library campaign. He now made it his mission to insure that Green River also benefited from Carnegie's largesse. Familiar with the logistics of the application process, he insured that everything was in order before the initial letter was even written. He was the one who wrote the

---

3 Parker, "Early Days" and letter from Robert Morris to Andrew Carnegie, Aug. 14, 1905.

4 Green River Historic Preservation Commission, "Self Guided Tour of Historic Green River."

support resolution city officials signed and he convinced county commissioners to donate a building site. He was the one who procured written assurances from the Union Pacific that it would transport construction supplies for the library at special reduced rates, thus insuring that Carnegie funds would suffice though all necessary materials would have to be imported to this desert region. He was the one who chaired the local library board formed for the purpose of pursuing an application, consisting of himself and two of his business associates, Mayor Hugo T. Gaensslen (a brewer, banker, and cattleman) and Thomas S. Taliaferro, Jr. (president and manager of the Green River Electric Light and Power Company).[5]

When Morris wrote Green River's initial inquiry letter to Carnegie on August 14, 1905, thorough documentation of the community's preparation for a grant was enclosed. All of Bertram's potential questions had been anticipated, and several of the steps that typically followed an inquiry and preceded a Carnegie commitment had been completed. Just four months later, in early December, Green River received a promise for $20,000.[6] Ground was broken the next spring. Morris's neat, detailed records relative to construction are preserved in the Green River Library Board's minutes with the building cost precisely what had been budgeted.

As the city celebrated the building's dedication on July 4, 1907, it also celebrated Robert Morris. He was proclaimed a local benefactor and awarded, in the words of the *Green River Star*, "the most cordial congratulations on all sides." More tangible rewards followed. Crediting Morris with more "backbone" than current council members, the *Star*'s editor proclaimed, "Mayor Robert C. Morris sounds just about right for Green River."[7] But higher office than mayor of Green River would cap Morris's career. That very autumn he was elected to the Wyoming State House of Representatives from Sweetwater County (county seat, Green River), then re-elected in 1909.[8]

Morris's efforts also secured him a permanent place in his boyhood community's memory and affection—a reward this roaming bachelor might have been especially happy to garner. Though Morris left Green River again to retire to Cheyenne in 1912, he is memorialized in the city's walking tour

5 Gasson, "Sweetwater County Library Association."

6 Letter from Robert Morris to Andrew Carnegie, Aug. 14, 1905, CCA; letter from James Bertram to Robert Morris, Dec. 8, 1905, CCA; "Library Board Minutes, Green River, Wyoming," June 30, 1907.

7 *Green River (WY) Star*, July 5 and Apr. 12, 1907.

8 Erwin, *Wyoming Historical Blue Book*, 753, 758.

Wyoming State Archives, Department of State Parks and Cultural Resources.

The new Green River Carnegie library.

brochure, which includes his house as number seven. The brochure gives a substantive biography of him, noting unequivocally, "Robert was responsible for the free county library system used in each county [and] the grants for the Carnegie libraries in Cheyenne and Green River." He is also credited two stops later, when visitors are invited to admire the community's still-standing Carnegie library, beautifully preserved and still serving Green River as the County Court building.[9]

Frank Norcross, Reno, Nevada

Frank Norcross of Reno, Nevada, seems to have been a man also genuinely convinced of the importance of public libraries, but he was younger, more ambitious, and more contentious than Morris. Under Norcross's direction, Reno's Carnegie library campaign functioned as a stage on which its leader demonstrated his prowess as he led his community to a symbolic victory in its long-standing quest for self-determination.[10]

Reno had been established in 1868 as a Central Pacific Railroad distribution center for surrounding ranches and for the Comstock mines. Despite its economic importance, however, the city had never possessed

9 Green River Historic Preservation Commission, "Self-Guided Tour of Historic Green River."

10 See Swetnam, "Battle for the Books," for an article based on this research.

municipal self-government because as seat of Washoe County its affairs were directed by county commissioners.[11] The county commission set property taxes, issued bonds, and, in one historian's judgment, "spent tax revenues as it pleased, hired, fired, named grand juries and generally ramrodded local matters in the county."[12] Washoe County commissioners were famously corrupt, indicted by state grand juries through the 1880s and 1890s for bribery and conspiracy (one review of contracts awarded declared "a looseness in this matter almost beyond belief"). The county was heavily in debt by 1895, and the *Reno Evening Gazette* blamed the current administration.[13] Still, the commissioners made no concessions to residents. "To even suggest . . . that primitive Reno might need better streets, sanitation systems or just a single park appeared frivolous to civic leaders, who held conservative opinions stressing public frugality, self-help, and laissez-faire individualism," reports Reno historian John Townley.[14] At the turn of the twentieth century, Reno was still dumping its raw sewage into the Truckee River,[15]

Self-interest appears to have driven such reluctance to invest in the city. The commissioners were all large landowners, and civic improvements would have meant higher property taxes. One, Grover Holcomb (an energetic foe of the city's Carnegie library application), was among "the most extensive landowners in the state," owning nine thousand acres on which he ran seven hundred head of cattle, and fifteen hundred sheep.[16] The largest landowner in the area, however, was the Central Pacific Railroad, a concern which

11 Reno's history is recounted in Barbara and Myrick Land's *Reno: A Short History*, Townley's *Tough Little Town on the Truckee*, and Rowley's *Reno: Hub of Washoe County*. Reno's lack of self-government mirrored the pattern in Nevada as a whole, for the state's legislature was dominated by lobbyists who insured that corporate needs were served by the law, see, Ostrander, *Nevada: The Great Rotten Borough*.

12 Townley, *Tough Little Town on the Truckee*, 175. Reno was not incorporated as a town until thirty years after its founding, and it had no privately owned utility company until that year (186).

13 For a discussion of the county commission's indictments and charges of malfeasance, see McDonald, *History of Washoe County*, lxii-lxx. Feelings against the commissioners ran so high that the *(Reno) Nevada State Journal* even blamed them for the city's crime problem, complaining that the Justice Court's "senile unconcern" and the prosecuting attorney's "utter[ ] incapabil[ity]" had made Reno "a rallying ground for the lowest specimens of humanity that exist in the west," Jan. 14, 1902.

14 Townley, *Tough Little Town on the Truckee*, 178.

15 McDonald, *History of Washoe County*, xiv.

16 These details come from the biographical sketch of Holcomb in Wren's *1904 History of the State of Nevada*, 499.

seems to have made it worth the commissioners' while to support its interests. Historians suggest that kickbacks and special rates for shipping were offered to the CP's particular friends, and the commissioners appear to have been among the latter, for they "decreed that no 'excessive' taxation would disturb prominent property owners, the Central Pacific in particular."[17]

Reno's citizens yearned for cultural amenities, including a public library. Indeed, coalitions of citizens had repeatedly petitioned county commissioners to institute a library during the early 1890s, but their requests were ignored. Granted, Nevada had as yet enacted no law allowing taxation for library purposes. But the commissioners could have suggested such legislation, had they wished.[18]

Into this picture of frustration stepped Frank Norcross, a young attorney with the education and the confidence necessary to challenge the status quo. Norcross was homegrown talent: he had been raised on a ranch near Reno and studied at the new University of Nevada.[19] Graduating with the university's first class in 1891, he briefly taught and served as principal of the Verdi School. Then he moved to Washington DC to work as a clerk in the census office (thanks to the patronage of Nevada Senator William Stewart) and continued his education at Georgetown Law School. He returned to Nevada in 1894 to practice law, soon gaining a high profile position as principal of Reno High School, superintendent of schools, and district attorney of Washoe County.

In 1895, Norcross acquired an additional responsibility. At a pro-public library rally in Reno, he was drafted to write enabling legislation to be presented to the state assembly then sitting.[20] The measure passed, but Norcross and his friends soon discovered that Nevada's legislators were actually no more sympathetic to the cause of public library development than the county commissioners. For the bill's language had been altered by "some kind friend" in a way that crippled its intent. Instead of ordering a dollar-based rate of taxation as Norcross had written, the bill as recorded contained a formula based on mills. Given the small population in all

17 Townley, *Tough Little Town on the Truckee*, 178.

18 John Hanlin, an early Reno librarian, describes early attempts to establish a community library in the *(Reno) Nevada State Journal*, Aug. 15 and 22, 1948. The news story about Reno's Carnegie library dedication also mentions this topic (*Reno) Nevada State Journal*, June 4, 1904.

19 For a biographical sketch of Norcross, see Scrugham, "Hon. Frank Herbert Norcross," 67–69.

20 This meeting is described in the *(Reno) Nevada State Journal*, June 4, 1904.

Courtesy of the Nevada State Museum, Carson City, Nevada.

Frank Norcross (left), the prime mover behind the Reno, Nevada, Carnegie library.

Nevada communities, that change meant that the amount that could be legally raised would have been insufficient to sustain any library. The bill had been sabotaged.[21]

Two years later Norcross himself sat in the state assembly, elected on a Populist ticket as a declared advocate of library legislation, and he "saw to it

21 Ibid. For the text of the 1895 law, see *Statutes of the State of Nevada Passed at the Seventeenth Session*, 79–81.

that the act was properly amended."[22] The revised legislation stipulated that if a majority of taxpayers or taxpayers holding a majority of taxable property were to sign a petition asking for a public library to be established, a levy of ten cents to fifty cents on each $100 worth of property would be made for library purposes after county commissioners verified the petition.[23] A larger community like Reno was now assured of being able to raise taxes sufficient for library purposes.

Triumphant advocates began gathering signatures on a petition, and on February 4, 1901, Norcross led the delegation which presented it to the Washoe county commissioners. But the fight was not to be won so easily. Furious at this challenge to their authority, the commissioners tried to stall, voting "that the whole matter of a free library petition be laid aside for one year."[24] Even as the press was reporting this development as a setback, Norcross procured a writ forcing the commissioners to act expeditiously. As a result, on February 23, 1901, the commission considered under protest what its minutes term "a petition purporting to be signed by a majority of the taxpayers of Reno School District."[25] During a heated hour and a half of debate, "many little episodes occurred that savored of anger," according to the *Nevada State Journal.* The commissioners resorted to challenging individual signatures and Norcross successfully defended them. With their minds already made up, however, the commissioners high-handedly dismissed the petition, registering their collective opinion "that the taxpayers who signed the petition do not know what is for their best interest."[26]

Norcross did not give up. At the time that the petition was disallowed, he was serving a second term in the state legislature, then in session. Just nine days later he introduced an amendment to his 1897 library law amendment designed to remove county officials from the process of library taxation. This new language permitted a district judge of any judicial district in Nevada to approve a petition requesting a library for any town. Once a judge verified a petition, the bill stipulated, "the said commissioners shall within ten days after said petition . . . levy a tax." Though conservative

---

22 Townley, *Tough Little Town on the Truckee*, 186–87.

23 For the text of the 1897 law, see *Statutes of the State of Nevada Passed at the Eighteenth Session*, 30.

24 "Minutes of the Washoe County Commissioners, Book F," Feb. 4, 1901.

25 Hamlin, *(Reno) Nevada State Journal*, Aug. 15, 1948.

26 Ibid., and *(Reno) Nevada State Journal*, Aug. 22, 1948.

legislators forced a compromise on the amount of tax allowed ("ten cents and no more"), the way was now clear for Reno's library.[27]

Norcross followed this victory with a letter to Andrew Carnegie, written November 14, 1901. Like Morris, he was familiar with the application process and anticipated problems, attaching a completed "Schedule of Questions," verifying Reno's population with census documentation, and attaching copies of his own new Nevada library act. Within a few months, Norcross was able to announce a $15,000 promise to a large pro-library crowd.[28] A sympathetic judge approved the city's new petition. Finally, on June 3, 1902, Washoe County commissioners grudgingly approved a support levy after a district attorney decreed that "all the requirements of the statute have been complied with, and, that being, the Board of County Commissioners have no option in the matter as to how they shall act. The language of the statute is mandatory and not optional."[29]

Reno's citizens celebrated with fervor. When ground was broken for the city's new Carnegie library, a joyful procession of club and lodge members (some dressed in regalia in acknowledgment of the occasion's importance) paraded the cornerstone through the streets. Norcross effectively managed the construction. When the library was finally completed and dedicated on June 1, 1904, he delivered the keynote address. Like Morris he was personally congratulated as the man whose brains, knowledge of the law, and sheer determination had allowed citizens to triumph over the coterie that had so long trampled on civic self-determination.[30]

Years of success followed for Frank Norcross, now a man known for accomplishing near-miracles. His law practice burgeoned and he was elected president of the Nevada State Bar Association. He was elected to both the US District Court and the Nevada Supreme Court. He became influential in state politics, the man who knew everybody, the consummate dealmaker. Ironically, Norcross gained so much power that years later he was accused of the sort of insider politics that he had fought at the turn of the

27 For the text of the 1901 law, see *Statutes of the State of Nevada Passed at the Nineteenth Session*, 99–100. At this point the legislation was head-spinningly termed "An Act to Amend an Act Entitled 'An Act to Amend an Act Entitled "An Act to Provide for Free Public Libraries and Other Matters Relating Thereto."'"

28 Letters from Frank Norcross to Andrew Carnegie, Nov. 14, 1901 and Feb. 17, 1902, CCA and *(Reno) Nevada State Journal*, Apr. 1, 1902.

29 "Minutes, Book F," June 3, 1902.

30 Norcross's speech is quoted in the *(Reno) Nevada State Journal*, June 4, 1904.

[Washoe County Library—correct credit line pending]

Reno's Carnegie Library cornerstone ceremony.

twentieth century. His bid for appointment to the US Circuit Court of Appeals failed amid allegations that while in office he had aided his former law partner unethically and later he was tarred as a member of the Wingfield machine, corrupted by his allegiance to Nevada's overlord, mining magnate and banker George Wingfield.[31]

All of that lay far in the future when a young Norcross determined to break the commissioners' hold on Reno and insure library service for its underserved citizens. Still, one can perhaps glimpse the stubborn taste for personal power that might presage such a future in the story of how Reno came to win its Carnegie library.

Clarence Clark, Evanston, Wyoming

Of the three men who gained local respect as prime movers in their communities' Carnegie library campaigns, US Senator Clarence D. Clark was the most experienced at turning favors into political capital. By 1902, when he interested himself in procuring a Carnegie library for Evanston, Clark stood firmly entrenched at the center of paternalistic, coterie-directed

31 Scrugham, "Hon. Frank Norcross," 67; Townley, *Tough Little Town on the Truckee*, 186; Ostrander, *Nevada: The Great Rotten Borough*, 139–49.

Courtesy of the Nevada State Museum, Carson City, Nevada.

Reno's completed Carnegie library.

Wyoming politics.[32] Though Clark had been born in New York, Evanston was his Wyoming hometown, the place he had settled in 1881 when he came west to work for the Union Pacific Railroad—both literally and through the favors he could provide as Sweetwater County Prosecutor. Clark's connections to the Union Pacific ran deep, for his brother, D. O. Clark, served for many years as first vice president of Union Pacific's Coal Division.

Clarence Clark took naturally to Wyoming politics from the earliest days of statehood, representing Evanston at the state's constitutional convention in 1888 so impressively that he was named "Orator of the Day." He was chosen as Wyoming's first Senator in 1890—and "chosen" is the correct word, for the office was awarded by the state legislature rather than by popular election in Wyoming. After a brief hiatus he regained the office in 1895, beginning a long career during which he did many favors for the men who continued to appoint him, wealthy railroad and mining executives and ranchers. Among the measures Clark supported were protective tariffs on coal and wool. Clark was an enemy of the Forest Service and of forest reserves, once remarking in the Senate that "conservation was fine, but that conservation never discovered the American continent, built cities, developed splendid farms, nor gave America its national standing and

32 Anderson's "The Political Career of Senator Clarence D. Clark" offers a detailed study of Clark's life and career.

greatness." His pet cause, though, was the Union Pacific Railroad. He never supported legislation potentially damaging to the Union Pacific, and he invariably voted for legislation to its advantage. He narrowly dodged accusations of graft, including allegations that he aided the Union Pacific in its effort to acquire known coal lands at dry-farm land prices.[33]

Clark "proved to be an expert" at keeping his Wyoming constituents happy. He was "always ready to receive a complaint or directive" from a special interest group, and he insured that his supporters were appointed to pork-barrel government positions.[34] He secured funding for a federal building and post office in Evanston, insuring that—in the words of a newspaper editor—he would become the "idol of his people," and man adored for "prov[ing] his love and interest for Evanston" through his benefactions.[35]

In 1902, however, potential trouble loomed for Clark as the political machine to which he belonged was challenged by Wyoming's liberal press. Contending that "Clark no longer served the requirements of a growing state" and that his party should "come forward with a man who would serve the people," a coalition of men brought pressure to sweep him out of office.[36]

Clark's campaign to secure a Carnegie library for Evanston began in the midst of this campaign, apparently on his own initiative, for no contemporary evidence suggest that citizens themselves were thirsting for such an institution. Evanston possessed no public library at the turn of the century, and neither local histories nor Carnegie Corporation archives record any grassroots effort to procure one.[37]

Clark's early inquiry letters to Carnegie were written on US Senate Committee on Railroad's letterhead, a not-so-subtle reminder of the potential power which Clark potentially held over Carnegie's own financial concerns.[38] The matter of a library grant for Evanston, Clark suggested heavy-handedly, was "of great interest to me personally," and he promised that "if you are in the least interested, I should be only too glad to furnish at any time all and

33 Ibid., 8–15, 18–26, 63–65.

34 *The (Evanston) Wyoming Press*, Feb. 7, 1903 and Anderson, "The Political Career of Senator Clarence D. Clark," 61.

35 *The (Evanston) Wyoming Press*, May 5, 1906.

36 Anderson, "The Political Career of Senator Clarence E. Clark," 50–51.

37 Dunn, "Unita County (Wyoming) Library, Evanston," credits Clark as the initiator of Evanston's bid for a public library.

38 Letter from Clarence Clark to Andrew Carnegie, Mar. 27, 1902, CCA. Clark was at the time a member of several other US Senate committees and might have used other letterhead had he wished.

Senator Clarence D. Clark, Benefactor of Evanston, Wyoming.

every detail of information that you may desire." Wyoming's complete congregational delegation, all the state Supreme Court justices, and the state's secretary of state and acting governor signed off on Clark's letter, registering their support. Though Clark did make sure that Evanston city officials were represented in this package—a brief letter from them registering interest in the project is included in the package with the other support letters—there could be no doubt that application actually came from a man to whom few said no.

While Evanston waited for a reply from Carnegie, the site question solved itself, for the Union Pacific abruptly offered the city land for the potential library.[39] While the site was not free, its cost was extremely reasonable, given its location diagonally across the street from the railway terminal—placement that insured that future structure would enhance Evanston's image with travelers. Though Clark's role in this transaction is not traceable, it can hardly be a coincidence that in no other Carnegie library community among the seventy-eight Intermountain West applicants was the Union Pacific so generous.[40]

On receipt of a $10,000 promise for Evanston, Clark thanked Carnegie, reminding him that "I, myself . . . feel a strong personal interest in the matter." He suggested, though, that the amount was too small, and asked for an increase as "purely a personal suggestion from me upon which I will

39 Letter from Donald McAteer to Andrew Carnegie, May 6, 1904, CCA.

40 Though, as Daniel F. Ring notes in "Men of Snap and Energy," the Northern Pacific offered a library building site to Billings, in eastern Montana.

Photo by author.

Juxtaposition of Evanston's Carnegie library (on left) and Union Pacific depot.

be exceedingly glad to have your favorable notice." Another $1,000 was promptly added.[41]

Once funds were released, Clark moved to center stage as "senior member" of the Board of Trustees of the Uinta County Public Library. He apparently did not involve others at all in the early steps of the application process, for when he left Evanston for another Senate term, city officials had no idea how to proceed and were forced to ask Franks what they should do next.[42] Clark's former secretary in Washington, DC and law partner, Benjamin Ausherman stepped in to negotiate the details of construction.[43]

The library's opening triggered a massive burst of positive publicity in which the *Wyoming Press* called Clark Evanston's "favorite son" and used the

---

41 Letter from James Bertram to C. S. Baker, Feb. 20, 1903, CCA; letter from Clarence Clark to Andrew Carnegie, Apr. 30, 1903, CCA; letter from James Bertram to B. N. Ausherman, Apr. 10, 1906, CCA.

42 Frank B. Smith wrote to Franks in December, 1904, "You wrote to Senator C. D. Clark, the senior member of our board exactly how we were to draw upon this fund—may I ask that you now instruct me fully for my guidance this coming year," letter from Frank B. Smith to R. A. Franks, Dec. 14, 1904, CCA.

43 A sketch of Ausherman's life, including his participation as a trustee of Evanston's Carnegie library, appears in the *(Evanston) Wyoming Press*, May 5, 1906.

occasion to review all the "good work" he had done on the community's behalf. Ausherman reminded the crowd who attended the dedication of Clark's contributions. He also adopted a patriarchal tone appropriate to the way the grant had been procured, spending much of his speech "forcibly and appropriately outlin[ing] the aims and objects of the institution" as if his listeners were children unable to imagine such things on their own.[44]

"How do you do it? Some Eastern senators now on the rack would appreciate instructions," a Senate colleague telegraphed to Clark after one of subsequent victories that stretched the Wyoming Senator's total career to twenty-two years of elected office. One answer seems to have been projects like Evanston's Carnegie library, standing as evidence of the Senator's "great foresight" in serving his constituents.[45]

Two Leaders Whose Personal Ambitions Failed

Robert Morris, Frank Norcross, and Clarence Clark were the real thing: men with the clout and personal skills able to see Carnegie public library building grant applications through to successful conclusions. In two other Intermountain West communities the inadequacies of lesser would-be leaders soon became apparent. Offering a low-comedy counterpoint to the men discussed above, these two individuals brought energy and charisma to their work and reaped both immediate benefits and brief mentions in community history books. Overblown egos, carelessness, and/or suspect behavior, however, eventually moved them out of the spotlight of their communities' Carnegie library applications even before the buildings were dedicated.

P. R. Keplinger, Rock Springs

When the Reverend P. R. Keplinger arrived in 1907 to take up his appointment as pastor of the Methodist Episcopal Church in Rock Springs, men of confident action were deeply needed to spark community development. Rock Springs had been blessed with abundant nearby coal deposits, but other crucial resources were in short supply. For more than a decade after the

44 *(Evanston) Wyoming Press*, Feb. 7, 1903, May 5, 1906, May 19, 1906. The library's paternalistic administration continued through its first decade, with Clark, Ausherman, and a wealthy associate of theirs serving as trustees, Dunn, "Uinta County (Wyoming) Library, Evanston," 2.

45 Anderson, "The Political Career of Clarence D. Clark," 20, 48, 50–59.

community's establishment, it didn't even have a potable water source; all water had to be imported in barrels from Green River. While that problem had been solved by the turn of the twentieth century, Rock Springs still had no reliable system of garbage disposal and no paved streets in 1907. Public safety was also a problem. Crowded with miners, with fully 40 percent of its commercial enterprises registered as saloons, Rock Springs experienced violent crime nearly every day. Indeed, its best-known historical event, a massacre of Chinese miners, had given the community a lasting reputation for out-of-control behavior.[46]

With an unreliable boom-and-bust tax base and a host of pressing social problems, even respectable citizens—like the group who wrote a vague inquiry letter to Carnegie in 1903 after establisheding a modest subscription library—lacked the ability to follow through on the projects they initiated.[47] Little help in solving these problems was forthcoming from Union Pacific or the mining companies. "The corporations controlling our mineral wealth have evinced little or no interest in their men," A. Kendall, Mayor of Rock Springs, complained.[48]

Keplinger entered Rock Springs ready to make a difference, whether out of a genuine interest in benighted Rock Springs and/or from an eagerness to demonstrate to Episcopal authorities that he deserved a more prestigious posting. He assumed his church on March 7, 1907, and within a week began submitting press releases promoting upcoming events to the *Rock Springs Miner*. On March 13, readers were informed that Keplinger would sing "The Holy City" at evening services and would preach a special children's sermon; on June 1, the church advertised a special song service tracing the history of popular hymns. No other clergymen were announcing their services in such circumstantial, proselytizing detail in Rock Springs at the time, and Keplinger's efforts certainly would have piqued the curiosity of what religiously inclined residents the community did house. But Keplinger had more ambitious plans than simply swelling his congregation. He was dreaming of a grand "institutional church" building that would

46 For a history of Rock Springs, see Rhode, *Booms and Busts on Bitter Creek*. The *Rock Spring (Wyoming) Miner*, Feb. 19, 1903 discusses the town's garbage and dust problems and for a sample of the almost daily reports of violence in this period, see the *Rock Springs (Wyoming) Rocket*, Dec. 19, 1907, which reports the stabbing of two Italian miners by a drunk and the consequent near-lynching of the assailant.

47 *Rock Springs (Wyoming) Miner*, Apr. 9, 1903.

48 Letter from A. Kendall to Andrew Carnegie, July 5, 1907, CCA.

house a host of public services, including a public library and reading room, a gymnasium, a kindergarten, and an employment bureau. Within four months of his arrival in Rock Springs, Keplinger submitted simultaneous queries to a number of philanthropists, including Carnegie, asking for an $18,000 donation for such a structure.[49] He enclosed several support letters in these requests, letters that made the request's agency very clear. "The self-appointed task of the Revd. P. R. Keplinger is one that appeals to every citizen of our town," wrote Kendall.[50]

When Carnegie did not reply within two weeks (he was in Scotland for the summer), Keplinger briskly followed up with a note asking for prompt consideration of his request. The answer did not come until months later on November 19, however, and it was disappointing. Carnegie was only interested in funding public libraries, Bertram wrote, not churches. The secretary did enclose a "Schedule of Questions," but he emphasized that city officials, not Keplinger, were the proper people to pursue such an application. Undaunted, Keplinger presented the form to Mayor Kendall, who completed and returned it, along with a cover letter which hints that the assertive clergyman was already wearing out his welcome in Rock Springs. "I am very pleased to note that you confine your library work strictly to the erection of free public library buildings not in connection with churches or other complications," Kendall told Bertram.[51] When Rock Springs' offer for a $12,500 library arrived, it was addressed to city officials, not to Keplinger. Still, the clergyman granted an interview to the local press, adopting the role of generous, disinterested benefactor. "Naturally Rev. Keplinger does not wish to see his plans fail," reported the *Rock Springs Rocket*, "and he is in no way discouraged with the fact that Mr. Carnegie's letter explains his work is confined to free public institutions. He agrees that should the great philanthropist look with favor upon the building of a library here it will be of untold benefit to the town, and he is ready to boost for the same."[52] Keplinger also sent a thank-you note to Carnegie which presumed proprietary interest. "I wish to commend you for your generous gift to our city," he wrote. "I thank you personally very much."[53] In this mailing Keplinger

---

49 Letter from P. R. Keplinger to Andrew Carnegie, July 6, 1907, CCA.

50 Letter from A. Kendall to Andrew Carnegie, July 5, 1907, CCA.

51 Ibid., Nov. 23, 1907.

52 *Rock Springs (Wyoming) Rocket*, Nov. 28, 1907.

53 Letter from P. R. Keplinger to Andrew Carnegie, Mar. 25, 1908.

stubbornly reiterated his appeal for funds to support an "institutional church." "I wish . . . to call your attention to the original request which led up to this gift," he wrote, requesting $15,000 for a multi-purpose church building—$2,500 more than the city had been offered for its Carnegie public library. Anyone familiar with James Bertram would have been able to predict the reply. "Mr. Carnegie," Bertram thundered as if speaking to the deaf, "has nothing to do with institutional churches . . . We are dealing with a public *Library Building* pure and simple."[54] Keplinger was forced to abandon his grand plan, and city officials gently but insistently shouldered him out of the Carnegie application that he had conceived. His name appears on no further Carnegie correspondence from Rock Springs. Instead he turned his energy to other causes during his four remaining years in town. He opened a night school for "foreigners," he imported several deaconesses (one from Chicago) to aid in church work, and he established an independent reading room in the church, an echo of his stubborn dream. He repaired church property at his own expense. He kept records and promoted himself through newspaper interviews, and along the way guaranteed himself a mention in a local history book associating him with the city's Carnegie library, though hardly the level of veneration a spirit like his might have craved.[55]

J. Challen Smith, Silverton, Colorado

J. Challen Smith was one of the most entertaining and enigmatic characters to appear in the history of Intermountain West Carnegie public library development. Smith called himself a clergyman, but if he had an actual affiliation it is not mentioned in any source this researcher was able to discover. No newspaper articles or other available records link him to a specific congregation. He may well have been a confidence man, or simply a man yearning to be thought important.

---

54 Ibid., and letter from James Bertram to P. R. Keplinger, April [?], 1908, CCA.

55 When Pastor Hubert Webster of the Rock Springs Methodist Episcopal Church compiled an article on his church's history for a local history anthology, he noted that his task was complicated by the sloppy record-keeping of early pastors. "The one exception in this case is the rather elaborate record left by Rev. P. R. Keplinger," he notes dryly in"History of the Methodist Episcopal Church," 354–58. Keplinger is mentioned in Miller, "Rock Springs Carnegie Library History." Keplinger, incidentally, was not the only energetic non-Mormon clergyman to initiate a small community's Carnegie library application. Baptist pastor Henry Cope began Dillon, Montana's application process, but voluntarily handed the project to city officials once he understood that Carnegie did not fund church development.

Some facts *are* clear about Smith. He appeared in Silverton, Colorado in 1904, having migrated from Alexandria, Indiana. In his previous home town he had documentably served on the library board and had been instrumental in procuring that town's Carnegie library.[56] He was married. He had a daughter. He spoke compellingly and exuded confidence.

Beyond that things get a bit fuzzy, for Smith seems to have moved to Colorado to avoid a scandal, leaving Alexandria under circumstances one Silverton historian terms "cloudy." A letter written to Smith from an acquaintance in Alexandria in reference to Silverton's Carnegie application cryptically alludes to such a problem in Smith's past with the statement, "I have often regretted the circumstances, but such things happen in the best of regulated families."

Whatever the Smith had done, he was looking for a fresh start in Silverton. Like so many other Intermountain West communities, it was exactly the sort of place where a man could reinvent himself, a town with a transient population and enough needs of its own that it wasn't likely to ask many questions of those who brought new energy. Silverton had been founded as a mining community in the early 1870s and its extreme isolation high in the rugged San Juan Mountains insured that it retained a provisional look and culture even into the early twentieth century. Across eleven-thousand-foot Red Mountain Pass, Silverton's nearest neighbor, Ouray, offered a striking cultural contrast; among other amenities, it had been given an "elegant" public library by a wealthy local philanthropist, where Silverton could only dream of such an institution.[57]

Smith had no sooner arrived in Silverton than he appointed himself as the man who would help Silverton reach parity in this regard, at least. He went from door to door introducing himself to his new neighbors, talking up a public library and collecting books and money. Within a year, he'd been so successful that the town was able to open its first library in a small wooden rented building. In a ceremony officially registering the community's gratitude, Smith's daughter Cornelia was issued the first library card.[58]

Elevated from anonymous newcomer to secretary of the new Silverton Public Library Board, Smith continued to push his fellow citizens onward.

56 Biographical details about Smith—insofar as they are known—are reported in Nossaman, "Silverton's Public Library," 6–7.

57 Bird, *Silverton Then and Now*, 2, 7, 25 and letter from J. Challen Smith to Andrew Carnegie, Apr. 16, 1904, CCA.

58 *Silverton (CO) Standard*, Apr. 16, 1904 and Nossaman, "Silverton's Public Library," 6.

Informing his fellow board members about Carnegie's program and assuring them of his own experience, he convinced them that an actual purpose-built public library was within Silverton's grasp, and that he was the man to win it. At their request, Smith applied to Carnegie on the community's behalf in April 1904 and received a $10,000 promise. "No one thing contributes more to the general tone and uplift of a community than a well-contained and well-conducted library," trumpeted the *Silverton Standard*, praising Smith as the "driving force behind" the application.[59]

But the new J. Challen Smith seems to have retained some of the ethics of the old J. Challen Smith, for he then made a questionable deal, and that deal was his undoing. Though local architects expressed interest in planning the building, Smith influenced the board to award the contract to the distant firm responsible for the Alexandria library—friends of his, judging by the tone of their correspondence. These Indiana architects were hardly the best choice. They lacked experience; though Smith didn't advertise this to his colleagues, the Alexandria building was the only library they'd ever designed.[60] More troubling was the fact that they'd never visited the interior West and had no sense of the difficulties mountain terrain and extreme weather might pose to construction. They also appear to have lacked basic competence. The plans for which they were paid proved unworkable, even though a Durango contractor experienced in mountain construction was engaged.[61] Construction was delayed by unanticipated costs and confusing blueprints. The absence of on-site architects and "questionable workmanship" stalled the work altogether. "The ghostly building stood unfinished through the 1905–06 winter," a historian writes, an unfortunate reminder that Silverton was not yet the well-conducted community it wanted to believe itself, and J. Challen Smith not the competent impresario he had made himself out to be.

In disgrace as quickly as he had come to local acclaim, Smith fled Silverton as he had fled Alexandria, submitting his letter of resignation from the library board in March 1906 from the town of Panoa, Colorado, eighty miles north. Construction on Silverton's library did begin again and the building was completed, but before those things happened Silverton's city

59 Letter from J. Challen Smith to Andrew Carnegie, Apr. 16, 1904, CCA; letter from James Bertram to J. Challen Smith, Jan. 10, 1905, CCA; *Silverton (CO) Standard*, Jan. 6, 1906.

60 Nossaman, "Silverton's Public Library," 7.

61 Epp, "Silverton."

fathers had to beg Carnegie for additional funds to complete the process. Even so, Smith's slipshod legacy remained to haunt the community. Eighty-five years later, restorers would get an expensive surprise when they discovered that the main floor supports had been framed for a mine tunnel rather than a normal building.[62]

All of these complications passed over Smith, however, for Silverton never heard of him again. Despite extensive searching, the only evidence this researcher has been able to recover about his subsequent career is an accidental find, the appearance of his name in a news story from Provo, Utah, a few years later. In this account, apparently undaunted and probably still up to something, Smith stands in a meeting and speaks enthusiastically in favor of a Carnegie library for his newest home town.[63]

The communities of the turn-of-the-twentieth-century interior West, these five applications reveal, were places where the boundaries between benefactor and confidence man, self-service and public service could blur. Carnegie himself would probably have been disappointed had he known the whole history of these applications, for he intended these grants to reward democratic initiative, not patriarchal direction. Still, as a benefactor himself he would have understood the impetus that drove Morris, Norcross, Clark, Keplinger, and Smith. He would have conceded that powerful, energetic, self-interested men will take action and others will be content to let them lead, especially where historical circumstances have accustomed people to believe that they cannot fully control their own destinies. Born in a Scotland that proclaimed its independent soul but suffered under colonialism, he would have even understood that such things happen in places that pride themselves—as Evanston's mayor proclaimed to him—in their "young and vigorous" nature, their "energetic" spirit.[64]

62 Nossaman, 7. The anecdote about the miss-framing of the Silverton library building was related to me when I visited Silverton in 1996 by a librarian who did not wish to be identified.

63 *Provo (UT) Daily Enquirer*, Apr. 17, 1907.

64 Letter from C. S. Baker to Andrew Carnegie, Feb. 7, 1902, CCA.

9

Contested Libraries

"It has engendered more bitterness than any question that has ever arisen within the town"

As PREVIOUS CHAPTERS OF THIS BOOK HAVE DOCUMENTED, most successful Carnegie library building grant applications from the Intermountain West encountered only temporary and ephemeral obstacles. Carnegie's own requirements delayed some, while economic obstacles and/or site selection posed difficulties in others. But in the vast majority of these interior West communities, citizens' belief in a public library's ability to serve common agendas insured that the work went forward as expeditiously as possible.

In four Intermountain West communities, however, Carnegie library applications encountered such bitter contention that their completion became doubtful for a time. In each, discussions touched deeper jealousies and social divisions that made Carnegie libraries into flashpoints for pre-existing factionalism. As citizens in these places debated their Carnegie libraries, they were also debating who would control the evolving physical shape of their communities, who would dominate local decision making.

Alturas, California

In Alturas, nearly everybody agreed that a Carnegie library grant was worth supporting. The trouble was that by the time the application was tendered, the community was so deeply fractured by resentment and jealousy that the application's details could not help but be caught in this spirit.

Alturas's Carnegie application might have looked like a typical boomtown project except for this rancor, for the community was coming rapidly into its own when it applied late in the first decade of the twentieth century. Prosperity had been long in coming. The earliest settlers had arrived around 1864 to homestead and ranch, but only after the Modoc Indian War of 1872–73 brutally cleared the area for Anglo development was the townsite (first called Dorris Bridge) established and made a county seat. Growth was initially slow, however, for Alturas was located deep within extreme northeastern California's lava country, lacking rail connections to the outside world. The closest incorporated communities lay many hours' travel away, and for thirty years Alturas went about its insular business as a market center for surrounding ranches.[1]

In 1908, though, the Nevada, California, and Oregon Railroad ("narrow, crooked, and ornery") began building through the region. The community's newspaper predicted that the area was "now at a transition stage," on the verge of growth and prosperity.[2] Like residents of the boom towns described in chapter 3, Alturas's city officials sought a Carnegie library as an appropriate addition to their presumably up-and-coming community, and they obtained a $7,500 promise in November 1908, which they managed to raise to $10,000.[3]

Soon, however, two developers—called with disrespectful familiarity only "Dunaway and Oliver" in the local newspaper—had blighted the community's optimistic mood.[4] The NC&O, these men argued, would certainly bypass Alturas unless a site for a railroad terminal was made available. Given the way the track was tending, the best zone would be just north of the original townsite. If the community would allow them to purchase this tract at a favorable rate, they would handle the negotiations.

Nervous city officials did grant that request, the land was donated, the NC&O constructed its terminal, and trains began stopping in Alturas's vicinity. Then Dunaway and Oliver revealed their ulterior motives. Rather than deeding all the land to the NC&O (as they had implied they would do), they kept most of it for themselves and began platting a town of their own, Alturas Heights, around the terminal. They convinced Modoc County officials that Alturas Heights, with its rail link, was destined to supplant Alturas as the region's business center, won the new county high school, and

---

1 The history of Alturas is discussed in Tierney, *History of Modoc County*, in "Looking Back: 100 Years of the Record," 3, and in Dorothy and Catherine Glaster, "History of Alturas."

2 Ibid., 9.

3 *Alturas (CA) Plaindealer*, Oct. 23, 1908.

4 The story of the developers' dealings with Alturas in reviewed in Ibid., July 2, 1909.

began lobbying for county and federal government buildings. Aggressive boosting drew new residents to Alturas Heights. Those invested in the old city center fumed that the developers had "cut the people's throats" and called the two "highwaymen."[5]

This resentment infected the site selection process for Alturas's Carnegie library. Since the community's Women's Improvement Club had established the town's pre-Carnegie library in 1906, it was appointed by city officials as the group of logical people to choose the new library's location.[6] What officials did not grasp, however, was that the club's current leadership had been assumed by the sort of educated newcomers described in chapter 6. These women lived in Alturas Heights and possessed no sentimental or material ties to old-town. Of the six sites offered, they chose the one most convenient to their homes, to the high school, and to the new business center whose promise had drawn their husbands: the one in the new addition.

A fracas erupted, fueled by long-time residents' sense that they were being literally marginalized.[7] Residents of the old town called the library site choice "but another move on the checker board" and protested that they "did not propose to be further taxed to boom the real estate of Dunaway and Oliver. They derided the site's physical properties, protesting at an angry public meeting that it was "out on a dry, desert, sagebrush flat," beyond the reach of "four-fifths" of the community's citizens. A petition to reject both the site and, retrospectively, the library grant itself gathered seventy-six signatures in forty minutes. "We are in favor of improvement and progress. But we seriously object to being longer exploited," signers agreed, "by a brace of buccaneers whose methods are those of the confidence man and the gold brick schemer."[8]

So long as "the library tangle" (as the *Plain Dealer* termed it) remained unresolved, the offer languished. "One would naturally suppose that on a proposition of such importance and unquestioned merit our citizens would stand as a unit, and that no dissension could possibly arise," wrote the editor. "Not so, however. On the contrary, it has engendered more bitterness than any question that has ever arisen within the town of Alturas."

---

5 Ibid.

6 Glaster and Glaster, "History of Alturas," 11.

7 See Ring, "Carnegie Libraries as Symbols for an Age," which notes that Carnegie libraries were perceived as important contributions to "Main Street's . . . permanence," 12.

8 *Alturas (CA) Plaindealer*, May 28 and July 2, 1909.

He urged that citizens pick a site, any site, so that the community did not lose Carnegie's funds.[9]

Only six years later, after the old town won the courthouse location in 1914, did the Carnegie library building campaign reignite. After a great deal of further discussion, a judge with old-Alturas sympathies raised enough money to buy the lot opposite the new courthouse and donated it for library purposes. Though Bertram complained about the lapse of years, Alturas's Carnegie library arose in the original town center, an acquisition that was enthusiastically celebrated in one quarter of the city, at least.[10]

Klamath Falls, Oregon

As with Alturas's application, the struggle to control the location of Klamath Falls, Oregon's, Carnegie library formed a subplot in long-time residents' struggle to retain their original city center's importance. In Klamath Falls's case, however, the conflict was more intimate, for the primary developer seeking to exploit the project was a familiar fellow citizen rather than a carpetbagger. Rebellious actions as well as bitter words marked this conflict.

The application began conventionally enough as a woman's club effort. Klamath Falls's Women's Library Club had established a small reading and club room in 1905, and the next year the town's old Methodist Church building was donated for library purposes.[11] The women collected an impressive number of books (more than 1,300) and approached Carnegie. Their letter appears to have miscarried, however, for no reply ever came.[12]

A few years later, in a period marked by expectations of growth inspired by Southern Pacific Railroad expansion and a federal irrigation project, the women decided to try again. Apparently assuming that Carnegie had previously ignored them because they seemed amateurish, they took pains to

9 Ibid., July 9, 1909.

10 Letter from James Bertram to Mrs. Nettie B. Harris, Jan. 26, 1915, CCA and Glaster and Glaster, "History of Alturas," 11.

11 The story of the library's establishment is told in Klamath County Historical Society, *The History of Klamath County, Oregon*, 44–45.

12 This initial letter is not in the archive of Carnegie correspondence, perhaps it was lost on its way to New York. Its existence is referenced in a letter from Mrs. O. A. Stevens to The Carnegie Library Corporation, [n.d.], CCA.

present a more polished image. Before submitting the initial inquiry letter, they circulated a petition, gathering enough signatures that county officials were authorized to levy an appropriate library tax on receipt of a Carnegie promise. They also chose one of those officials—County Judge William S. Worden, the husband of one of their members—as spokesman for the community's revived Carnegie application. A good negotiator, Worden secured an offer of $10,000 within a year. The supplemental levy was summarily approved, and Klamath Falls seemed assured of a library.[13]

Like Alturas's Dunaway and Oliver, however, Worden had his own agenda, and by the time the promise arrived in 1911 he was already enmeshed in scandal over another public building. During his 1910 campaign for re-election as judge, Worden promised to replace Klamath Falls's outdated courthouse. What he hadn't told voters was that he intended to replace it with a courthouse located far from the current community center, on land donated by the Hot Springs Development Company, a concern planning a new addition. Though the Hot Springs Addition project was in its early stages, a new courthouse would give the area an appearance of being the most important point in the area, providing a substantial advantage over old Klamath Falls in attracting new settlers. It was common knowledge that Worden had invested heavily in this scheme.

When the judge's plan for the new courthouse (and the building's expensive architecture) was revealed after his election, accusations of conflict of interest began immediately. Businessmen with commercial interests in Klamath Falls's downtown protested to Oregon's governor. They would donate an appropriate site for the new courthouse, they said. But the governor supported Worden. They followed up by requesting that the old courthouse be remodeled in preference to constructing a new one. That communication was also ignored, as was a petition for Worden's recall.[14]

There was more of the same insult to old Klamath Falls to come, for Worden had determined to build the new Carnegie library in the Hot Springs Addition too, on a lot adjoining the new courthouse.[15] Carnegie archives reveal that by then he'd learned enough to anticipate complaints. Before Worden announced his choice of library site to the public, he secured

13 Klamath County Historical Society, *The History of Klamath County, Oregon*, 44–45.

14 Drew details Worden's involvement in the Hot Springs Addition project and his vexed political career in *The Great Courthouse Battle*. See also, Klamath County Historical Society, *The History of Klamath County, Oregon*, 44–45.

15 Worden references this placement in a letter to R. A. Franks, June 25, 1913, CCA.

written confirmation from Bertram that local government agencies had the right to make such decisions. "The point which the County Court desires to make," Worden wrote in his inquiry, "is to ascertain whether the locale of the site shall be left to it or somebody else. You are probably aware that in cases like this there are often numerous sites offered, and sometimes a conflict of opinion and feeling arises, and it is the desire of the County Court to be immune from any interference in this matter after it once starts construction of the building."[16] Bertram had no way of knowing the lively local back-story, and he confirmed the point.

Once the prospective Carnegie library's location was announced, however, Bertram was deluged with protest letters from Klamath Falls which argued that the site had been chosen "in the interests of speculators, and not for the convenience of those who will want to take advantage of its benefits." A high school teacher termed the Hot Springs site "practically inaccessible" and a merchant pointed out that the location was a mile from the town center, not accessible in winter, and eight blocks from the nearest store. The town's postmaster informed Carnegie that it would be dangerous for school children to cross the large irrigation ditch which separated the site from the developed part of Klamath Falls.[17]

Correspondents explicitly accused Worden of conflict of interest. One woman's club member, who termed herself an original settler and noted that her husband had helped survey the city's streets, protested that Worden had explicitly betrayed the club's trust. The women who initiated the application, she informed Carnegie, had assumed that the library would be constructed near the center of town. "Imagine our chagrin," she wrote, "now we understand the motive of the judge."[18] Another citizen registered his opinion that "the people here do not feel that they should be taxed for the promotion of the sale of outlying vacant lots." Worden, he said, was "do[ing] his utmost to promote the real estate propositions of the Klamath Development Company to the detriment of the town and country."[19] Worden countered

16 Letter from W. S. Worden to James Bertram, Mar. 27, 1913, CCA.

17 Letter from Annie B. Appletation to The Carnegie Corporation, Oct. 25, 1913, CCA and letter from H. Bowen to The Carnegie Corporation, Oct. 24, 1913, CCA.

18 Letter from Mrs. O. A Stevens to The Carnegie Library Corporation, n.d., CCA. No records suggest how Mrs. Worden responded to this controversy, but it seems likely that she no longer attended women's club meetings.

19 Letter from C. K. Brandenburg to The Carnegie Corporation, Oct. 24, 1913, CCA and letter from [ill.] Roberts to Carnegie Corporation, Oct. 24, 1913, CCA.

by soliciting twenty letters in favor of the Hot Springs site, one of which maligned protesters as "petty" and "not progressive."[20]

Unmoved by all arguments, Bertram stood firmly by Carnegie policy, which was not to interfere in local site selection. Standard practice said that the local authorities responsible for library service could choose a library's location while the county judge had authority over this library's funding. Therefore this county judge could pick any site he thought suitable. Plans for the city's new Carnegie library in the Hot Springs Addition went forward.

The city's women protested that they would not turn the 6,000 books in the extant city library over to the Carnegie library unless the latter were constructed near the old downtown. When Worden ignored their threat they decided to boycott the very project they had begun, voting to maintain their old library as a separate institution. The Carnegie library might be the county library, they said, but their library would be Klamath Falls's city library. They abolished the subscription fees they had been charging to insure the widest possible competitive patronage.[21]

Thus Klamath Falls, which had possessed no public library a decade earlier, found itself with two in 1914. Worden's triumph was short-lived, for voters swept him out of office the next year in favor of a candidate determined to economize. While the Hot Springs Addition Carnegie library had opened for business at that point, the Hot Springs Courthouse was still under construction, and new County Judge Marion Hanks sustained lawsuits which blocked further spending on project. The partial structure stood empty for the next fourteen years, a "symbol of pride and discontent," until cracks in the foundation inspired its demolition in 1927.[22]

Klamath Falls's Carnegie library flirted temporarily with a similar fate, for Hanks also shut the institution, remarking that it was "an unnecessary expense upon the taxpayers of this county to keep said building open and pay a salary to a Librarian for the little benefit same would be to the taxpayers at this time." It reopened a year later, but the women of Klamath Falls continued adamantly to maintain their city library downtown. Only in 1926, after the municipality decided to consolidate its library service in the more modern and efficient building, did the city books move to Klamath Falls's Carnegie library. The story was not quite over even then, though, for

20 Letter from W. S. Worden to The Carnegie Corporation, Nov. 18, 1913, CCA.

21 Klamath County Historical Society, *The History of Klamath County, Oregon*, 44.

22 Drew, *The Great Courthouse Battle*, 39, 55.

county officials promptly removed *their* books from the structure and set up a new, specifically county library. The Klamath Falls area once again had two public libraries, which did not merge until 1969.[23]

Missoula, Montana[24]

Missoula, Montana's, residents had been at war over their community's center of gravity for years by the time controversy broke out over the location of that city's promised Carnegie library. In this case an overt class struggle added fuel to the fire.

Missoula's original town center had been constructed north of the Bitterroot River around 1864. Soon wealthy men bought up land south of the river, planning to establish a rival town between Missoula and Montana's rich Bitterroot Valley to the south in hopes that farmers and ranchers would stop short to conduct their business. In the 1880s two lawyers, W. J. Stephens and W. M. Bickford, platted their own street grid on a plan different than the old city's and announced a new town called South Missoula.[25]

Their scheme was disrupted, however, when another southside landowner with loyalties to the original townsite laid out a grid on his own land—one in which streets matched up with Missoula's. When the time came to bridge the river, the span's south end touched his property, not the Stephens-Bickford addition. Without convenient access from the north, Stephens and Bickford's South Missoula never incorporated, remaining a neighborhood of the parent city. By the turn of the twentieth century, however, it had become a very prosperous neighborhood indeed. Developers had lured the state university with a land donation, and the substantial homes of professors and other professionals surrounded campus. Downtown held Missoula's industry and its working people, while the south side tended toward the leafy and genteel.

Missoula's diversified economy (fueled by nearby mining and agriculture, Northern Pacific rail shops, county government, and the university) contributed to prosperity and the community established a tax-supported public library in 1894. In 1902, the institution's board took initial steps

23 Klamath County Historical Society, *History of Klamath County, Oregon*, 45.

24 Ring's "Carnegie Libraries as Symbols for an Age," includes a brief discussion of the controversy discussed in this section (p. 12).

25 Kroelbel recounts Missoula's history in *Missoula the Way It Was* and his discussion of the Stevens-Bickford addition and southside development appears on pages 68–75.

to procure a Carnegie building by organizing a local Carnegie Public Library Grant Building Commission.[26] With thoughtful diplomacy, the Commission was built to include representation from both north and south of the Bitterroot River, including W. M. Aber, a professor at the University of Montana, and the town's mayor, a businessman who resided on the north side.[27] These men secured a $12,500 grant and a tax levy was in place by early 1903.

Contentious negotiation began, however, as soon as the committee had to decide on a site. Mayor Stevens strongly favored two city-owned lots downtown at Pine and Pattee Streets,[28] while other committee members championed the county-owned courthouse square, also north of the river, as an alternative. Stevens declared the square inappropriate and made what proved to be an offer that invited, rather than prevented, further dissention: anyone who didn't like the idea of a public library at Pine and Pattee was welcome to come forward and offer the donation of another lot.[29]

Within a few days Mrs. Marcus Daly, the widow of a Montana mining magnate, offered a site on Missoula's south side. "Residents of South Side are After Public Library," the *Missoulian* warned. Confirming the editor's prediction that they would make "strenuous efforts," wealthy southsiders pledged to contribute $5,000 if the library were sited in their neighborhood, thus insuring "a more pretentious edifice" than Carnegie's mere grant would allow. They had challenged north side residents to match the amount if they could. "Business portion of city residents [were] expected to protest," the newspaper predicted.[30]

This also proved an accurate assessment. The library site, one north-sider wrote to the *Missoulian*, was "not on the block to be sold to the highest bidder." "The library should be for rich and poor alike," another argued.[31] Southside residents, a proponent of a downtown location suggested, were puffed

26 Letters from A. W. Stevens to Andrew Carnegie, Apr. 25, 1902 and Jan. 7, 1903, CCA and letter from Mrs. L. J. Knopf, Mrs. W. R. McBride, and Mrs. Kenneth Ross to Andrew Carnegie, Jan. 15, 1903, CCA.

27 The commission is described in a letter from W. M. Aber to Andrew Carnegie, Feb. 21, 1903 and Koelbel identifies Aber as a faculty member in *Missoula the Way It Was*, 75.

28 *Missoulian (Missoula, MT)*, Jan. 18, 1903.

29 Ibid., Jan. 22, 1903.

30 Ibid., Jan. 24, 1903.

31 Ibid., Jan. 25, 1903.

"with location pride," seeking "an opportunity to have that pride increase." An editorial by north-sider P. D. Shipperns reminded readers that Carnegie had not promised a library necessarily to "beautify" the south side, nor one "to be auctioned to the wealthiest residents." Most library users, he said, "do not come from the 400, nor do they hail from shaded avenues or stone and marble fronts . . . Ninety-nine and one-hundredths of library readers come from the poor and middle classes, from the laborers and mechanics, from the factories and the great mercantile establishments." Therefore, Missoula's Carnegie library should be centrally located to serve such people.[32]

As protracted debate ensued, the editor of the *Missoulian* counseled citizens to "get a move on" before Carnegie lost patience.[33] Finally Abers called an open commission meeting, and fifty people attended to argue their positions. South-siders argued that they had only public good in mind and north-siders made what one of them called a "workingman's stand." "Build the library on the south, but the books should stay north of the river," the city's fire chief remarked, suggesting that the south-siders were more concerned with show than with substance.[34]

A location north of the river was eventually selected, and old Missoula—like old Alturas—celebrated this apparent evidence that democracy still worked.

Provo, Utah

The site of Provo's Carnegie public library building was also contested between an older working class neighborhood and a newer and more wealthy one, but in this most complicated case, religion as well as class entered the mix. Since Provo possessed a substantial gentile population, one might assume that this application was touched by the same kind of Mormon-non-Mormon antagonism that characterized Salt Lake City's and Ogden's main library applications. That assumption would be wrong, however, for the religious fault lines in Provo's Carnegie application opened as rank-and-file Mormons' protested high-handedness by their own elite leaders.[35]

---

32 Ibid., Feb. 1, 1903.

33 Ibid., Jan. 20, 1903.

34 Ibid., Mar. 14, 1903.

35 Provo's Carnegie library application thus offers a useful corrective to the gentile stereotype of Mormons as slavish and naïve followers of their leaders. Evidence within Mormon culture further challenges this assumption. Several kinds of LDS narratives,

Provo had long contained a diverse population by the time its Carnegie library application began. Though the city was established as a Mormon community in 1850, a Methodist seminary had been established in the city in 1886 and a Congregationalist academy in 1887. Gentiles came to staff the State Hospital, and "various women's organizations" worked together to organize a Civic Improvement League. Mormon church news shared space in the local newspaper with accounts of Protestant events.[36] From the start, Carnegie application leaders invited many segments of the city's population to claim ownership in the process—indeed, the spirit of this application resembles Eureka's and Price's more than it does Salt Lake City's and Ogden's. This early Utah Carnegie application began when city officials, Mormon at the time, approached Carnegie in 1902, years before the formation of the Utah Library-Gymnasium Commission. Rather than pursuing the application in a manner that would identify it unilaterally with LDS interests, these men delegated J. W. N. Whitecotton, a Congregationalist lawyer and the Provo City Attorney, to write the initial inquiry letter to Carnegie.[37] The rhetoric which began appearing in the Provo Enquirer to prepare the way for the project diplomatically blended appeals. "A public library affords a place where boys who now run the streets can find a snug corner and a pleasant book," explained an editorial in a vein that would appeal to LDS readers, then quickly invoked generic local pride and to the interests of all who sought to rise through self-education: "A public library adds character and weight to a city . . . it is the workingman's friend, the book-lover's delight and the students' necessity."[38]

When Carnegie replied, however, Provo's Carnegie library leaders realized that they'd been premature in working to muster local support, for Utah's extant state library legislation was inadequate to satisfy Carnegie's stipulations. The largest tax which the city was allowed to collect for library

---

for example, acknowledge the fallibility of leaders. One is a genre of jokes which features J. Golden Kimball, a down-to-earth church official who always gets the better of his more pretentious colleagues (Wilson, "The Paradox of Mormon Folklore," 40–53). Another is a personal history, in which stories are told of ancestors who righteously corrected flawed authority figures (Swetnam, *Lives of the Saints*, 93).

36 Miller and Moffett, *Provo, Story of a People in Motion*, 14, 37 and *Provo (UT) Daily Enquirer*, March 23 and Apr., 1907.

37 Letter from J. W. N. Whitecotton to Andrew Carnegie, May 20, 1902, CCA. The *Provo (UT) Daily Herald*, June 2, 1916, identifies Whitecotton as a Congregationalist.

38 *Provo (UT) Enquirer*, Dec. 21, 1904.

purposes would never support a gift that would allow an adequate building. While officials debated what they might do, Dr. Fred Taylor, a Mormon, circulated a petition to establish an interim reading room. After 425 citizens signed to support a levy (only two are said to have refused), Provo's modest new city library opened for business.[39]

The institution proved a great success, and three years later, in 1905, Taylor pleaded its cause to Carnegie. While Bertram expressed admiration for the institution, he reiterated that a grant could not be considered without a 10 percent pledge, noting that "until your law changes or your valuation doubles I cannot consider the question."[40]

Bertram's suggestion about legislative reform resonated with Taylor (in later correspondence he told Bertram with gratitude that the hint "has been of value to us and to the entire State of Utah"[41]). He enlisted men from Salt Lake City, Ogden, and Cache County also frustrated over the state's restrictions on public library funding, and together they brought pressure to bear on the state legislature. Legislation was unanimously approved on March 5, 1907 that significantly raised the ceiling for library tax.[42] Taylor promptly submitted a certified copy of the new law to Bertram, and Provo received a $17,500 promise.[43] The city council unanimously increased the extant tax levy, and citizens determined to "all work together in the good cause and have a library," as the local newspaper suggested.[44]

Unanimity broke down, however, when the library board had to choose a site. The two best suggestions were only half a mile apart, but one was on the city's east side, the other on the west side, and Provo's east and west sides had long been quarreling. The west side had seemed destined as the city center. In Provo's earliest days the original public square was sited in that district, and in 1852 the young community's leaders broke ground there for a meeting house. In 1855, however, Brigham Young advised the people to halt construction and relocate the meeting house to higher ground on the east side, disappointing those who had invested in

39 Ibid.

40 Letter from James Bertram to Fred W. Taylor, Jan. 23, 1905, CCA.

41 Letter from Fred Taylor to Andrew Carnegie, Mar. 25, 1907, CCA.

42 Hepworth, *Carnegie Libraries*, 33.

43 Letter from Fred W. Taylor to Andrew Carnegie, Mar. 25, 1907, CCA and letter from James Bertram to Fred W. Taylor, Apr. 8, 1907, CCA.

44 *Provo (UT) Enquirer*, Apr. 17, 1907.

the original plat. "In the change lay the germ of the sectional controversy that was to make itself vigorously manifest half a century later," wrote a local historian in 1924.[45]

Development followed relocation. Brigham Young University (BYU) was built on Provo's east side, along with a courthouse in 1872 and a Utah Southern Railroad depot in 1873. The location of Provo's main post office was not as certain, for during the nineteenth century a game of neighborhood musical chairs ensued, with the institution located first on the west side, then moved to the east, then the west again, then the east.[46]

Around the time of the city's Carnegie library application a new skirmish was raging, one that "almost ripped the town asunder at the time and precipitated one of the bitterest community battles it ever saw," according to one of the principles.[47] The Denver and Rio Grande Railroad had proposed to build a second railway station in Provo's east side. Though the city council approved this location, Mayor Thomas N. Taylor vetoed it as inconvenient. Taylor was a west-sider both in terms of his home and in terms of his hereditary family business (a furniture, appliance, and dry goods store, established in 1866).[48] Two terminals would confuse passengers, he suggested. Instead Provo itself should erect a union station which could be used by both the Denver and Rio Grande and the Union Pacific Railroads, on the west end of town.[49]

Both railroads registered interest in this scheme. In 1907, the same year that Utah's library legislation was emended and a Carnegie promise received in Provo, Taylor attempted to sweeten the deal for the city council, raising $6,000 from west side residents to purchase a station site that could be deeded to the city.[50]

An open hearing attended by city council members, railroad representatives, and citizens revealed how strongly Provo's citizens felt about the location of their proposed union station.[51] Enthusiastic west-enders led by Taylor spoke in favor of the west-side. Angry east-enders rallied around one

45 Wilson traces the history of the city's east/west division in *Provo, Utah*, 333–35.

46 Ibid., 333.

47 Taylor, "The Life and Times of T. N. T.," 68.

48 Ibid., 19–25, 30.

49 Wilson identifies this idea as Taylor's in *Provo, Utah*, 335.

50 Taylor, "The Life and Times of T. N. T.," 70.

51 Ibid., 68.

of east Provo's richest and most powerful men, Jessie Knight, demanding that the station be moved east. The council finally agreed by one vote to sustain the west side location. The action, however, was legally challenged, and a judge called for a popular referendum.[52]

In the interim before the referendum on the station's location took place, feelings became even more heated as west-enders realized that the Mormon Church was corporately lobbying for their opponents. The stake presidency in Provo published a pamphlet urging people to vote for the east end. Church President Joseph F. Smith voiced his preference that a rail station be located in eastern Provo. Personal pressure was brought to bear on T. N. Taylor, by church authorities, in particular by BYU president and library board member George H. Brimhall, who had been Taylor's professor. Himself a Mormon bishop, T. N. Taylor resented the Church's name being used in support of what looked like self-interest. Words grew heated, and Brimhall "made some statements [Taylor] did not think he should have made." "I told him," Taylor reported in his autobiography, "that if I'm what he claimed, I had no right to be a bishop." He would resign, Taylor fumed, but he "would not throw down the people who looked to [him] to carry on the fight." Church leaders even tried to influence Taylor through his mother, advising her that her son was "going against the church authorities" and she should straighten him out.

Taylor stood firm in his insistence that the depot be built on the west side, and west-enders, tired of their neighborhood "being a dumping ground," raised their voices. BYU wanted everything in town, they avowed, and some of them publicly declared that they would not send their children to school there, even if the choice deprived them of a college education. In return BYU faculty began to boycott Taylor's store.[53]

Thus nerves were already raw about one public building's location when Carnegie offered a public library building grant to Provo. The library board seemed equally balanced between sections of the city. East-enders included Brimhall, Dr. Fred Taylor, and William Roylance, who had run for public office with an anti-west-side-railway-station agenda. West-enders included S. P. Eggertsen and Maud Taylor (T. N. Taylor's wife). But Jessie Knight

52 The situation was so volatile that a judge was brought in from Salt Lake City, since Provo's federal judge was a known east-side advocate. When west-enders attempted to retain a railroad attorney to plead their case, the man proclaimed that "he would resign first" rather than become embroiled in the controversy, see, Ibid., 70–71.

53 Ibid., 68–72 and Taylor, "George Taylor and His Friends," 118–19.

tipped the balance by offering to donate a large and favorable east-side site, and it was selected.[54]

Maud Taylor then publicly joined her husband's campaign, writing a letter to the editor co-signed by her fellow east-end board members. The proposed library site had been chosen, she suggested, because privileged citizens used to dominating the common people considered only their own self-interest. The new library's site would greatly limit the good it could do because it was too far from west-end schools "which well represent the common people." "Just because there is more wealth east of Academy [A] venue does not say that books are more needed by them than the people farther west," she protested.[55] Her collaborator S. P. Eggertsen sounded these themes directly to Carnegie. "The sight [sic] selected is very unsatisfactory to the majority who need it most," he wrote, urging Carnegie to endorse a "central" location "for the benefit of all."[56] West-enders attempted to enlist Provo's city council in a veto of the library's location, igniting such fierce debate that when adjournment time came at 11:00 p.m., the regular business of the month had not been transacted. Ultimately, however, "after the council had exhausted itself in the contention," the verdict was that "the action of the library board was legal and without recourse."[57]

This decision stood, and Provo's east-end did become the Carnegie library's home —though the west-enders won the railroad station, after a referendum whose difference was only forty votes in a city of ten thousand.[58] This latter victory apparently did not assuage hard feelings, for news stories reporting the library's dedication identify no west-end board members as speaking or serving on the celebration committee. Thomas Taylor complained for many years that the majority of Provo's school children were not taking advantage of the Carnegie library because of its distance from their homes.[59]

So convinced was Taylor of the need for a west-end library that when he died a widower he deeded his home to the city for use as a branch library.

---

54 Board members neighborhood alliances have been determined by consulting Polk's *Provo City Directory, 1917–18* (the earliest available in the Provo City Library). Knight's offer is noted in Taylor, "The Life and Times of T.N.T.," 70.

55 *Provo (UT) Daily Herald*, May 4, 1907.

56 Letter from S. P. Eggertsen to Andrew Carnegie, May 4, 1907, CCA.

57 *Provo (UT) Daily Herald*, May 7, 1907.

58 Wilson, *Provo, Utah*, 337.

59 *Provo (UT) Daily Enquirer*, Dec. 2, 1908.

Once again his neighborhood loyalty was undermined, however, for after six years city officials closed the institution, arguing that a branch library was not worth the upkeep.[60]

But lovers of the underdog will be happy to know that Taylor's neighborhood has had the last laugh in public library matters (at this writing, at least). Eventually the city outgrew its Carnegie library building, and that structure was decommissioned. With land at a premium on the east side, the city looked elsewhere for a new building site. Today's Provo Public Library is located on the west side, just a few blocks from the still-standing Thomas Taylor home.

The debates over Carnegie library locations in these four communities demonstrate just how volatile intramural civic rivalries could be in the turn-of-the-twentieth-century interior West. Jealous of their dignity, concerned about class privilege, understanding that their communities' physical shapes could deeply impact their personal futures, citizens with competing interests saw potential trespass or advantage in every local decision. In Provo and Missoula, Klamath Falls and Alturas, Carnegie libraries came to stand not as symbols of the common values which united people, but as reminders of what divided them.

60 Taylor, "The Life and Times of T.N.T.," 29.

10

Conclusion

THIS PROJECT BEGAN MORE THAN TWENTY YEARS AGO with a series of questions. What drove ordinary citizens of the turn-of-the-twentieth-century Intermountain West to become advocates for public libraries? Who were those supporters? Can those of us who value books and reading today learn anything from them that we can use? Or was the region so different then, so filled with idealists willing to sacrifice for cultural enrichment that we can only regard the time and place with envy?

The answers, it turns out, are complex, for the turn-of-the-twentieth-century Intermountain West was a much more culturally diverse place than stereotypes might suggest. No more culturally hegemonic than the region is now, it included big dangerous cities and small rowdy towns as well as upstanding communities where saloons were banned and religious leaders dominated local decision making. It counted cosmopolitan people among its citizens, including Mary Beatty, speaker of six languages, and Yale-educated Benjamin Fowler, a man who associated familiarly with the most powerful politicians in America. It was also home to Ray Gundmunsen, who could not spell Bertram's name, and to tax protesters who contended that the services a library would provide did not justify its expense. Mormon librarian Jean Brown lived in the interior West, as did rabidly anti-Mormon librarian Zoe Faddis, shifty J. Challen Smith, public-service-minded Robert Morris, and delinquent Ligerwood Red.

Even within middle-class Anglo culture, values and priorities varied tremendously. Some applicants could imagine nothing more desirable than growth and change. Others struggled to maintain their insular culture. Some Westerners believed that an aggressive, can-do spirit was the way to move their town forward, others waited for improvements to come to them. Some were driven by money, others by faith. The priorities in Prosser couldn't have been more different than the priorities in Preston had the towns been four thousand rather than four hundred miles apart, despite the fact that their Anglo-American citizens physically looked a great deal alike.

Nor was the region a democratic paradise. Gender, class, religious affiliation, and race all counted in the balance of local power. Minnie Howard would not have been able to bring pressure on Pocatello city officials had she been a farmer's wife, and had she been a small-town Latter-day Saint, she wouldn't even have imagined that she might do so. The library board in Yuma would have ignored a Hispanic voice. Strong personalities like Frank Norcross shaped local opinions and priorities. Blatant self-interest drove William Worden.

Citizens of the Intermountain West became intensely political animals when they negotiated local Carnegie library support. They formed coalitions that lobbied, bullied, and manipulated their fellow citizens. On occasion even the most upright of them stretched the truth, as the ladies of Boise did. The people who sought Carnegie libraries were every bit as concerned with personal advantage as Carnegie himself had ever been.

Carnegie library history also suggests that the turn-of-the-twentieth-century Intermountain West was a place deeply divided by fear. On occasion library applications opened the wounds of intramural class rivalries, as they did in Missoula and Provo. More often they were inspired by anxiety about outsiders. Citizens of boom towns jealously contested with citizens of rival boom towns. Mormons looked suspiciously at gentiles while gentiles looked suspiciously at Mormons. Rowdies and recent immigrants were labeled as dangerous and Hispanics as hopelessly backwards.

Yet these Westerners *were* idealistic, in a sense. They dreamed dreams for their own futures and their communities' futures, and they engaged in the political process to help those dreams come true. They contributed their own time and money, sometimes in impressive quantities. They generated the energy to galvanize their fellow citizens. They donated months and years of their lives to working through Carnegie's requirements. They believed that it was the responsibility of citizens work for the greater municipal good. To read their stories is to meet a variety of characters—sometimes quirky and manipulative characters with outdated priorities, but frequently the kind of activist citizens who make life in a particular place worth living.

Granted, few of these people who advocated for Carnegie public library building grants a hundred years ago evoked the pure joy of reading. And yet they did believe deeply in the influence of libraries. Carnegie libraries were not simply pleasant, bland institutions in their supporters' eyes, but practical ones, catalysts that could make a wide range of things happen. They were institutions that functioned as powerful symbols both internally and externally, buildings that stood as proud testimony to "who we are."

Therein, I believe, lays the positive answer to the quest that ultimately inspired this book. For those library supporters a hundred years ago did indeed employ a tactic that those of us who advocate for grassroots support of cultural institutions today can use: they aligned their campaigns with concerns that seemed immediately relevant to their particular time and place.

We can do the same, for, as Carnegie library history suggests, libraries' potential significance is protean. We can ask ourselves what our neighbors are worried about at the moment of what pleases them about community life. We can note how our communities are promoting themselves and explain how libraries will strengthen outsiders' perception of them. In times of transition or growth, we can tie libraries symbolically to the coattails of current aspirations.

Carnegie library history suggests that institutions so-promoted retain their power as community symbols for a long time. True, about a dozen Intermountain West Carnegies have been torn down, including one of the very "Let's Talk About It" sites that inspired this study, which disappeared as this book was being written. But the great majority still exists, tenaciously maintained as the municipal landscape around them has changed.[1] Some have become arts centers, government office annexes, chamber of commerce offices, or professional offices, and a handful rest securely on the National Register of Historic Places.

Twenty or so are still used as libraries. A few of these have been swallowed by expanded architecture, as in Rock Springs, but librarians are still delighted to indicate the space they occupy. More often the original Carnegie sections remain distinctive in enlarged libraries, and these are often put to special use. I like to think that Minnie Howard would be delighted by the fact that Pocatello's librarians—women no less idealistic

1 Jones includes a chart noting Carnegie libraries' fates in *Carnegie Libraries Across America*, 128–66.

Photo by author.

Marshall Public Library, Pocatello, Idaho, showing the original Carnegie building, now library offices, on the right.

and hard-working in the cause than she and her friends—have affectionately claimed the original Carnegie library section of the Marshall Public Library for their own offices.

Perhaps the sweetest of all the still-operating Carnegie libraries are the ones in small towns, standing essentially as they were originally constructed, absurdly grand little buildings on quiet streets. The motives that inspired them proved to be merely wishful thinking. None of the former boom towns where a functioning Carnegie library stands have become a Queen City and a few are even less populated than they were at the time of their application. Neither have Carnegie libraries prevented the migration of youth from Mormon agricultural villages out into the larger, morally compromised world. Yet these libraries still embody community spirit, and any citizen who knows anything about local history will proudly point them out to a visitor.

Coming across one of those small town Carnegies was the highlight of my long work on this project. To spend a day working at a wooden desk in an original Carnegie library's cool interior, the summer heat or winter glare

Wyoming State Archives, Department of State Parks and Cultural Resources.

Delta Public Library.

outside signified only by a shaft of sunlight across the desk's corner, was to spend a day blissfully out of time. It was always evident, though, that those libraries were not museums; they were places still being used for the purposes for which they were designed. Once I was startled by an explosion of school children rushing in for story hour, dressed in bright ski jackets that reminded me that this was not 1920. On another day, a young man in low-rider pants took a seat across the table from me and dove into a novel. All of these working Carnegie libraries have computers and copy machines and current magazines and newspapers on the magazine rack. All are living institutions, testifying that their hometowns are still far-seeing enough to appropriate funds for library service.

If we can find a way to tap into such community pride today, we will be a long way down the road toward popular support for libraries. For people still worry about who they are, individually and communally; they evaluate their present situations and imagine their futures. In a time and place that parallels our own in uncertainty, division, and possibility, public libraries once helped people reach toward their dreams. They still can.

Bibliography

1. Primary Sources

A. Corporate Papers

Carnegie Corporation Archives (CCA) Rare Book and Manuscript Library, Butler Library, Columbia University, New York, NY.

B. Library Board Minutes

Boise, ID
Green River, WY
Parowan, UT
Prescott, AZ
Twin Falls, ID

C. County Commission Minutes

Washoe County, NV

D. Newspapers

Alturas Plaindealer (Altruas, CA), 1908–9.
Arizona Daily Miner (Prescott, AZ), 1902–5.
Arizona Daily Star (Tucson, AZ), 1899–1901.
Arizona Gazette (Phoenix, AZ), 1904.
Arizona Republican (Phoenix, AZ), 1941, 1943.
Baker City Herald (Baker City, OR), 1909.
Baker City Morning Democrat (Baker City, OR), 1907–8.
Beaver City Weekly Press (Beaver, UT), 1913–15.
Box Elder News (Brigham City, UT), 1912.
Carbon County News (Price, UT), 1912.
Coeur d'Alene Evening Press (Coeur d'Alene, ID), 1913.
Deseret News (Salt Lake City, UT), 1918, 1948, 1963.
Eastern Oregonian (Pendleton, OR), 1913.
Ellensburg Evening Record (Ellensburg, WA), 1910.
Enterprise Record-Chieftain (Enterprise, WA), 1911–13.
Ephraim Enterprise (Ephraim, UT), 1912–15.
Eureka Reporter (Eureka, UT), 1908–9.
Franklin County Citizen (Preston, ID), 1914.
Garland Globe (Garland, UT), 1907–14.
Goldfield Tribune (Goldfield, NV), 1909.
Grand Junction Daily Independent (Grand Junction, CO), 1899.
Green River Star (Green River, WY), 1907.

Hood River Glacier (Hood River, OR), 1912–13.
Hood River News (Hood River, OR), 1912–13.
Idaho Statesman (Boise, ID), 1902, 1927, 1939.
Iron County Record (Cedar City, UT), 1912–13.
Kalispell Bee (Kalispell, MT), 1904.
La Grande Weekly Observer (La Grande, OR), 1911–12.
Lewiston Tribune (Lewiston, ID), 1905.
Manti Messenger (Manti, UT), 1910–12.
Milton Eagle (Milton, OR), 1905–8.
Missoulian (Missoula, MT), 1903.
Mount Pleasant Pyramid (Mount Pleasant, UT), 1916–17.
Mountain Home Republican (Mountain Home, ID), 1905–8.
Nampa Leader-Herald (Nampa, ID), 1906.
Nevada State Journal (Reno, NV), 1902–4, 1948.
New York World, 1909.
Ogden Standard (Ogden, UT), 1901–3.
Panguitch Progress (Panguitch, UT), 1915.
Pasco Express (Pasco, WA), 1909.
Pocatello Tribune (Pocatello, ID), 1906–8, 1980.
Prosser Record (Prosser, WA), 1906–10
Provo Daily Enquirer (Provo, UT), 1904–7.
Provo Daily Herald (Provo, UT), 1907, 1916.
Ravalli Republican (Hamilton, MT), 1914–15.
Reno Evening Gazette (Reno, NV), 1921.
Rock Springs Miner (Rock Springs, WY), 1903.
Rock Springs Rocket (Rock Springs, WY), 1903–7.
Salt Lake City Herald (Salt Lake City, UT), 1899, 1918.
Salt Lake Tribune (Salt Lake City, UT), 1900, 1948.
Silverton Standard (Silverton, CO), 1904–6.
Spokane Chronicle (Spokane, WA), 1901–5.
Spokane Spokesman-Review (Spokane, WA), 1901–2, 1909.
Springville Independent (Springville, UT), 1906, 1924.
Steamboat Pilot (Steamboat, CO), 1907–10.
Sunnyside Sun (Sunnyside, WA), 1909–11.
The Dalles Weekly Chronicle (The Dalles, OR), 1905, 1910.
Toole Transcript (Toole, UT), 1909–10.

Twin Falls Times (Twin Falls, ID), 1913–15.
Walla Walla Union (Walla Walla, WA), 1903–4.
Wenatchee Republic (Wenatchee, WA), 1909.
Wenatchee World (Wenatchee, WA), 1909.
Wyoming Press (Evanston, WY), 1903–6.
Yuma Daily Sun (Yuma, AZ), 1921.

2. Books, Articles, Government Documents, Theses

Alexander, Thomas G., and James B. Allen, *Mormons and Gentiles: A History of Salt Lake City*. Boulder, CO: Pruett Publishing, 1984.
Altbach, Edith H., *Women in America*. Lexington, MA: D. C. Heath and Co., 1974.
Anderson, Albert G., Jr., "The Political Career of Senator Clarence D. Clark". Master's thesis, University of Wyoming, 1953.
Anderson, Nels, *Desert Saints: The Mormon Frontier in Utah*. Chicago: University of Chicago Press, 1942.
Antrei, Albert C., ed, *The Other 49ers: A Topical History of Sanpete County, Utah, 1849–1983*. Salt Lake City: Western Epics, 1982.
Arrington, Leonard, *Great Basin Kingdom: An Economic History of the Latter-day Saints 1830–1900*. Cambridge, MA: Harvard University Press, 1958.
———, and Melvin A. Larkin. "The Logan Tabernacle and the Temple," *Utah Historical Quarterly* 41 (Summer 1973): 301–14.
Augst, Thomas, "Introduction: American Libraries and Agencies of Culture," *American Studies* 42 (Fall 2001): 5–22.
Ayres, Mary C., *History of the Durango Public Library*. Durango, CO: Durango Public Library, 1947.
Ballou, Irving, *Early Klickitat Valley Days*. Goldendale, WA: *Goldendale Sentinel*, 1938.
Bair, Amos W., *History of Richmond, Utah*. Richmond Bicentennial Committee, 1976.
Baker County Historical Society, *The History of Baker City*. Taylor Publishing, 1986.
Beal, Franke, "History of Garland, Utah," March 1928, no. 10 in *Series of Seminar Papers, Written Under the Direction of Dr. Joel E. Ricks, Department of History, Utah State Agricultural College, Logan for the Undergraduate Seminar in Historical Method, 1928–50*. Logan: Utah State University, 1957.
Benton, Carolyn French, *The Complete Club Book for Women*. Boston: Colonial Press, 1915.
Blair, Karen J., *The Clubwoman as Feminist: Womanhood Redefined, 1868–1914*. New York: Holmes and Meier, 1980.
Bobinski, George S., *Carnegie Libraries: Their History and Impact on American Public Library Development*. Chicago: American Library Association, 1969.
Boehringer, C. Louise, "Mary Elizabeth Post—High Priestess of Americanization," *Arizona Historical Review*, no. 2 (July 1929): 92–100. Clipping, Yuma County (AZ) District Library, "Biography" file folder.
Bollinger, Edward T., and Frederick Bauer, *The Moffat Road*. Denver: Sage Books, 1962.
Boorstin, Daniel, *The Americans: The National Experience*. New York: Random House, 1967.

Breckenridge, Sophanisba P., *Women in the Twentieth Century: A Study of Their Political, Social, and Economic Activities*. New York: McGraw-Hill, 1933.

Brenchley, Ralph Reed, "Preston, Idaho: A History of Its Founding and Economic Life." Master's thesis, Utah State University, 1968.

Buchanan, James E., *Phoenix: A Chronological and Documentary History*. Dobbs Ferry, NY: Oceana Publications, Inc., 1978.

Bufkin, Don, "From Mud Village to Modern Metropolis," *Journal of Arizona History* 22 (Spring 1981): 63–98.

Burley Chapter, Idaho Writers League, *The History of Cassia County and Burley*. Burley, ID, 1952.

Burley Chapter, League of Women Voters, *Know Your Town*. Burley, ID, n.d., pamphlet, Burley Public Library.

Burroughs, John Rolfe, *Steamboat in the Rockies*. Fort Collins, CO: Old Army Press, 1974.

"Caldwell, Revisited," *The News-Tribune (Caldwell, ID)*, n.d., Caldwell Public Library, "Caldwell, Idaho," clipping file.

Campbell, Bruce L. and Eugene E. Campbell, "Pioneer Society." In *Utah's History*, edited by Richard D. Poll, 275–94. Provo, UT: Brigham Young University Press, 1978.

Campbell, Eugene E., "Early Colonization Patterns." In *Utah's History*, edited by Richard D. Poll, 133–52. Provo, UT: Brigham Young University Press, 1978.

Carbon County Chapter, Daughters of Utah Pioneers, *Centennial Echoes from Carbon County*. Price, UT: Daughters of Utah Pioneers, 1948.

Centennial Book Committee, *Ephraim's First 100 Years, 1854–1954*. Ephraim, UT, n.d., Ephraim Public Library.

Clark, Mary R., and Patricia Lyn Scott. "From Schoolmarm to State Superintendent: The Changing Role of Women in Education, 1847–2004." In *Women in Utah History: Paradigm or Paradox?*, edited by Patricia Lyn Scott and Linda Thatcher, 223–48. Logan: Utah State University Press, 2005.

Cleverley, J. Michael, "The Development of an Urban Pattern." In *Utah's History*, edited by Richard D. Poll, 54562. Provo, UT: Brigham Young University Press, 1978.

Conlin, Joseph R., *Bacon, Beans, and Galatines: Food and Foodways on the Western Mining Frontier*. Reno: University of Nevada Press, 1986.

Cottingham, F. C., "History of Nampa and Vicinity," *The Nampa Messenger*, Nov. 29, 1911.

Cox, Cheryl, and Lexie French., *Second Stories: Historical Narratives of Idaho Falls Women*. Harrisburg, PA: Graphic Experience, 1986.

Crowe, Rosalie, and Sidney Brinckerhoft, eds., *Early Years: A Graphic History of Life on the American Nile*. Flagstaff, AZ: Northland Press, 1976.

Crowder, David, *Tales of Eastern Idaho*. Idaho Falls: KID Broadcasting Company, 1981.

David, Homer, *Moscow at the Turn of the Century*. Moscow ID: Latah County Historical Society, 1979.

Derr, Jill Mulvay, "Scholarship, Service, and Sisterhood: Women's Clubs and Associations, 1877–1977." In *Women in Utah History: Paradigm or Paradox?*, edited by Patricia Lyn Scott and Linda Thatcher, 249–94. Logan: Utah State University Press, 2005.

Deverell, William, ed., *A Companion to the American West*. Oxford: Blackwell, 2004.

"The Dewey Dynasty," *Nampa Press-Tribune*, Feb. 11, 1983.

The Doctrine and Covenants of the Church of Jesus Christ of Latter-day Saints, Containing Revelations Given to Joseph A. Smith, Jr., the Prophet, With Some Additions By His

Successors to the Presidency of the Church. Salt Lake City: Church of Jesus Christ of Latter-day Saints, 1979, c. 1949.

Doherty, Deborah V., *Delta, Colorado: The First 100 Years*. Delta, CO: The Delta County Independent, 1981.

Downing, Andrew, *History of the Carnegie Public Library in Phoenix, Arizona*. Phoenix, AZ: n.p, 1914.

Drew, Harry J., *The Great Courthouse Battle*, Klamath County Museum Research Papers, n.d., no. 7, Klamath Falls, OR.

Driggs, Howard, "The Utah Library-Gymnasium Movement," *Improvement Era* 12 (May 1909): 510–16.

Ditzion, Sidney, *Arsenals of a Democratic Culture: A Social History of the American Public Library Movement in New England and the Middle Atlantic States from 1850–1900*. Chicago: American Library Association, 1947.

Dwyer, Robert J., *The Gentile Comes to Utah: A Study of Religious and Social Conflict, 1862–1890*. Salt Lake City: Western Epics, 1971.

Eide, Henry, *Oregon Trail*. Chicago: Rand McNally, 1973.

Elkins, Stanley, and Eric McKitrick, "A Meaning for Turner's Frontier: Democracy and the Old Northwest." In *Turner and the Sociology of the Frontier*, edited by Richard Hofstadter and Seymour Martin Lipset, 120–51. New York: Basic Books, 1968.

Elsensohn, Sr. M. Alfreda, *Pioneer Days in Idaho County*, vol. 1. Caldwell, ID: The Caxton Printers, 1947.

Eliel, Frank, *Our Little Old Home Town, Dillon, Montana*. N.p., n.d., pamphlet, Dillon Public Library.

Elwood, Henry, *Kalispell, Montana, and the Upper Flathead Valley*. Kalispell, MT: Thomas Printing, 1980.

Erwin, Marie H., *Wyoming Historical Blue Book: A Legal and Political History of Wyoming 1868–1943*. Denver, CO: Bradford-Robinson Press, 1946.

Evans, Max J., "A History of the Public Library Movement in Utah." Master's thesis, Utah State University, 1971.

"Federated Women's Clubs Turn 100 Years Old," *Delta County Independent*, April 25, 1900.

Fiege, Mark, *Irrigated Eden: The Making of an Agricultural Landscape in the American West*. Seattle: University of Washington Press, 1999.

Finley, Mary Chase, *A History of Springville*. Springville, UT: Art Publishing Company, n.d.

Foy, Leslie T., *The City Bountiful: Utah's Second Settlement from Pioneers to Present*. Bountiful, UT: Horizon Publishing, 1975.

French, Hyram T., *History of Idaho: An Account of Its Historical Progress, Its People, and Its Principal Interests*. Chicago: Lewis Book Publishing, Inc., 1914.

Fritzen, Mary Jane, *Idaho Falls, City of Destiny*. Idaho Falls, ID: Bonneville County Historical Society, 1991.

Gardner, Hamilton, *History of Lehi, Including a Biographical Section*. Salt Lake City, UT: Deseret News, 1913.

Garfield County Chapter, Daughters of Utah Pioneers, *Golden Nuggets of Pioneer Days: A History of Garfield County*. Panguitch, UT: Garland County News, 1949.

Garrison, Dee, *Apostles of Culture: The Public Librarian and American Society, 1876–1920*. New York: The Free Press, 1979.

Gellatly, John A., *History of Wenatchee, The Apple Capital of the World*. Wenatchee, WA, 1958.

Gentry, Jim, *In the Middle and On the Edge*. Twin Falls, ID: College of Southern Idaho, 2007.

Gittins, H. Leigh, *Pocatello Portrait: The Early Years, 1878–1928*. Moscow: University of Idaho Press, 1983.

Green River Historic Preservation Commission, "Self Guided Tour of Historic Green River," Green River, WY, n.d., pamphlet, Green River Public Library.

Greenwood, Annie Pike, *We Sagebrush Folks*. New York: D. Appleton-Century, 1934, reprinted with intro. by Susan H. Swetnam. Moscow: University of Idaho Press, 1998.

Greever, William, *Bonanza West: The Story of Western Mining Rushes*. Norman: University of Oklahoma Press, 1963.

Gregg, Jacob Ray, *Pioneer Days in Malheur County*. Los Angeles: Lorrin L. Morrison, 1950.

Groebli, Katharine Elizabeth, "The Housing Problem in Salt Lake City." Master's thesis, University of Utah, 1915.

Groefsema, Olive, *Elmore County: Its Historical Gleanings*. Caldwell, ID: Caxton Printers, 1949.

Haarsager, Sandra, *Organized Womanhood: Cultural Politics in the Pacific Northwest, 1840–1920*. Norman: University of Oklahoma Press, 1997.

Hall, Sharlott, "The First Woman's Club in Arizona" *Yavapai Magazine* 22 (April 1932): 8, 18.

Harris, Chauncy, *Salt Lake City: A Regional Capital*. Chicago: University of Chicago Library, 1940.

Hart, Arthur A., *Life in Old Boise*. Boise, ID: Boise City Celebrations, 1989.

Harwood, Don W., "The Economic History of Smithfield, Utah, 1859–1940," no. 47 in *Series of Seminar Papers, Written Under the Direction of Dr. Joel E. Ricks, Department of History, Utah State Agricultural College, Logan for the Undergraduate Seminar in Historical Method, 1928–50*. Utah State University, 1957.

Hayden Heritage Center, *History of West Routt County*. N.p.: Curtis Media, 1995.

Hellenic Orthodox Church of the Assumption, Price, Utah. N.p.: n.d. Pamphlet, Price Public Library.

Hepworth, Bobbee McGee, "Carnegie Libraries in Utah." Master's thesis, Brigham Young University, 1976.

Hine, Robert V., *Community on the American Frontier: Separate but Not Alone*. Norman: University of Oklahoma Press, 1994.

History of Smithfield. Smithfield, UT, 1927, Smithfield Public Library.

Hodsett, Vernetta Murchison, *The Golden Years: A History of the State Federation of Women's Clubs, 1905–55*. Caldwell, ID: Caxton, 1955.

Hood River County Historical Society, *History of Hood River, 1852–1987*, 2 vols. Hood River, State: Hood River County Historical Society, 1987.

Horton, Alice, *Beautiful Bonneville: County of Contrasts*. Logan, UT: Herff Jones, 1989.

Idaho Digest and Blue Book, 1935. Caldwell: Caxton, 1935.

Idaho Writers League. *Tsceminicum*. N.p.: n.d. Pamphlet, Lewiston Public Library.

"John Larsen." In *Progressive Men of Southern Idaho*, 286–87. Chicago: A. W. Bowen and Company, 1904.

Johnson, G. Wesley, Jr., "Directing Elites: Catalysts for Social Change." In *Phoenix in the Twentieth Century: Essays in Community History*, 17–20. Norman: University of Oklahoma Press, 1993.

Johnson, Welburn K., "Cedar City: A Study of Regional Functions of an Urban Center." Master's thesis, University of Utah, 1956.

Jones, Barbara, "'The Center of Light and Helpfulness': Buhl, Minnesota, Public Library's Impact on the Early Twentieth-Century Iron Range," *Journal of the West* 30 (July 1991): 53–62.

Jones, Theodore, *Carnegie Libraries Across America: A Public Legacy*. New York: John Wiley and Sons, Inc., 1997.

Journal of Discourses by Brigham Young, His Two Counselors, The Twelve Apostles, and Others. Reported by G. D. Watt, J. V. Long, 26 vols. Salt Lake City: Church of Jesus Christ of Latter-day Saints, 1967.

Judy, Clarence G., "A History of Preston, Idaho." Master's thesis, Brigham Young University, 1961.

Kissane, Leedice, *Pocatello Memories*, 2 vols. Pocatello: Idaho State University Press, 1995.

Klamath County Historical Society, *The History of Klamath County, Oregon*. N.p.: Taylor Publishing, 1984.

Koelbel, Leonora, *Missoula The Way It Was: A Portrait of an Early Western Town*. Missoula, MT: Gateway Printing, 1972.

Land, Barbara and Myrick, *Reno: A Short History*. Reno: University of Nevada Press, 1995.

Larson, T. A., *History of Wyoming*, rev. ed. Lincoln: University of Nebraska Press, 1978.

———. "Idaho's Role in America's Woman Suffrage Crusade," *Idaho Yesterdays* 18 (Spring 1974): 2–15.

———. "The Woman's Rights Movement in Idaho," *Idaho Yesterdays* 16.1 (Spring 1972): 2–15, 18–9.

Lehi Centennial Commission, *Lehi Centennial History, 1850–1950*. Lehi, UT: Free Press, 1950.

Longsdorf, Hilda Madsen, *Mt. Pleasant, 1859–1939*. Salt Lake City: Stevens and Wallis, 1939.

Luckingham, Bradford, "The Promotion of Phoenix." In *Phoenix in the Twentieth Century: Essays in Community History*, edited by G. Wesley Johnson, 83–91. Norman: University of Oklahoma Press, 1993.

Lyon, T. Edgar, and Glen M. Leonard, "The Churches in the Territory." In *Utah's History*, edited by Richard D. Poll, 317–55. Provo, UT: Brigham Young University Press, 1978.

Mabry, Jonathan B., et al., *Tucson at the Turn of the Century: The Archaeology of a City Block*. Tucson: Center for Desert Archaeology, 1994.

Mackell, Jan, *Red Light Women of the Rocky Mountains*. Albuquerque: University of New Mexico Press, 2009.

Madsen, Brigham D., *Corinne: The Gentile Capital of Utah*. Salt Lake City: Utah State Historical Society, 1980.

Madsen, C. H., ed., *Carbon County: A History*. N.p., 1947, Price Public Library.

Madsen, Carol Cornwall, "Decade of Detente," *Utah Historical Quarterly* 63 (Fall 1995): 298–319.

Magie, Dian, *Carnegie Free Library 1900–1990: A Resource Document*. Tucson: Pima Paths Council, n.d.

Manning, Leslie A., "The Public Library in the American West: A Bibliographic History," *Journal of the West* 30 (July 1991): 90–91.

Marker, Joe L., *Eagle Rock, U.S.A. (Now Idaho Falls, Idaho)*. Idaho Falls, ID, 1980.

Martin, Robert Sidney, ed., *Carnegie Denied: Communities Rejecting Carnegie Library Construction Grants 1898–1925*. Westport, CT: Greenwood Press, 1993.

Mawn, Geoffrey P., "Phoenix, Central City of the Southwest, 1870–1920." PhD dissertation, Arizona State University, 1979.

May, Dean L., *Three Frontiers: Family, Land, and Society in the American West, 1850–1900.* New York: Cambridge University Press, 1994.

May, Pete, *100 Golden Years*. Goldendale, WA: Goldendale Centennial Corp., 1972.

McCormick, John S., *Salt Lake City: The Gathering Place*. Woodland Hills, CA: Windsor Publications, 1980.

McCune, Alice Paxman, *History of Juab County, 1847–1947*. Springville, UT: Juab County Daughters of Utah Pioneers, 1947.

McDonald, Russell W., *History of Washoe County: Introduction to the Washoe County Code.* Reno, NV: Board of County Commissioners of Washoe County, 1982.

McNeal, William H. *History of Wasco County, Oregon*. The Dalles, OR, 1953.

Meinig, David W., "Spokane and the Inland Empire: Historical Geographic Systems and a Sense of Place." In *Spokane and the Inland Empire: An Illustrated Pacific Northwest Anthology*, edited by David H. Stratton, 17–23. Pullman: Washington State University Press, 1991.

Miller, Marilyn McMeen and John Clifton Moffett, *Provo: A Story of People in Motion.* Provo, UT: Brigham Young University Press, 1974.

Monroe, Anne Shannon, "When Women Will," *Good Housekeeping*, Nov. 1921, 104–9.

"Mrs. Bowerman's Address" *The Idaho Clubwoman* 3 (Sept. 1912): 6–9.

Mueller, Gene, *Natives, Migrants, and Immigrants: Lewiston's Cultural Heritage and Early Society*. Boise, ID: Association for the Humanities in Idaho, 1980.

"Murray City Library." In *The History of Murray*, edited by Murray City Corp., 38–41. Salt Lake City: Sheelwright Printing, 1976.

Murray, Keith A., *The Modocs and Their War*. Norman: University of Oklahoma Press, 1984.

Nasaw, David, *Andrew Carnegie*. New York: Penguin, 2006.

Nelson, Lowry The *Mormon Village: A Pattern and Technique of Land Settlement*. Salt Lake City: University of Utah Press, 1952.

Nossaman, Allen, "Silverton's Public Library: 30 Years in Coming," *Silverton (CO) Standard*, April 12, 1984, 6–7.

Notarianni, Philip F. "Italianite in Utah: The Immigrant Experience." In *The Peoples of Utah*, edited by Helen Papanikolas, 303–31. Salt Lake City: Utah State Historical Society, 1976.

———. *Tale of Two Towns: The Social Dynamics of Eureka and Helper, Utah*. PhD dissertation, Utah State University, 1980.

———. "The Tintic Mining District." In *From the Ground Up: The History of Mining in Utah*, edited by Colleen Whitley, 242–58. Logan: Utah State University Press, 2006.

———."Utah's Ellis Island: The Difficult 'Americanization' of Carbon County," *Utah Historical Quarterly*, 47 (Spring 1979): 178–93.

Parsons, Katherine Barrette, *History of Fifty Years: Ladies Literary Club, Salt Lake City, 1877–1927*. Salt Lake City: Arrow Press, 1927.

Olsen, Gilbert, "Richmond: 1885–1908," no. 77 in *Series of Seminar Papers, Written Under the Direction of Dr. Joel E. Ricks, Department of History, Utah State Agricultural College, Logan for the Undergraduate Seminar in Historical Method, 1928–50*, Utah State University, 1957.

Orr, Maryde Faley, "Development of the Walla Walla Public Library." Master's thesis, University of Washington, 1953.

Ostrander, Gilmon *Nevada: The Great Rotten Borough, 1859–1964*. New York: Alfred A. Knopf, 1966.

Paker, Stanley W., *Goldfield: Boom Town of Nevada*. Las Vegas: Nevada Publications, 1982.

Papanikolas, Helen, "The Exiled Greeks." In *The Peoples of Utah*, 409–35. Salt Lake City: Utah State Historical Society, 1976.

———. "From Babylon to Babylon: Immigration from the Middle East." In *The Peoples of Utah*, 385–405. Salt Lake City, UT: Utah State Historical Society, 1976.

———. "The New Immigrants." In *Utah's History*, edited by Richard D. Poll, 447–62. Provo, UT: Brigham Young University Press, 1978.

———. "Women in the Mining Communities of Carbon County." In *Carbon County: Eastern Utah's Industrialized Island*, edited by Philip F. Notarianni, 80–102. Salt Lake City, UT: Utah State Historical Society, 1981.

Parker, Jerri Kim, "Early Days of Green River Schools." Master's thesis, University of Wyoming, 1990.

Parsons, Katherine Barrette, *History of Fifty Years: Ladies Literary Club*. Salt Lake City: Arrow Press, 1927.

Passet, Joanne E., *Cultural Crusaders: Women Librarians in the American West 1900–1917*. Albuquerque: University of New Mexico Press, 1994.

Paul, Rodman, *Mining Frontiers of the Far West, 1848–1880*. New York: Holt, Rinehart and Winston, 1963.

Peters, Afton, "History of the Brigham City (Utah) Library," no. 82 in *Series of Seminar Papers, Written Under the Direction of Dr. Joel E. Ricks, Department of History, Utah State Agricultural College, Logan for the Undergraduate Seminar in Historical Method, 1928–50*. Utah State University, 1957.

Peterson, Levi S., *Juanita Brooks: Mormon Woman Historian*. Salt Lake City: University of Utah Press, 1988.

Pierson, Jay Dexter, "The Growth of a Western Town: A Case Study of Yuma, Arizona 1915–1950." Master's thesis, Arizona State University, 1987.

Powell, Allan Kent "Coal Industry." In *From the Ground Up: The History of Mining in Utah*, edited by Colleen Whitley, 126–41. Logan: Utah State University Press, 2006.

———. *Utah History Encyclopedia*. Salt Lake City: University of Utah Press, 1994.

Rodewald, Evelyn, "Palouse: Boom or Bust? 1900–20." *Bunchgrass Historian: The Whitman County Historical Society Quarterly* 10 (Summer 1982): 20–35.

Richards, Dee, *Steamboat Round the Bend*. Steamboat Springs, CO: The Steamboat Press, 1995.

Richards, Susan, "Carnegie Library Architecture in South Dakota and Montana: A Comparative Study," *Journal of the West* 30 (July 1991): 69–78.

Ring, Daniel F., "Carnegie Libraries as Symbols for An Age: Montana As a Test Case," *Libraries and Culture* 27 (Winter 1992): 1–19.

———. "Men of Energy and Snap: The Origins and Early Years of the Billings Public Library," *Libraries and Culture* 36 (2001): 397–412.

———. "The Origins of the Butte Public Library: Some Further Thoughts on Public Library Development in the State of Montana," *Libraries and Culture* 28 (Fall 1993): 430–44.

———. "Outpost of New England Culture: The Ladies Literary Association of Kalamazoo, Michigan," *Libraries and Culture* 32 (Winter 1997): 38–56.

Ronda, James P., "Passion and Imagination in the Exploration of the American West." In *A Companion to the American West*, edited by William Deverell, 53–76. Oxford: Blackwell, 2004.

Rowley, William D., *Reno: Hub of Washoe County*. Woodland Hills, CA: Windsor Publications, Inc., 1984.

Ryder, Sarah L., "Ellensburg Public Library," *Library News Bulletin* 4 (Jan. 1936): 15–16.

Scott, Anne Firor, *Natural Allies: Women's Associations in American History*. Urbana: University of Illinois Press, 1992.

———. "Women and Libraries," *The Journal of Library History, Philosophy, and Comparative Librarianship* 21 (Spring 1986): 400–5.

Scrugham, James G., ed., *Nevada: A Narrative of the Conquest of a Frontier Land*, 3 vols. Chicago: American Historical Society, Inc., 1935.

Sermon, Suzanne, "Beyond Simple Domesticity: Organizing Boise Women, 1866–1920." Master's thesis, Boise State University, 1996.

Sewall, May Wright, "An Historical Gem," Yavapai Magazine, 13.5 (April 1932): 4–5.

Shamberger, Hugh A., *Historic Mining Camps of Nevada: Goldfield*. Sparks, NV: Western Printing and Publishing, 1982.

Sheller, Roscoe, *Sunnyside at Sixty*. Sunnyside, WA, 1962.

Shelley, George F., Early History of American Fork: With Some History of the Later Days. American Fork, UT: American Fork City, 1945.

Shera, Jesse H., *Foundations of the Public Library: The Origins of the Public Library Movement in New England, 1629–1855*. Chicago: University of Chicago Press, 1949.

Smith, Dean, *The Goldwaters of Arizona*. Flagstaff, AZ: Northland Press, 1986.

Smith, Duane A., *Rocky Mountain Boom Town: A History of Durango*. Albuquerque: University of New Mexico Press, 1980.

Smith, Karen, *The Magnificent Experiment: Building the Salt River Reclamation Project 1890–1917*. Tucson: University of Arizona Press, 1986.

Stark, Charles A., Jr. "Wallace . . . City of Old-Timers . . . and Millionaires," *Spokane (WA) Spokesman-Review*, June 1, 1958.

Statutes of the State of Nevada Passed at the Eighteenth Session of the Legislature, 1897. Carson City: Nevada State Printing Office, 1897.

Statutes of the State of Nevada Passed at the Nineteenth Session of the Legislature, 1901. Carson City, NV: Nevada State Printing Office, 1901.

Stauffer, Suzanne M., "'She Speaks as One Having Authority': Mary E. Downey's Use of Libraries as a Means to Public Power," *Libraries and Culture* 40 (2005): 38–62.

Stephens, Esther J., "Delta." In *Colorado Public Libraries 1876–1976, Historical Sketches*, edited by Tertu Maija Barsch. Denver: Colorado Department of Education, 1977.

Stimson, William, *A View from the Falls: An Illustrated History of Spokane*. Spokane, WA: Windsor Press, 1985.

Sturgis, Cynthia Jane, "The Mormon Village in Transition: Richfield, Utah as a Case Study, 1910–30." Master's thesis, University of Utah, 1978.

Sunnyside Museum and Historical Association, *The Sunnyside Story*. Prosser, WA: Perfect Printing, 1982.

Swetnam, Susan H., "Battle for the Books," *Nevada Magazine* 63.3 (June 2003): 24–26.

———. *Lives of the Saints in Southeast Idaho: An Introduction to Mormon Pioneer Life Story Writing*. Moscow: University of Idaho Press, 1990.

———. "Pro-Carnegie Library Arguments and Contemporary Concerns in the Intermountain West," *Journal of the West* 30 (July 1991): 63–8.

"Table of Knowledge," *Idaho Falls Post-Register*, Sept. 15, 1990.

Tars, William, *The American West: A Treasury of Stories, Legends, Narratives, Songs, and Ballads of Western America*. Cleveland, OH: The World Publishing Co., 1946.

Taylor, Thomas Sterling, *The Life and Times of T.N.T. [Thomas N. Taylor], As Told to Theron H. Luke*. Salt Lake City, UT, 1959.

"The Facts About Union Oregon and Tributary Country," *Eastern Oregon (Union) Republican*, (ca.1911). Clipping enclosed in a letter to Andrew Carnegie from Mary L. Hill, Apr. 3, 1911.

Toney, Ken L., *The Prescott, Arizona Story*. Phoenix: Toney Publishing Company, 1964.

Tooele County Chapter, Daughters of Utah Pioneers, *History of Tooele County*. Salt Lake City: Publishers Press, 1961.

Townley, John M., *Tough Little Town on the Truckee: Reno 1868–1900*. Reno: Great Basin Studies Center, 1983.

Trafzer, Clifford E., *Yuma: Frontier Crossing of the Far Southwest*. Wichita: Western Heritage Books, 1980.

Turner, Faith, *The Golden Dream: Being a Story of the Beginnings of the Public Library System in Boise, Idaho*. Boise: *The Idaho Statesman*, 1955.

Twin Falls Historical Society, *The First Hundred Years, 1811–1911*. Twin Falls, ID: *Times-News* Publishing, n.d.

Tyer, Pearl, "Idaho's Twenty Years of Woman Suffrage," *The Outlook*, Sept. 16, 1916, 35–39.

Underwood, Kathleen, *Town Building on the Colorado Frontier*. Albuquerque: University of New Mexico Press, 1987.

United Methodist Centennial Committee, *The United Methodist Church: The First Century of the Church in Utah*. Salt Lake City, 1970.

US Bureau of Education, *Statistics of Libraries and Library Legislation in the U.S.,1895–1896*. Washington, DC: US Government Printing Office, 1897.

US Department of Agriculture, *Summary of Climatological Data for the United States, By Sections, Sections 1–36, Western States*. Washington, DC: US Government Printing Office, 1920.

Van Slyck, Abigail A., *Free to All: Carnegie Libraries and American Culture, 1890–1920*. Chicago: University of Chicago Press, 1995.

Van Wagoner, Richard S., *Lehi: Portrait of a Utah Town*. Lehi, UT: Lehi City Corporation, 1990.

———. *Mormon Polygamy: A History*. Salt Lake City: Signature Books, 1989.

Wall, Joseph Frazier, *Andrew Carnegie*. New York: Oxford University Press, 1970.

Wall, Ronald G., *A History of Carbon County*. Salt Lake City: Utah State Historical Society, 1997.

Wallowa County Museum Board, *The History of Wallowa County, Oregon*. Wallowa County, OR, 1983.

Warrum, Noble, ed., *Utah Since Statehood*, 3 vols. Chicago: S. J. Clarke Publishing Co., 1919.

Watson, Paula D., "Founding Mothers: The Contribution of Women's Organizations to Public Library Development in the United States," *The Library Quarterly* 64 (July 1994): 233–69.

Watt, Ronald G., *A History of Carbon County*. Salt Lake City, UT: Utah State Historical Society, 1997.

Webster, Hubert, "History of the Methodist Episcopal Church of Rock Springs." In *Rock Springs—A Look Back: Glimpses of Early Day Happenings and Events in the Lives of its First Settlers*, edited by Thomas P. Cullen, 354–58. Portland, OR, 1991.

Weiner, Melissa Ruffner, *Prescott: A Pictorial History*. Virginia Beach, VA: The Donning Company, 1981.

———. *Prescott Yesterdays*. Prescott, AZ: Primrose Press, 1978.

Wells, Merle, *Boise: An Illustrated History*. Woodland, CA: Windsor Press, 1982.

West, Elliott, *The Last Indian War: The Nez Perce Story*. New York: Oxford University Press, 2009.

———. *The Saloon on the Rocky Mountain Mining Frontier*. Lincoln: University of Nebraska Press, 1979.

Wheeler, Denice, *The Feminine Frontier: Wyoming Women 1850–1900*. N.p., 1987.

White, Richard, *It's Your Misfortune and None of My Own: A History of the American West*. Norman: University of Oklahoma Press, 1991.

Whitley, Colleen, ed., *From the Ground Up: The History of Mining in Utah*. Logan: Utah State University Press, 2006.

Wiegand, Wayne, "The Development of Librarianship in the United States," *Libraries and Culture* 24 (Winter 1989): 99–109.

Wilson, Margaret Gibbons, *The American Woman in Transition: The Urban Influence 1870–1920*. Westport, CT: Greenwood Press, 1979.

Wilson, William, "The Paradox of Mormon Folklore," *BYU Studies* 17 (Autumn 1976): 40–53.

Wilson, William M., *Provo, Utah: Early Pictorial Provo; Early History of Provo*. N.p., 1924.

Woodford, Frank, "Second Thoughts on Writing Library History," *Journal of Library History, Philosophy, and Comparative Librarianship* 1 (Jan. 1966): 34–42.

Worster, Donald, *Rivers of Empire: Water, Aridity, and the Growth of the American West*. New York: Pantheon Books, 1985.

Wren, Thomas, *1904 History of the State of Nevada: Its Resources and People*. New York: Lewis Publishing, 1904.

Wrobel, David M., *Promised Lands: Promotion, Memory, and the Creation of the American West*. Lawrence: University Press of Kansas, 2002.

———. *The End of American Exceptionalism: Frontier Anxiety from the Old West to the New Deal*. Lawrence: University Press of Kansas, 1993.

Youngs, William T., *The Fair and the Falls: Transforming an American Environment*. Cheney: Eastern Washington University Press, 1966.

Zanjani, Sally, *Goldfield: The Last Gold Rush on the Western Frontier*. Athens, OH: Swallow Press, 1992.

Zarbin, Earl, "In Pursuit of a Reservoir." In *Phoenix in the Twentieth Century: Essays in Community History*, edited by Wesley Johnson, Jr., 139–53. Norman: University of Oklahoma Press, 1993.

———. *Salt River Project: Four Steps Forward, 1902–1910*. Phoenix: Salt River Project, 1986.

Zeidner, Robert F., "From Babylon to Babylon: Immigration from the Middle East." In *The Peoples of Utah*, edited by Helen Papanikolas, 385–405. Salt Lake City: Utah State Historical Society, 1976.

Unpublished Sources

Cottingham, F. G., "History of Nampa and Vicinity," bound typescript, 1911, RNW/BIRD/979.823., Nampa, Idaho Public Library. .

Dunn, Ella, "Uinta County (Wyoming) Library, Evanston," typescript, n.d., file, 3690-00, Unita County (Evanston) Library. .

Epp, Irene, "Silverton," typescript, n.d., Colorado Public Libraries file, Silverton (Colorado) Public Library.

Gasson, Grace, "Sweetwater County Library System," typescript, n.d., "Green River" binder, Sweetwater County (Green River, Wyoming) Public Library.

Gengler, Rita, "Spokane's Public Libraries 1880–1956," n.d., typescript, Spokane (Washington) Public Library, Northwest Room.

Gertz, Earl R., Jr., "Biography of Mrs. B. A. Fowler," typescript, n.d., "Biographical" file B 10 F-30, Arizona Historical Foundation, Hayden Library, Tempe, Arizona.

Gipson, Lina M., "A History of the Library and Reading Room Movement in Caldwell," typescript, n.d., "Carnegie Public Library–History" file, Caldwell (Idaho) Public Library.

Glaster, Dorothy, and Catherine E. Glaster, "History of Alturas," typescript, n.d., "Alturas History" file, Modoc County (Alturas, California) Library.

Haydon, Curtis, Letter to Jennie Wood, June 23, 1913 (not included in CCA), "Correspondence with Carnegie Corporation 1911–1914" file, Caldwell (Idaho) Public Library.

Henshaw, Virginia C., "General Federation of Women's Clubs Centennial Gift to the Nation/World," Sept. 1993, typescript "prepared for the Federated Women's Clubs of Delta, Colorado," n.d., binder, item #93.27.14, Delta County (Colorado) Historical Society Museum.

Hodgin, Gordon V., "A Historical Narrative of the Delta Public Library—80 Years 1909–1989," typescript, n.d., "Delta Public Library" file, Delta County (Colorado) Historical Society Museum.

"History of Washington #804 [sic]," photocopy, Local History Collection, Ellensburg, (Washington) Public Library.

Jones, Walter R., "Evanston, Wyoming: A Brief History," typescript, n.d., "Evanston History" file, 1800-00, Unita County (Evanston, Wyoming) Public Library.

Kenneke, Mrs. E. H., "History of the Nampa Women's Club," typescript, n.d., "Women's Century Club Scrapbook, 1900–1966," Nampa (Idaho) Public Library.

Manifold, Pearl, as told to Howard Spencer, "My Memories of Yuma's Free Reading Room and Rest Room for Men and Women 1914–21," typescript, n.d., "Yuma Library History" file, Yuma County (Arizona) District Library.

Miller, Shirley, "Rock Springs Carnegie Library History," typescript, n.d., "Green River" binder, Sweetwater County (Evanston, Wyoming) Public Library.

"Miss Ethel Bear, Aug. 16, 1972," clipping, Obituary file, Delta County (Colorado) Historical Society Museum.

"Modoc County Free Library Building," typescript, n.d., "Libraries" file, Modoc County (Alturas, California) Library.

"Mrs. Warren Truitt," typescript, "Moscow" file, Idaho State Historical Society, Boise.

Oyler, Beth, Compiler, "Events in the History of the Salt Lake City Free Public Library As Appearing in Salt Lake Newspapers," typescript, n.d., "Salt Lake City Public Library" binder, U-020-098, Salt Lake City (Utah) Public Library.

"Program of General Meetings, The Women's Club of Delta, Colorado, 1915–16," booklet, Delta County (Delta, Colorado) Historical Society Museum.

"Secretary's Record of the Round Table Club, Idaho Falls, Idaho, 1909–[1915]," manuscript minutes, n.d., Idaho Collection item #367R, Idaho Falls (Idaho) Public Library.

Taylor, Clarence D., "George Taylor and His Family, 1838–1926, Thomas Nickolls Taylor," typescript, n.d., Special Collections, Provo (Utah) Public Library.

"Thomas Taliaferro, Jr.," typescript, n.d., "Green River" binder, Sweetwater County (Evanston, Wyoming) Library.

Uhland, Lucile, "Progress," typescript, n.d., Marshall Public Library (Pocatello, Idaho).
Ward, Cora, "A Manuscript on Lewiston, Idaho," typescript, Seattle, WA, 1957, Lewiston (Idaho) Public Library.
"Washington (State) Wenatchee Public Library," typescript, n.d., "Wenatchee Public Library" file, Wenatchee (Washington) Public Library.
Westover, William H., "Yuma Public Library," typescript, "Yuma, Library History" file, Yuma County (Arizona) District Library.

Index